HARVARD ECONOMIC STUDIES

Volume 158

The studies in this series are published under the direction of the Department of Economics of Harvard University. The department does not assume responsibility for the views expressed.

Consumption Behavior and the Effects of Government Fiscal Policies

Randall P. Mariger

Harvard University Press

Cambridge, Massachusetts, and London, England   1986

WITHDRAWN

This book is printed on acid-free paper, and its binding materials have
been chosen for strength and durability.

Library of Congress Cataloging-in-Publication Data

Mariger, Randall P., 1954 –
    Consumption behavior and the effects of government
fiscal policies.

    (Harvard economic studies ; v. 158)
    Bibliography: p.
    Includes index.
    1. Consumption (Economics) — United States.
2. Consumers — United States.   I. Title.   II. Series.
HC110.C6M287   1986   339.4'7'0973   85-17550
ISBN 0-674-16635-3 (alk. paper)

To the memory of Susan Lee Campbell, who was a passenger on the Korean airliner shot down by Soviet forces over the Sea of Japan on September 1, 1983. She was a bright, energetic person and a dear friend.

Acknowledgments

Of the many people who aided me in this endeavor, I am most indebted to Dale Jorgenson. He stimulated my interest in the topic and offered many helpful suggestions. I am also grateful to Alan Auerbach, Martin Feldstein, Benjamin Friedman, Jerry Green, David Jones, Laurence Kotlikoff, and Lawrence Summers for carefully reading parts of an early version of the manuscript and making valuable comments.

Contents

Consumption Behavior and the Effects
of Government Fiscal Policies

1 Introduction

For more than twenty years the life-cycle theory of consumption (Modigliani and Brumberg, 1954) has provided the popular framework for analyzing important economic issues. Among these issues are the following: (1) How does an unfunded social security system affect the size of the capital stock? (2) How do government fiscal policies affect the consumption-investment mix? (3) Is a consumption tax "superior" to an income tax? (See, for example, Auerbach and Kotlikoff, 1983b; Diamond, 1965; Eisner, 1969; Feldstein, 1974, 1978; and Kotlikoff, 1979a.)

In recent years evidence has arisen suggesting that the life-cycle consumption theory has serious deficiencies. Kotlikoff and Summers (1981) find that it cannot account for the size of the U.S. capital stock; White (1978) finds that it cannot explain the amount of aggregate annual savings in the United States; and Atkinson (1971) and Oulton (1976) find that it cannot explain the degree of inequality of wealth in Britain. In addition, Hall and Mishkin (1982) and Hayashi (1984) conclude that the life-cycle consumption theory explains only part of the sensitivity of consumption to contemporaneous income for a cross section of households.

These studies bring into question two fundamental assumptions underlying the life-cycle consumption theory — namely, that there are no planned bequests and that human capital is marketable. As is demonstrated in Chapter 3, these assumptions have important implications for the effects of government fiscal policies on the real economy.

A primary objective of this study is to test whether liquidity constraints and planned bequests are prevalent. To do so, I fit a life-cycle consumption model that incorporates liquidity constraints, but no planned bequests, to data on a cross section of U.S. families in 1962–63. The estimated model, in conjunction with estimates of alternative models, enable me to make inferences about the respective effects of liquidity constraints and social security wealth on consumption. As Barro (1974) has shown, the effect of social security on consumption yields indirect evidence pertaining to the prevalence of planned bequests. I also examine the fit of the model for various subsamples to uncover evidence directly relating to planned bequests. Among the findings discussed are the following:

(1) The consumption model fits the data very well and the parameter estimates are reasonable. The model explains more than 60% of the consumption variance for families with net worth less than $250,000 in 1963, and who constitute 94.2% of the sample and represent 99.1% of the U.S. population in 1963.

(2) Liquidity constraints have an important effect on consumption. I estimate that liquidity-constrained families make up 19.4% of the population of families represented in the sample. These families were responsible for 16.7% of total consumption undertaken by the population sampled.

(3) Social security wealth is indistinguishable from other forms of wealth in its effect on consumption. Furthermore, I conclude it is 95% certain that, in any period, each dollar of net social security receipts has at least 60% as great an effect on consumption as does one dollar of ordinary net noninterest income.[1]

(4) There is evidence that families with net worth exceeding $250,000 in 1963 intend to leave bequests. These families represent 0.9% of the population in 1963 and held approximately 30% of the total wealth in that year.

(5) For families in the lower 99.1% of the wealth distribution, the model explains the consumption behavior of all age groups quite well. In particular, there is no evidence that older families, for whom the desire to leave a bequest would be most evident, consume significantly less than the model predicts.

The models I estimate are rigorously derived, assuming that families maximize the expected value of intertemporal utility subject to the appropriate constraints. To my knowledge, these are the first estimates of a reasonable structural consumption model.[2] The advantage of estimating a structural model is made evident in the latter half of this study, where I utilize the estimated model to simulate the effects of government fiscal policies on the real economy. For this purpose I simulate policy-induced consumption changes for the population of families represented by the sample as well as a hypothetical population of families. Clearly, these tasks require a structural consumption model. My simulations suggest the following:

(1) A 10% incremental tax on labor income immediately decreases the consumption of families represented by the sample by 18.4% of the incremental tax revenue. This change would only be 25% as large if no families were liquidity constrained.

(2) A 10% incremental tax on labor income, followed by an anticipated reduction in the rate of tax on labor income ten years later that keeps the present value of the government's revenue constant, immediately reduces consumption by 9.0% of the initial incremental tax revenue. This consumption change would be only 20% as large if no families were liquidity constrained. The lagged effects of this policy are significant in spite of liquidity constraints. Over nine years consumption falls by 33.4% of the initial incremental tax revenue.

(3) Eliminating the social security system in the United States would increase the steady-state capital stock by at least 6.5% and possibly by as much as 31.3%. This increase is generally *larger* when liquidity constraints are imposed than when they are not.

(4) Life-cycle savings are not nearly large enough to explain the size of the U.S. capital stock.

The latter three sets of findings are implied by simulations for a hypothetical population of families.

I conclude from these simulations that the short-run effects of government fiscal policies on aggregate demand, while significantly greater than they would be in the absence of liquidity constraints, are still rather small. In the longer term, however, government fiscal policies have a significant effect on capital intensity.

The organization of the remaining chapters is as follows. Chapter 2 presents the theoretical framework that underlies the entire study. I begin with a simple life-cycle consumption model introduced by Yaari (1964) which, in the spirit of Modigliani and Brumberg (1954), assumes perfect capital markets and no planned bequests. This model then is generalized in two directions. First, it is extended to the case where net worth must exceed some arbitrary level, which may vary over time, in each period. The solution to the agent's problem is expressed in a form that is empirically applicable. Second, the model is adapted to the case where the family cares about its descendants. Chapter 3 motivates this study and draws heavily on the material in Chapter 2. It begins by demonstrating the important implications of liquidity constraints and intergenerational transfers for the effects of government fiscal policies on the real economy. The second part of the chapter critically evaluates the recent empirical evidence concerning liquidity constraints and intergenerational transfers. It is concluded that our current knowledge of these phenomena is quite limited. Chapter 4 presents the consumption model that serves as the basis for my empirical investigations. This model incorporates liquidity constraints, but no planned bequests, and is applicable to a family. The data used to estimate the parameters of the model are discussed in Chapter 5. Chapter 6 contains a stochastic specification of the model and a discussion of my estimation procedure. The empirical results are reported in Chapters 7 and 8. Chapter 7 presents the parameter estimates for my preferred model, tests the model's robustness, and examines the effects of liquidity constraints on consumption. Chapter 8 generalizes the Chapter 7 model specification to the case where intergenerational transfers may be operative. It tests the implications of this model for the effect of social security on consumption and finds that the Chapter 7 specification cannot be rejected. Evidence directly relating to planned bequests is also presented. Chapters 9, 10, and 11 contain the simulation results. Chapter 9 investigates the effect of liquidity constraints on the lifetime consumption profiles of various families; Chapter 10 studies the effect of temporary taxes on aggregate consumption; and Chapter 11 simulates the steady-state equilibrium of various economies with and without a social security system like the one currently in place in the United States. Finally, Chapter 12 summarizes my findings.

2 The Theoretical Framework

Modern consumption theory extends the static theory of the consumer to an intertemporal setting to explain an agent's choice of consumption, and perhaps leisure, over time. This theory has spawned a variety of models I refer to as choice-theoretic consumption models. In these models: (1) The objects of choice are made explicit; (2) a monotonically increasing and strictly concave utility function is postulated to represent preferences for the objects of choice; (3) constraints facing the agent are made explicit; and (4) the agent is assumed to make choices that maximize expected utility, subject to the constraints imposed. Normally the objects of choice are real consumption expenditure, and perhaps leisure, in each period of the agent's planning horizon.

A special class of choice-theoretic consumption models, which until recently have been the accepted paradigm in consumption theory, are life-cycle models. These models evolved from the model of Modigliani and Brumberg (1954) and tend to share the following characteristics.

(1) The agent is rational and attempts to maximize his expected utility derived from his family's consumption, and perhaps leisure, over his planning horizon.

(2) The agent's planning horizon is the lifetime of himself and his spouse — parents and mature children are not provided for.

(3) The agent has access to perfect insurance and capital markets.

Friedman's permanent income model (Friedman, 1957) shares many of the insights of Modigliani and Brumberg's life-cycle model but is different in some important respects. In particular, Friedman did not specify the length of the horizon and suggested that younger households may have difficulty borrowing against their future labor earnings. These complications forced him to leave his model largely unspecified.[1]

As pointed out in Chapter 1, the second and third assumptions underlying the life-cycle consumption theory have come under close scrutiny in recent years. This chapter investigates how the behavioral implications of the theory are altered when these assumptions are relaxed. We begin with a presentation of a prototype life-cycle model that was first introduced by Yaari (1964) and includes the Modigliani and Brumberg and the Friedman models as special cases. This model is generalized in Section 2.2 to the case where borrowing is restricted. Then, in Section 2.3, a model that allows for planned bequests is presented. All these models assume that the intertemporal utility function has an additive form and depends only on real consumption expenditure in each period. The implications of these assumptions are explored in Appendix A.

This chapter contains the basic theoretical framework that underlies the remainder of the book. In particular, the model of Section 2.2, which allows for liquidity constraints, is the basis for the empirical model of Chapter 4. The Yaari model of Section 2.1, in turn, is the basis for the model of Section 2.2. The properties of these models, therefore, are investigated in some detail. In addition, the results given in Section 2.3 concerning planned bequests are extremely useful for determining how the empirical model, which assumes no planned bequests, would reveal their existence. I refer to this material when devising tests for planned bequests in Chapter 8.

This chapter, with the exception of Section 2.2.3, assumes no uncertainty. The effect of uncertainty on consumption is discussed in Chapter 4.

2.1 A Prototype Life-Cycle Consumption Model

Yaari (1964) develops a consumption model in which the agent faces no uncertainty. He considers two cases, one where the agent derives utility from bequests left to her descendants and one where she does not. The latter case is reviewed here and a discussion of the bequest problem is delayed until Section 2.3. Yaari's continuous time framework is translated to a discrete time framework to facilitate comparability with other models that are presented later.

2.1.1 The General Model

Yaari makes the following assumptions:

(1) The agent's lifetime (horizon) is certain to be $T + 1$ periods long.

(2) The rate of return on investments in each period is certain and equal to that which must be paid on borrowed funds.

(3) Noninterest income in each period is certain and exogenous.

(4) Preferences for lifetime consumption are represented by a utility function of the form

$$V_0(C_0, C_1, \ldots, C_T) = \sum_{i=0}^{T} \alpha(i,0)U(C_i),$$

where C_i is real consumption expenditure in period i, $U(C_i)$ is a monotonically increasing and concave function giving the level of utility experienced in period i, $\alpha(i,0)$ is a subjective discount factor, and time is measured relative to the time the agent is age 0.

(5) The agent must be solvent at the end of period T.

(6) The agent is rational and maximizes lifetime utility subject to the constraints he faces.

The second argument of the subjective discount factor denotes the period in which the optimal consumption plan is formulated, here assumed to be period 0. This dependence is allowed so that later I may discuss the question of whether the agent continues to follow the plan formulated at time 0 as he ages. For now the reader is advised to ignore the dependence of α on its second argument.

Under these assumptions, the agent's problem is

$$\underset{\mathbf{C}}{\text{Max}} \ V_0(\mathbf{C}) = \sum_{i=0}^{T} \alpha(i,0)U(C_i) \tag{2.1}$$

subject to

$$A_{T+1} \equiv [P(T,0)]^{-1} \sum_{i=0}^{T} P(i,0)(YL_i - C_i) \geq 0 \tag{2.2}$$

$$\leftrightarrow \sum_{i=0}^{T} P(i,0)C_i \leq W_0 \equiv \sum_{i=0}^{T} P(i,0)YL_i,$$

$$\mathbf{C} \geq \mathbf{0}, \tag{2.3}$$

where

$$\mathbf{C} = [C_0, C_1, \ldots, C_T], \tag{2.4}$$

$$P(i,0) = \prod_{j=0}^{i-1} (1 + R_j)^{-1}, \quad \text{for } i = 1,2, \ldots, T, \tag{2.5}$$

$$= 1, \quad \text{for } i = 0,$$

and R_i, YL_i, and A_i are, respectively, the real net rate of return, real net noninterest income, and real net worth, in period i. The agent is insatiable so that (2.2) holds with equality. Also, it is assumed that the marginal utility of consumption in any period becomes infinite as consumption in that period approaches zero,

$$\lim_{X \to 0} U'(X) = \infty, \tag{2.6}$$

so that (2.3) is not a binding constraint so long as there exist positive consumption vectors that satisfy (2.2), which is clearly true as long as $W_0 > 0$.

An interesting implication of the budget constraint is that the income stream only affects consumption through its impact on W_0, full wealth in period 0. In other words, any two income streams yielding the same value of W_0 result in the same optimal consumption plan. This observation may seem trivial but it is at the heart of the permanent income hypothesis which states that current income is an important determinant of current consumption only insofar as it reflects "permanent income" which, by definition, is closely related to W_0. An immediate implication of this hypothesis is that the time profile of consumption does not passively follow the time profile of income, as the earlier measured income theories of consumption maintained.

Returning to our problem, we note that under assumption (2.6), (2.1) is a simple constrained maximization problem. Furthermore, since the lifetime utility function is strictly concave in **C** and the budget constraint is convex in **C**, the Kuhn-Tucker necessary conditions for the maximum of (2.1) subject to (2.2) and (2.3) are also sufficient. Denoting the optimal consumption levels by a superscript asterisk[*], these conditions are

$$\frac{\alpha(i,0)U'(C_i^*)}{\alpha(k,0)U'(C_k^*)} = \frac{P(i,0)}{P(k,0)} = \prod_{j=k}^{i-1} (1 + R_j)^{-1}, \tag{2.7}$$

$$i > k; \; i,k = 0,1, \ldots ,T,$$

$$\sum_{i=0}^{T} P(i,0)C_i^* = W_0, \tag{2.8}$$

which simply state that the ratio of the marginal utilities of C_i and C_k is equal to the ratio of their respective prices and that all available resources are expended.

The model implies that consumption in each period is a normal good. To see this, note that an increase in W_0 must increase consumption in at least one period by virtue of (2.8). But, assuming the subjective discount factors and interest rates remain constant, (2.7) requires that the ratios $U'(C_i^*)/U'(C_k^*)$, all i and k, remain unchanged so that consumption in all periods must increase.

It is apparent from (2.7) and the fact that marginal utility diminishes that an increase in $\alpha(i,0)/\alpha(k,0)$, other things equal, increases C_i^* and decreases C_k^*.

Changes in interest rates, conversely, have ambiguous effects on the optimal consumption plan. Suppose, for instance, that $P(i,0)/P(k,0)$ increases. Equation (2.7) requires that C_i^* decrease and C_k^* increase if W_0 is held constant. But $P(i,0)$ and $P(k,0)$ also enter (2.8) and it is impossible to determine the effect on consumption without knowing more about the utility function and the effect of $P(i,0)$ and $P(k,0)$ on W_0.

This ambiguity of the effect of interest rates on consumption is due to the possibility that the resulting income effects may offset the substitution effects of such changes. The reduction in interest rates over the interval $[k,i-1]$, which increases $P(i,0)/P(k,0)$, makes consumption in period i (the later period) more expensive relative to consumption in period k, and the resulting substitution effect decreases C_i^* and increases C_k^*. The direction of the income effect depends on whether the agent would have been a net debtor or a net creditor during the interval $[k,i-1]$ if interest rates had not changed. This, in turn, depends on preferences as well as the time profile of the noninterest income stream. If the agent would have been a debtor, then the reduction in interest rates enriches her and, since consumption in each period is a normal good, C_k^* must rise but C_i^* may rise or fall. Otherwise C_i^* must fall and C_k^* may rise or fall.

2.1.2 Dynamic Consistency

Yaari's formulation of the agent's problem assumes that the agent plans his lifetime consumption at the beginning of life and follows that plan thereafter. An interesting question, first posed by Strotz (1955–56), is whether the agent will continue to follow the original plan as he ages. To answer this question it is necessary to specify how preferences change with time. Recall that at time 0 preferences are represented by

$$V_0(C_0,C_1, \ldots ,C_T) = \sum_{i=0}^{T} \alpha(i,0)U(C_i). \tag{2.9}$$

It is natural to assume preferences in period 1 are represented by

$$V_1(C_1,C_2, \ldots ,C_T) = \sum_{i=1}^{T} \alpha(i,1)U(C_i),$$

which is (2.9) without the first term and, possibly, with different discount factors. Let the optimal consumption plan formulated at time 0 be denoted $\mathbf{C}_0^* = (C_{0,0}^*, C_{1,0}^*, \ldots ,C_{T,0}^*)$ and let $A_{1,0}^* =$

$(YL_0 - C^*_{0,0})(1 + R_0)$ be the net worth of the agent at the beginning of period 1 when following plan $\mathbf{C}^*_0$. Then the problem faced by the agent at the beginning of period 1 is

$$\underset{\mathbf{C}_1}{\text{Max }} V_1 = \sum_{i=1}^{T} \alpha(i,1)U(C_i), \tag{2.10}$$

subject to

$$\sum_{i=1}^{T} P(i,1)C_i \le W_1 \equiv A^*_{1,0} + \sum_{i=1}^{T} P(i,1)YL_i,$$

where

$$P(i,1) = \prod_{j=1}^{i-1} (1 + R_j)^{-1}, \quad \text{for } i = 2,3, \ldots ,T,$$
$$= 1, \quad \text{for } i = 1.$$

Let the solution to this problem be denoted $\mathbf{C}^*_1 = (C^*_{1,1}, C^*_{2,1}, \ldots , C^*_{T,1})$. We wish to determine under what circumstances the agent is dynamically consistent so that $(C^*_{1,0}, C^*_{2,0}, \ldots , C^*_{T,0}) = \mathbf{C}^*_1$.

The necessary and sufficient conditions for $\mathbf{C}^*_1$ to be the solution to (2.10) are entirely analogous to those given in (2.7) and (2.8):

$$\frac{\alpha(i,1)U'(C^*_{i,1})}{\alpha(k,1)U'(C^*_{k,1})} = \frac{P(i,1)}{P(k,1)} = \prod_{j=k}^{i-1} (1 + R_j)^{-1}, \tag{2.11}$$
$$i > k, \, i,k = 1,2, \ldots ,T,$$

$$\sum_{i=1}^{T} P(i,1)C^*_{i,1} = W_1. \tag{2.12}$$

It is readily apparent that if

$$\alpha(i,1) = \beta\alpha(i,0), \quad i = 1,2, \ldots ,T; \, \beta \ne 0, \tag{2.13}$$

then the agent's plan formulated at time 0, which satisfies (2.7) and (2.8), must also satisfy equations (2.11) and (2.12). Hence (2.13) is a sufficient condition for the agent to be dynamically consistent between periods 0 and 1. It is apparent that this condition is also necessary for dynamic consistency.

We conclude that for dynamic consistency to hold over the agent's lifetime, the subjective discount factors on future utility levels must all change proportionately from one planning period to the next so that the relative importance put on utility levels experienced in future periods does not change with time.

An important class of discount factors is those where the discount on utility experienced in a future period i depends only on the elapsed time until period i occurs and, perhaps, the date i itself:

$$\alpha(i,t) = f(i, i - t), \qquad i = t, t + 1, \ldots, T. \tag{2.14}$$

In this case dynamic consistency requires that $i - t$ enter the discount factor exponentially:

$$\alpha(i,t) = \delta(i)(1 + \rho)^{-(i-t)}, \qquad i = t, t + 1, \ldots, T \tag{2.15}$$

where ρ and the function $\delta(i)$ are arbitrary.

It is important to point out that in cases where the agent is not dynamically consistent, as here defined, our method of solving the agent's problem is inappropriate. This is because the agent will take into account his actual future behavior when deciding his current consumption and not that behavior which, from his present perspective, appears to be optimal. The appropriate method of solution, therefore, is dynamic programming (Pollak, 1968). The consumption plan so derived will be such that the agent adheres to it as he ages and, in this sense, the agent will always be dynamically consistent. The question of dynamic consistency, therefore, has no behavioral significance but instead addresses the issue of what optimization technique is appropriate.

Dynamic consistency is not necessary for rationality, but it does lead to simpler consumption models. For this reason, and because discount factors satisfying (2.14) are intuitively appealing, it is nearly universal that discount factors of the form (2.15) are assumed in choice-theoretic consumption models.

2.1.3 The Proportionality Hypothesis

Thus far, the Yaari model has led us to the following conclusions:

(1) Full wealth in period 0, W_0, completely summarizes all the information about the agent's earnings stream that is relevant to her consumption decisions.

(2) Full wealth and consumption in each period are positively related.

(3) An increase in $\alpha(i,0)/\alpha(k,0)$, other things equal, causes C_i^* to rise and C_k^* to fall.

(4) Changes in interest rates have an ambiguous effect on the optimal consumption plan. The effect of such changes depends on preferences as well as the time profile of net noninterest income.

(5) The discount factors on utility experienced in future periods must satisfy (2.13) for the agent to be dynamically consistent.

Not much more can be said without making further assumptions. To this end, one may either assume something about the within-period utility function, $U(\cdot)$, and derive the implications for the optimal consumption plan, or assume something about the optimal consumption plan and derive the implications for the within-period utility function. Yaari takes the latter approach and shows that the proportionality hypothesis proposed by Modigliani and Brumberg (1954) and by Friedman (1957)—that $b_i^* \equiv C_i^*/W_0$, $i = 0,1, \ldots ,T$, are independent of W_0—implies that the within-period utility function takes either of the two forms:

$$U(C_i) = (1/\gamma)C_i^\gamma, \qquad \gamma < 1; \gamma \neq 0, \tag{2.16}$$

$$U(C_i) = \log(C_i), \tag{2.17}$$

where (2.17) is the limit of (2.16) as γ approaches zero. This is a direct implication of (2.7), which requires that

$$\frac{U'(b_i^* W_0)}{U'(b_k^* W_0)} = \text{constant}, \quad \text{all } W_0 > 0, \qquad i,k = 0,1, \ldots ,T,$$

so that $U'(X)$ must be a homogeneous function.

The logical justification given by Modigliani and Brumberg and by Friedman for the proportionality hypothesis is compelling. Why should the relative consumption levels experienced over the years of an agent's life change with his overall capacity to consume?[2] Furthermore, the proportionality hypothesis yields a relatively simple model of consumption and is a natural starting point for any empirical study of consumption. For these reasons nearly all choice-theoretic consumption models assume the proportionality hypothesis to be valid.

It is constructive to solve the Yaari model under the assumption that the proportionality hypothesis holds. Since (2.17) is a limiting form of (2.16), we assume the within-period utility function has the form (2.16). Utilizing conditions (2.7) and (2.8), we arrive at the solution

$$C_j^* = \frac{[P(j,0)\alpha(0,0)/\alpha(j,0)]^{1/(\gamma-1)}}{\sum_{i=0}^{T} \{[P(i,0)^\gamma \alpha(0,0)/\alpha(i,0)]^{1/(\gamma-1)}\}} W_0, \tag{2.18}$$

$$j = 0,1, \ldots ,T.$$

We assume, as is typical, that the discount factors take the form

$$\alpha(j,0) = (1 + \rho)^{-j}, \tag{2.19}$$

which is a special case of (2.15) and ensures that the agent is dynamically consistent. Utilizing (2.19) and the definition of $P(j,0)$ in (2.5), (2.18) may be expressed as:

$$C_j^* = \frac{\left[\delta_{j,0} \prod_{i=0}^{j-1} (1 + R_i)\right]}{\left[1 + \sum_{i=1}^{T} \delta_{i,0}\right]} W_0, \quad \text{for } j = 1, 2, \ldots, T, \quad (2.20)$$

$$= W_0 \Big/ \left(1 + \sum_{i=1}^{T} \delta_{i,0}\right), \quad \text{for } j = 0,$$

where

$$\delta_{i,0} = \prod_{k=0}^{i-1} [(1 + R_k)^\gamma/(1 + \rho)]^{1/(1-\gamma)}, \quad i = 1, 2, \ldots, T.$$

It is immediately apparent that the proportionate change in consumption between periods j and $j + 1$ is

$$(C_{j+1}^*/C_j^*) = [\delta_{j+1,0}(1 + R_j)/\delta_{j,0}] \quad (2.21)$$

$$= [(1 + R_j)/(1 + \rho)]^{1/(1-\gamma)}, \quad j = 0, 1, \ldots, T - 1,$$

which is most revealing of the logic underlying choice-theoretic consumption models. A large gross interest rate in period j makes C_{j+1} cheaper relative to C_j, thereby increasing the former relative to the latter. A larger gross rate of time preference, conversely, makes utility experienced in period $j + 1$ less important to intertemporal utility than utility experienced in period j, thereby decreasing C_{j+1}^* relative to C_j^*. The net impact of these two factors is given by their ratio raised to the power $1/(1 - \gamma)$. Recall that γ is the exponent on consumption in the within-period utility function and determines the degree of concavity of the intertemporal utility function. A large value of γ implies a larger consumption growth rate if R_j exceeds ρ and a smaller growth rate otherwise. This is in accord with our intuition, in that a large value of γ implies that marginal utility diminishes slowly and consumption is very responsive to relative prices. In other words, a high γ implies a high degree of intertemporal substitutability in consumption. A small value of γ, conversely, implies that the agent's consumption is relatively unresponsive to relative prices. In fact, an infinitely negative value of γ implies a zero growth rate of consumption regardless of the values of R_j and ρ.

The foregoing discussion suggests a close relationship between γ and the intertemporal elasticity of substitution.[3] In fact, it is easily shown that this elasticity is $1/(1 - \gamma)$.

The optimal consumption plan given in (2.20) may be converted to a contingent plan where C_j^* depends on full wealth in period j, W_j, rather than full wealth in period 0. To this end, note that

$$W_j = \left[\prod_{k=0}^{j-1} (1 + R_k)\right]\left[W_0 - \sum_{k=0}^{j-1} P(k,0)C_k^*\right]. \tag{2.22}$$

Equations (2.20) and (2.22) make it possible to express W_0 as a function of W_j. Substituting this expression back into (2.20) would give the desired result. Alternatively, our choice of discount factors ensures that the agent is dynamically consistent so that she may resolve her problem at any time and arrive at the same result for the remainder of her consumption plan. In particular, if the agent resolves her problem in period j, the solution for period j consumption is

$$C_j^* = W_j \Big/ \left(1 + \sum_{i=j+1}^{T} \delta_{i,j}\right), \qquad j = 0,1, \ldots ,T, \tag{2.23}$$

where

$$\delta_{i,j} = \prod_{k=j}^{i-1} [(1 + R_k)^\gamma/(1 + \rho)]^{1/(1-\gamma)}, \tag{2.24}$$

$$i = j + 1, j + 2, \ldots ,T,$$

which is the desired result.

2.1.4 The Modigliani and Brumberg and Friedman Models

Both Modigliani and Brumberg and Friedman assume the proportionality hypothesis to be valid, so that in the Yaari framework the utility function must take either of the two forms (2.16) or (2.17). In addition, Modigliani and Brumberg assume that the agent desires a flat consumption stream,[4] and Friedman assumes that the agent consumes a constant portion of his full wealth in each period.[5] This section demonstrates that each of these properties of the optimal consumption plan can be generated by the Yaari model. In so doing, it is assumed that the within-period utility function and the subjective discount function have the forms (2.16) and (2.19), respectively.

First consider the Modigliani and Brumberg hypothesis. It implies that the growth rate of consumption is zero throughout the agent's lifetime. It was established in the previous subsection that $\gamma = -\infty$ is a sufficient condition for the optimal consumption plan to have this property regardless of the pure rate of time preference and the time profile of interest rates. It is apparent from (2.21) that an alternative possibility is that the interest rate in each period is equal to the pure rate of time preference, in which case the growth rate of consumption is zero for any value of γ.

The Friedman hypothesis, that the propensity to consume out of full wealth is independent of the agent's age, is easiest to analyze under the assumption that interest rates remain constant over the agent's lifetime. In this case (2.24) becomes

$$\delta_{i,j} = \delta^{i-j},$$

where

$$\delta = [1/(1 + R)][(1 + R)/(1 + \rho)]^{1/(1-\gamma)},$$

and (2.23) simplifies to

$$C_j^* = [(1 - \delta)/(1 - \delta^{T-j+1})]\, W_j, \quad \text{for } \delta \neq 1; j = 0,1, \ldots ,T, \quad (2.25)$$
$$= [1/(T - j + 1)]\, W_j, \quad \text{for } \delta = 1; j = 0,1, \ldots ,T.$$

It is apparent from (2.25) that the propensity to consume out of full wealth increases with the agent's age unless δ is less than one and the agent's time horizon is infinite. In this case, $C_j^* = (1 - \delta)W_j$, $j = 0,1, \ldots ,\infty$, and $1 - \delta$ is equal to Friedman's k (that is, the propensity to consume permanent income) multiplied by $R/(1 + R)$.[6]

An interesting reference case is where $\gamma = -\infty$ so that $\delta = 1/(1 + R)$ and $C_j^* = R*W_j/(1 + R)$, $j = 0,1, \ldots ,\infty$, which implies that full wealth and consumption remain constant over time and Friedman's k is equal to one. If δ is greater than $1/(1 + R)$, then k is less than one and consumption grows over time. Alternatively, a δ less than $1/(1 + R)$ yields a k greater than one and a declining consumption profile.

2.2 A Consumption Model with Liquidity Constraints

The Yaari model implies that lifetime full wealth summarizes everything about the agent's income stream that is relevant for consumption decisions. This conclusion hinges on the assumption that borrowing is unrestricted provided the agent is solvent at the time of death.

In the following we consider a situation where the agent is required to have some minimal level of net worth, which may vary over time, in each period. Restrictions of this type would obtain, for example, if creditors require that all loans be fully secured with collateral, in which case the minimal level of net worth is zero in every period. It is argued in Chapter 4, however, that the minimal levels of net worth are positive and vary with time. This section, therefore, presents a general model where the minimal levels of net worth are arbitrary.

We begin with a statement of the agent's problem and a discussion of its treatment in the previous literature. Section 2.2.2 establishes three propositions that render the model tractable in all cases for which the model is tractable in the absence of liquidity constraints. Section 2.2.3 discusses the case where lifetimes are uncertain. Finally, Section 2.2.4 addresses the question of how liquidity constraints, as here formalized, are likely to affect consumption behavior.

2.2.1 Statement of the Problem

Consider an agent currently aged t, with net worth A_t, and who lives to age T with certainty. Her problem is to choose a consumption plan for the remainder of her life, say $\mathbf{C}^*(t,T) = (C_t^*, C_{t+1}^*, \ldots, C_T^*)$, that maximizes

$$V[\mathbf{C}(t,T)] = \sum_{i=t}^{T} \alpha(i,t)U(i,C_i)$$

subject to the constraints

$$A_i \equiv P(i,t)^{-1}[A_t + \sum_{j=t}^{i-1} P(j,t)(YL_j - C_j)] \geq B_i, \qquad (2.26)$$

$$i = t+1, t+2, \ldots, T+1,$$

where $\mathbf{C}(i,j) = (C_i, C_{i+1}, \ldots, C_j)$, $i \leq j$, denotes an arbitrary consumption vector over the interval $[i,j]$ and B_i denotes the minimal level of net worth in period i. The discount factors are defined in (2.5). The minimal levels of net worth are arbitrary aside from the requirement that they be nonstochastic.

The agent's decision problem is very similar to the Yaari problem of the last section. The only differences are that the within-period utility function is time dependent, so as to facilitate the derivation of our empirical model in Chapter 4, and net worth is constrained in all periods, not just period $T + 1$ as in the Yaari model.

Yaari does address the problem presented here in another study (Yaari, 1965) which concerns the effect of lifetime uncertainty on consumption. In that study Yaari considers the case where the minimal levels of net worth are always zero because creditors will not extend loans for which there is a positive probability of default. He derives necessary and sufficient conditions that determine the optimal consumption plan. My contribution is that I give an operational procedure for solving these conditions for the optimal consumption plan.

Unlike Yaari's, my results are derived for the case of lifetime certainty. Section 2.2.3 demonstrates that uncertain lifetimes are easily allowed for provided the agent is one individual with no dependents, the case considered by Yaari.

2.2.2 The Solution

THE FIRST PHASE OF THE OPTIMAL CONSUMPTION PLAN

Consider the partition of $C^*(t,T)$, $[C^*(t,v),C^*(v+1,T)]$, where v is the first date that (2.26) is a binding constraint. (Normally, $v+1$ is the earliest date that net worth equals its minimal allowable level.) The objectives of this subsection are to characterize the solution $C^*(t,v)$ for given v and to determine v.

This task requires additional notation. Let q be an arbitrary date such that $t \leqslant q \leqslant T$. Define:

$$C(t,q) = (C_t, C_{t+1}, \ldots, C_q),$$

$$A(C(t,q)) = \{A_{t+1}[C(t,q)], A_{t+2}[C(t,q)], \ldots, A_{q+1}[C(t,q)]\}$$

where

$$A_i[C(t,q)] = P(i,t)^{-1}\left[A_t + \sum_{j=t}^{i-1} P(j,t)(YL_j - C_j)\right],$$

$$i = t+1, t+2, \ldots, q+1,$$

and A_t is predetermined;

$$V[C(t,q)] = \sum_{i=t}^{q} \alpha(i,t)U(i,C_i),$$

$$B(t,q) = (B_{t+1}, B_{t+2}, \ldots, B_{q+1}),$$

$$S^u(t,q) = \{C(t,q)|A_{q+1}[C(t,q)] \geqslant B_{q+1}\},$$

$$C^u(t,q) = [C^u_t(t,q), C^u_{t+1}(t,q), \ldots, C^u_q(t,q)]$$
$$= \{C'(t,q)|C'(t,q) \in S^u(t,q); V[C'(t,q)] \geqslant V[C(t,q)],$$
$$\text{for all } C(t,q) \in S^u(t,q)\},$$

$$A^u(t,q) = A[C^u(t,q)].$$

$C(t,q)$ is an arbitrary consumption vector for the interval $[t,q]$; $A[C(t,q)]$ is the net worth vector over the interval $[t+1, q+1]$ corresponding to the consumption plan $C(t,q)$; $V[C(t,q)]$ is the portion of intertemporal utility in period t due to $C(t,q)$; $B(t,q)$ is the vector of minimum net worth levels over the interval $[t + 1,q + 1]$; $S^u(t,q)$ is the set of consumption vectors over the interval $[t,q]$ that do not violate the constraint on net worth in period $q + 1$; $\mathbf{C}^u(t,q)$ maximizes $V[\mathbf{C}(t,q)]$ subject only to the constraint on net worth in period $q + 1$; and $\mathbf{A}^u(t,q)$ is the net worth vector over the interval $[t + 1,q + 1]$ corresponding to the consumption plan $\mathbf{C}^u(t,q)$. Note that the concavity of the preference function and the fact that $S^u(t,q)$ is a convex set ensure that $\mathbf{C}^u(t,q)$ is unique.

The following proposition characterizes the first phase of the optimal consumption plan, $\mathbf{C}^*(t,v)$, for a given v.

Proposition 2.1: $\mathbf{C}^*(t,v) = \mathbf{C}^u(t,v)$.

Remarks: The intuition for the proposition can be seen as follows. It is given that the optimal consumption plan is such that $A^*_{v+1} = B_{v+1}$. This, in addition to the fact that the intertemporal utility function is additive, implies that $\mathbf{C}^*(t,v)$ maximizes $V[\mathbf{C}(t,v)]$ subject to the constraints on net worth in *all* periods of the interval $[t + 1, v + 1]$. But, by assumption, the constraints are only binding in period $v + 1$ so that $\mathbf{C}^*(t,v)$ maximizes $V[\mathbf{C}(t,v)]$ subject only to the constraint on net worth in period $v + 1$. That is, $\mathbf{C}^*(t,v) = \mathbf{C}^u(t,v)$.

Proof: We prove the proposition for the normal case where $v + 1$ is the first date that net worth is equal to its minimal allowable level (that is, $\mathbf{A}[\mathbf{C}^*(t,v - 1)] > \mathbf{B}[t,v - 1]$). The general proof is a straightforward extension of the proof that follows and is sketched in Appendix B.

Suppose, contrary to the proposition, that $\mathbf{C}'(t,v) \in S^u(t,v)$ and $V[\mathbf{C}'(t,v)] > V[\mathbf{C}^*(t,v)]$. If $\mathbf{A}[\mathbf{C}'(t,v)] \geq \mathbf{B}(t,v)$ then the plan $[\mathbf{C}'(t,v),\mathbf{C}^*(v + 1,T)]$ is feasible and, because the intertemporal utility function is additive, $V[\mathbf{C}'(t,v),\mathbf{C}^*(v + 1,T)] > V[\mathbf{C}^*(t,T)]$ so that $\mathbf{C}^*(t,T)$ cannot be optimal. If instead $\mathbf{A}[\mathbf{C}'(t,v)] \leq \mathbf{B}(t,v)$, then (assuming $\mathbf{A}[\mathbf{C}^*(t,v - 1)] > \mathbf{B}(t,v - 1)$) the convexity of $S^u(t,v)$ ensures that there exists a plan $\mathbf{C}^+(t,v) = k\mathbf{C}'(t,v) + (1 - k)\mathbf{C}^*(t,v)$, for $k \in \,]0,1[$, such that $\mathbf{A}[\mathbf{C}^+(t,v)] \geq \mathbf{B}(t,v)$ and, by concavity of the preference function, $V[\mathbf{C}^+(t,v)] > V[\mathbf{C}^*(t,v)]$. It follows that $[\mathbf{C}^+(t,v),\mathbf{C}^*(v + 1, T)]$ is feasible and dominates $\mathbf{C}^*(t,T)$ so that the latter plan cannot be optimal.

The proposition indicates that once the cutoff date, v, is known, the first phase of the optimal consumption plan is the solution to an optimization problem with one equality constraint. The following proposition determines v.

Proposition 2.2: The first cutoff date, v, is the maximum s such that $\mathbf{A}^u(t,s) \geq \mathbf{B}(t,s)$.

Proof: Suppose, contrary to the proposition, that there exists a p such that $\mathbf{A}^u(t,p) \geq \mathbf{B}(t,p)$, $p > v$. This situation is illustrated in Fig-

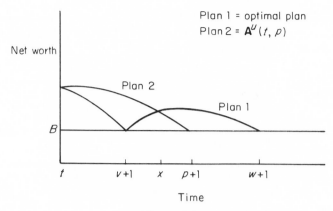

Figure 2.1

ure 2.1. The figure illustrates a net-worth path corresponding to each of two consumption plans. Plan 1 is the optimal plan and plan 2 is $C^u(t,p)$, $p > v$, which by assumption does not violate the constraints on net worth. For diagrammatic simplicity the minimal levels of net worth are assumed to be time-invariant at B.

Let $C_i^+(q,r)$ denote consumption plan i, $i = 1,2$, over the interval $[q,r]$. Assuming there exists a date x such that $A_x[C^*(t,T)] = A_x^u(t,p)$ (the general proof is given in Appendix B), we will show that the plan $[C_1^+(t,x-1), C_2^+(x,p)]$ is preferred to $C_2^+(t,p)$ over the interval (t,p), thereby contradicting the supposition that plan 2 is the most preferred plan on the interval (t,p) that results in $A_{p+1} = B_{p+1}$.

Consider the consumption plans $C_1^+(t,x-1)$ and $C_2^+(t,x-1)$. Both plans are feasible and they each begin and end with the same levels of net worth. Therefore $C_1^+(t,x-1)$ must yield a higher level of utility on the interval $(t,x-1)$ than $C_2^+(t,x-1)$ if plan 1 is to be optimal as hypothesized. It immediately follows that $[C_1^+(t,x-1), C_2^+(x,p)]$ is preferred to $C_2^+(t,p)$.

If it is possible to find $C^u(t,s)$ for an arbitrary s, then Proposition 2.2 gives an operational, but computationally burdensome, method of finding the first cutoff date. Simply compute the net worth path over the first phase of the consumption plan for all possible values of the first cutoff date and let v be the futuremost cutoff date that does not lead to a violation of the constraints on net worth. The following proposition suggests a much simpler alternative procedure.

Proposition 2.3: The maximum s such that $A^u(t,s) \geqq B(t,s)$ is the maximum s that minimizes $C_t^u(t,s)$.

Propositions 2.2 and 2.3 imply that the first cutoff date is the futuremost cutoff date that minimizes current consumption.

Remarks: The strategy of the formal proof is most easily explained with reference to Figure 2.2. Again, for diagrammatic simplicity the minimal levels of net worth are assumed to be time-invariant at B. The figure shows two net worth paths. $\mathbf{A}^u(t,v)$ is the net worth path corresponding to $\mathbf{C}^u(t,v)$, the optimal consumption plan over the interval $[t,v]$. $\mathbf{A}^u(t,p)$, $p \neq v$, is the net worth path corresponding to $\mathbf{C}^u(t,p)$. It is assumed, contrary to the proposition, that $C_t^u(t,p) < C_t^u(t,v)$. Our strategy is to show that this assumption leads to a contradiction. Since the Kuhn-Tucker necessary conditions hold with equality for each plan on the interval $[t, \text{Min}(p,v)]$, we are able to show that $p > v$, and $\mathbf{A}^u(t,p)$ lies above $\mathbf{A}^u(t,v)$ in each period of the interval $[t+1,v+1]$. (The figure is drawn to be consistent with each of these findings.) This implies that the date w, defined as the earliest date that $A_{w+1}^u(t,p) \leq B_{w+1}$, is such that $v+1 < w+1 \leq p+1$. It then is shown that $\mathbf{C}^u(t,w)$, $w > v$, is feasible, which contradicts Proposition 2.2.

To prove the proposition, it is helpful to refer to partitions of the vectors $\mathbf{C}^u(t,s)$ and $\mathbf{A}^u(t,s)$ for $s \geq t$. Define

$$\mathbf{C}^u(t,s,q,r) = [C_q^u(t,s), C_{q+1}^u(t,s), \ldots, C_r^u(t,s)],$$

$$\mathbf{A}^u(t,s,q,r) = [A_{q+1}^u(t,s), A_{q+2}^u(t,s), \ldots, A_{r+1}^u(t,s)], \qquad t \leq q \leq r \leq s.$$

Proof: The first step of our proof is to show that

$$\mathbf{C}^u(t,s,t,q) \geq \mathbf{C}^u(t,r,t,q) \tag{2.27}$$
$$\text{or} \quad \mathbf{C}^u(t,s,t,q) \leq \mathbf{C}^u(t,r,t,q), \qquad t \leq q < r \leq s.$$

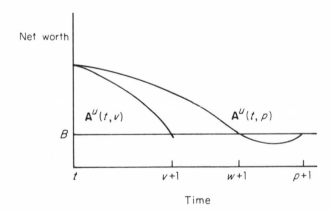

Figure 2.2

This follows from the fact that the Kuhn-Tucker necessary conditions, for each of the plans referenced in (2.27), require that

$$\partial V/\partial C_j = (\partial V/\partial C_k) \sum_{i=j}^{k-1} (1 + R_i), \qquad t \leqslant j < k \leqslant q.$$

This condition, in addition to the facts that the intertemporal utility function is additive and marginal utility is diminishing, implies (2.27).

We now prove the proposition. Suppose, contrary to the proposition, that $C_t^u(t,p) < C_t^u(t,v)$, where v satisfies Proposition 2.2. If $p < v$ then (2.27) requires that $\mathbf{C}^u(t,p) < \mathbf{C}^u(t,v,t,p)$ and $A_{p+1}^u(t,p) > A_{p+1}^u(t,v) \geqslant B_{p+1}$, which contradicts the fact that the consumer is insatiable (that is, $A_{p+1}^u(t,p) = B_{p+1}$). If instead $p > v$, then (2.27) implies that $\mathbf{C}^u(t,p,t,v) < \mathbf{C}^u(t,v)$ so that $\mathbf{A}^u(t,p,t,v) > \mathbf{A}^u(t,v) \geqslant \mathbf{B}(t,v)$. Let w be the first date such that $A_{w+1}^u(t,p) \leqslant B_{w+1}$. Since $\mathbf{A}^u(t,p,t,v) > \mathbf{B}(t,v)$ and $A_{p+1}^u(t,p) = B_{p+1}$, it follows that w exists and $v + 1 < w + 1 \leqslant p + 1$. By condition (2.27), $\mathbf{C}^u(t,w) \leqslant \mathbf{C}^u(t,p,t,w)$ and $\mathbf{A}^u(t,w,t,w-1) \geqslant \mathbf{A}^u(t,p,t,w-1) \geqslant \mathbf{B}(t,w-1)$. It follows that $\mathbf{C}^u(t,w)$, $w > v$, is feasible, which contradicts Proposition 2.2.

Corollary: Let q be the earliest date that $A_{q+1}^u(t,T) \leqslant B_{q+1}$. Then $v = T$ if $q = T$, and $v \geqslant q$ if $q < T$.

Proof: The first part of the corollary follows directly from Proposition 2.2. If $q < T$, Proposition 2.3 requires that $C_t^u(t,T) > C_t^u(t,v)$ and, by condition (2.27), $\mathbf{C}^u(t,T,t,v) > \mathbf{C}^u(t,v)$ so that $A_{v+1}^u(t,T) < A_{v+1}^u(t,v) = B_{v+1}$. It follows that $v \geqslant q$.

LATER PHASES OF THE OPTIMAL CONSUMPTION PLAN

Once the first phase of the optimal consumption plan is found, the second phase is found in an entirely analogous manner. The only differences are that the initial period becomes $v + 1$ rather than t and the initial level of net worth, A_{v+1}, is B_{v+1}. In this way, all phases of the optimal consumption plan are determined sequentially.[7]

SUMMARY

The main results of this subsection are summarized below.

(1) The effect of the constraint $A_i \geqslant B_i$, with $i = t + 1$, $t + 2, \ldots, T + 1$, is to break up the family's lifetime into one or more distinct intervals such that the constraints are binding only in the final period of each interval.

(2) Given the first interval, $[t,v]$, the optimal consumption plan for the interval, denoted $\mathbf{C}^u(t,v)$, is the solution to a maximization problem with one equality constraint.

(3) If, for a given v, it is possible to solve for $\mathbf{C}^u(t,v)$, then v is easily found. Simply compute $C_t^u(t,s)$, the level of current consumption associated with $\mathbf{C}^u(t,s)$, for $s = t + 1, t + 2, \ldots, T$, and set v equal to the value of s that calls for the smallest amount of current consumption.

(4) Once the first cutoff date is found, the next cutoff is found in the exact same way. The only difference is that the initial period becomes period $v + 1$ and the initial level of net worth becomes B_{v+1}.

These findings imply that it is possible to explicitly solve for $\mathbf{C}^*(t,T)$ in all cases where it is possible to solve for the optimal consumption plan in the absence of liquidity constraints. This is because, in the absence of liquidity constraints, $B_{T+1} = 0$ and the optimal consumption plan is $\mathbf{C}^u(t,T)$. If it is possible to find $\mathbf{C}^u(t,T)$ then it is also possible to find $\mathbf{C}^u(t,s)$, where $s = t + 1, t + 2, \ldots, T$, which is all that is necessary in order to find $\mathbf{C}^*(t,T)$.

2.2.3 The Case of Uncertain Lifetimes

Consider an individual with no dependents who is currently age t and who lives to age τ, a stochastic integer in the range $[t + 1, T]$. Following Yaari (1965), we assume that the agent chooses the consumption plan that maximizes

$$_t E \left[\sum_{i=t}^{\tau} \alpha(i,t)U(i,C_i) \right]$$

subject to the constraints given in (2.26). It is assumed that the minimal levels of net worth are nonnegative so that creditors are assured repayment of any outstanding loans.

Let the probability of living to age i, given survival to age t, be denoted $PR(i|t)$. It is assumed that the agent's age is the only variable that is relevant to the probability distribution of τ. This implies that the optimal consumption plan, $\mathbf{C}^*(t,T)$, is contingent *only* on survival in each period. It follows that $\mathbf{C}^*(t,T)$ maximizes

$$V^e[\mathbf{C}(t,T)] = \sum_{i=t}^{T} PR(i|t)\alpha(i,t)U(i,C_i) \qquad (2.28)$$

subject to the constraints in (2.26). In other words, $\mathbf{C}^*(t,T)$ maximizes the expected value of the nonoptimal objective function subject to the constraints.

The agent's problem is identical in form to the one considered in the previous subsection. The results given there apply, therefore, to this case provided the intertemporal utility function is defined by (2.28).[8]

For a multiple-person family, however, uncertain lifetimes complicate the family's optimization problem considerably.[9] These complications, which are present regardless of whether borrowing is restricted, are discussed in Chapter 4.

2.2.4 The Effect of Liquidity Constraints on Consumption

How are liquidity constraints likely to affect the optimal consumption plan? To answer this question it is necessary to distinguish between two qualitatively different kinds of liquidity constraints: (1) Those arising because of the desire to consume earlier than income is received and (2) those arising because of a desire to acquire assets.

First, consider liquidity constraints arising for the first reason. These are more likely to arise the more noninterest income is concentrated in the later years of life, and the greater is the family's impatience.

Assuming the family desires a relatively smooth consumption profile, the first consideration suggests that the net worth accumulation path, corresponding to the optimal consumption plan, commonly looks like the one given in Figure 2.3. As before, it is assumed that the minimal levels of net worth are time-invariant at B. Between times t and w the household, whose net worth path is illustrated in the diagram, would like to borrow against its relatively plentiful future income to increase its current consumption but cannot. (The interval $[t,w]$ is made up of a sequence of single-period consumption phases and the first cutoff date, v, is period $t + 1$.) Therefore, the family consumes its disposable income in excess of the discounted change in the minimum level of net worth in each period of the interval $[t,w]$. Note that there is no desire to move resources forward within this interval because it is assumed that the

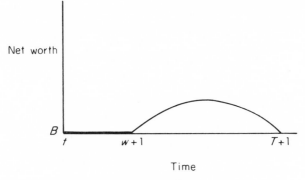

Figure 2.3

family's marginal rate of time preference is decreasing owing to increasing income (consumption). At time w, however, income has increased to the point where the household wishes to move some resources forward to the retirement years when earnings are low. This continues until retirement, at which time the household begins to draw upon its accumulated net worth.

In this scenario there are only two regimes. The family is either liquidity constrained and consumes its entire disposable income in excess of the discounted change in the minimum level of net worth (interval $[t,w]$) or the family is an unconstrained lifetime planner (interval $[w + 1,T]$). This is in accord with the popular belief that unless a family consumes its entire income, it is not liquidity constrained (for example, Thurow, 1969). But, as is evident from the model developed above, at any point in time there are as many possible regimes associated with liquidity constraints as there are periods remaining in a family's life, each regime corresponding to a different cutoff date. The example depicted in the diagram illustrates only two regimes: when the cutoff date is one period in the future and when it is equal to T.

In what circumstances would the family be liquidity constrained and have a multiperiod horizon? Figure 2.4, which illustrates the situation, is helpful for answering this question. The family whose net-worth path is illustrated in the figure is consuming less than its income during the interval $[t,q]$ so that it may consume more than its income during the interval $[q + 1,w]$. It is also true that the consumption plan $\mathbf{C}^u(t,w + 1)$ results in $\mathbf{A}^u(t,w + 1) \not\geqq \mathbf{B}(t,w + 1)$ (Proposition 2.2) so that adding one more year to the plan results in a movement of resources backward from period $w + 1$ to earlier periods. The situation, therefore, is such that the family would like to move resources forward from the interval

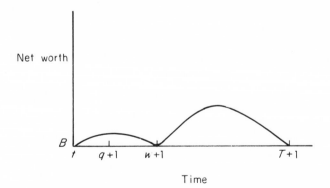

Figure 2.4

$[t,q]$ and backward from period $w + 1$ to finance additional consumption during the interval $[q + 1,w]$. Assuming that noninterest income is increasing throughout the interval $[t,w]$, it must be that consumption "needs" are unusually high during the interval $[q + 1,w]$. A likely possibility is that family size is unusually large during this interval.[10]

A net worth profile like that in Figure 2.4 also can result from an atypical time profile of net receipts. Consider, for example, a family exactly like the one whose net worth path is illustrated in Figure 2.3, except that it receives a windfall in period p, where $t < p \leqslant w - 1$. If the windfall is large enough so that it is allocated to more than one period's consumption, but small enough so that it does not affect consumption subsequent to period q, where $q \leqslant w$, then the net worth path for this family is identical to the one given in Figure 2.3 except that it spikes in period $p + 1$ and falls back to the minimum allowable level in period $q + 1$. Hence, at time p the family is liquidity constrained and has a multiperiod horizon.

So far we have only considered liquidity constraints that arise because of the desire to move relatively plentiful future resources backward to the less prosperous early phase of the life cycle. But when lifetimes are uncertain, liquidity constraints may become binding late in life as well. Consider the case of the previous subsection, where the agent is one individual with no dependents and an uncertain lifetime. In this case the agent maximizes expected utility where the expectation is taken over the date of death. So, late in life when the conditional probability of surviving becomes smaller, the agent's effective rate of time preference is becoming larger, and this encourages earlier consumption.[11] If not faced with the net worth constraints prior to period $T + 1$, the agent may be inclined to borrow against future income (most probably an annuity or pension if there is any at all), and gamble that he will not live to period T, after which his net worth must not be less than $B_{T+1} > 0$. In this case the constraints on net worth become binding. Furthermore, since the desire to borrow against future income will increase as the conditional probability of living gets smaller, these late-life constraints will result in a sequence of single-period consumption phases beginning at some age q and ending at age T. Consumption in each of these periods is equal to income in excess of the discounted change in the minimum level of net worth, and net worth coincides with its minimum allowable level beginning in period $q + 1$. It is clear that an elderly family with no noninterest income will not be liquidity constrained.

The second type of liquidity constraint, that arising because of the desire to acquire an asset, say a home, also leads to a short multiperiod horizon. Figure 2.5 illustrates this situation. The home is purchased in

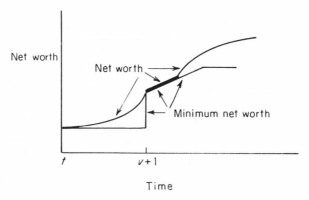

Time

Figure 2.5

period v and the required level of net worth in this period rises by the amount of the down payment. The family chooses the date v so as to trade off the benefits of earlier ownership of the home against the cost of having to acquire the down payment more quickly. After the purchase date the minimum level of net worth continues to rise according to the rate at which the family is required to acquire equity in the home. The constraint may be binding for some time after the purchase but eventually income is sufficiently high so that the family accumulates net worth for retirement at a rate exceeding the required rate.

SUMMARY

The main results of this subsection are summarized below.

(1) Liquidity constraints are most likely to be effective (a) the more labor income is concentrated late in life, and (b) the greater the agent's taste for early consumption.

(2) Liquidity constraints may be effective but not result in a family consuming all its available resources. Cases where a family is liquidity-constrained and still has a multiperiod horizon are (a) when the family is temporarily large or it is anticipated that the family will become temporarily large, (b) when the family receives some sort of a windfall, and (c) when the family wishes to accumulate a down payment to purchase an asset. We expect that these situations are quite common.

(3) The popular notion that liquidity constraints lead a family to consume all its available resources is likely to be valid in those cases where (a) the family is young and family size is not expected to change appreciably, or (b) the family is old and receiving pension or annuity income.

2.3 A Consumption Model with Planned Bequests

In recent years many models have been formulated that allow for endogenous bequests. There have been two basic approaches: to include bequests as a choice variable in the intertemporal utility function (see, for example, Yaari, 1965; and Blinder, 1975), and to include the lifetime utility levels experienced by the agent's descendants in her lifetime utility function (see, for example, Barro, 1974; Bevan, 1979; Drazen, 1978; Laitner, 1979; and Shorrocks, 1979). The first approach is far simpler but leads to the unrealistic conclusion that bequests left to one's children are independent of their earning capacity. The second approach has much more potential for yielding useful conclusions. We consider a model of this sort below.

UNILATERAL INTERGENERATIONAL ALTRUISM

Consider a family with one agent per generation. Let V_i represent the total utility of agent i, where i denotes the generation. It is assumed that V_i is a monotonically increasing and concave function of utility derived from agent i's lifetime consumption and the total utility of his child:

$$V_i = V_i[U_i(\mathbf{C}_i), V_{i+1}], \tag{2.29}$$

where each generation lives $T + 1$ periods and $\mathbf{C}_i = (C_{i0}, C_{i1}, \ldots, C_{iT})$. Note that (2.29) is not completely general since V_i is independent of V_{i-1}, the total utility of agent i's parent. This is nearly always assumed in models of this type. The shortcomings of this assumption are discussed below.

It is assumed that labor income and the rate of return in each future period are known and that each agent i receives a nonnegative gift, say I_i, from her parent at age 0. The consumption feasibility set for agent i, conditional on her net transfer, is

$$S_i(W_i') = \left\{ \mathbf{C} \in R^{T+1} + \mid \sum_{j=0}^{T} P[j, i(T+1)] C_j \leq W_i' \right\},$$

where

$$P[j, i(T+1)] = \prod_{k=i(T+1)}^{i(T+1)+j-1} (1 + R_k)^{-1}, \quad \text{for } j = 1, 2, \ldots, T,$$

$$= 1, \quad \text{for } j = 0,$$

$$W_i' = W_i + TR_i,$$

$$W_i = \sum_{k=0}^{T} P[k, i(T+1)] YL_{ik},$$

$$TR_i = I_i - P[T, i(T+1)] I_{i+1},$$

and YL_{ik} is net noninterest income of agent i when age k. Notice that the subscripting conventions have changed slightly now that more than one agent (generation) is being considered. Consumption and noninterest income now have two subscripts identifying the generation and age, respectively. Also, the interest rate is identified by time measured relative to the date that generation 0 is age 0.

Given the time profile of labor income and interest rates, the budget constraint for agent i's consumption is entirely determined by adjusted full wealth, W_i', which is ordinary full wealth plus net intergenerational transfers, TR_i. This assumes, of course, that there are no borrowing restrictions. This assumption is discussed below.

For a given W_i', agent i maximizes $U(\mathbf{C}_i)$ subject to the constraint that $\mathbf{C}_i \in S_i(W_i')$. A theorem by Fama (1970)[12] implies that there exists a monotonically increasing and strictly concave function, Z_i, defined as

$$Z_i(W_i') = \underset{\mathbf{C}_i \in S_i(W_i')}{\text{Max}} U_i(\mathbf{C}_i).$$

Agent i's problem may now be written

$$\underset{I_{i+1}}{\text{Max}} \; V_i(Z_i(W_i'), V_{i+1}) \quad \text{subject to } I_{i+1} \geq 0, \tag{2.30}$$

where

$$V_{j+1} = V_{j+1}[Z_{j+1}(W_{j+1}'), V_{j+2}],$$
$$W_j' = W_j + I_j - P[T, j(T+1)]I_{j+1}, \qquad j = i, i+1, i+2 \ldots,$$

and agent i's receipt from her parent, I_i, is predetermined.

It is apparent that the solution to (2.30) entails successive nonnegative transfers from one generation to the next and that transfers affect each generation's consumption plan entirely through their effect on adjusted full wealth.

To solve problem (2.30) it is necessary to specify the functions $V_i(\cdot)$ and $U_i(\cdot)$, $i = 0, \ldots$. Fortunately this is not necessary since most of the useful results that can be obtained from such an exercise may be gleaned from the structure of the problem itself. Note, however, that the appropriate method of solving problem (2.30) is dynamic programming. This is because agent i cannot choose the appropriate bequest without knowing the dependence of V_{i+1} on her bequest given that all future agents behave optimally. This necessitates working backward as in the method of dynamic programming.

It is common in the literature to assume that V_i and $U_i(\mathbf{C}_i)$ are additive and that the within-period utility function is of the isoelastic form (see, for example, Bevan, 1979; Laitner, 1979; and Shorrocks, 1979). As is established in Section 2.1.3, these assumptions lead to consumption plans for each generation that satisfy the proportionality hypothesis. An immediate implication is that intergenerational transfers have the effect of shifting the consumption profile of each generation by the factor W_i'/W_i.

Returning to the general problem (2.30), note the following important implications:

(1) For any succession of generations that are linked by positive intergenerational transfers, the composite consumption plan of these generations is dependent on their joint full wealth and not its distribution over the constituent generations (Barro, 1974).

(2) The optimal transfer between generations i and $i + 1$ is more likely to be positive: (a) the larger W_i is relative to W_{i+1}, (b) the smaller $P[T,i(T + 1)]$ is (the higher are interest rates in the interval $[i(T + 1),i(T + 1) + T]$, and (c) the more weight which is given to V_{i+1} relative to Z_i in the utility function V_i.

(3) When the optimal transfer between generations i and $i + 1$ is positive, the conditions stated in (2) have the effect of making the transfer larger.

(4) Net transfers are likely to have a full wealth elasticity greater than one. This is necessarily true in cases where the proportionality hypothesis holds. This is a direct consequence of implication (1). Consider a succession of k generations linked by positive transfers. Then if one such generation, say generation i, experiences an increase in full wealth of $a\%$, then the composite full wealth of the k generations goes up by less than $a\%$ (assuming at least one other generation has a positive full wealth) and the consumption of each of the k generations therefore increases by less than $a\%$. It follows that generation i increases its net transfer by more than $a\%$.

(5) In a cross section one would expect a positive relationship between full wealth across generations of a family. But if earning capacity regresses toward the societal mean, the elasticity of net transfers with respect to full wealth in a cross section is likely to be greater than one (Bevan, 1979).

Note that if implication (5) is true, then the proportionality hypothesis, applied to a single generation, will not be valid. A given change in a generation's full wealth will cause less than a proportionate change in present value of lifetime consumption. It may remain true, however, that a generation's relative consumption levels over time will be independent of its full wealth.

RECIPROCAL INTERGENERATIONAL ALTRUISM

The reader is warned not to confuse the case where bequests are zero in the above model with the case where intergenerational transfers are not operative. Intergenerational transfers are operative so long as there is a net flow of resources from parents to children or from children to parents. The above model does not allow for the possibility that the net flow of resources is from children to parents. This is a serious shortcoming of the model since it suggests that intergenerational transfers are more likely to be inoperative than they would be in a model with reciprocal altruism between parents and children. The reason is clear: Those cases where bequests are likely to be zero in the above model—where children are wealthy relative to their parents and interest rates are low—are precisely those cases where transfers are likely to flow from children to their parents.

An intergenerational consumption model that allows for reciprocal altruism is quite complex. It is apparent, however, that such a model would not be inconsistent with any of the five implications of the unilateral altruism model that are listed above.

LIQUIDITY CONSTRAINTS

The above model assumes there are no borrowing constraints. I argue here that this is appropriate for cases where intergenerational transfers are operative. In so doing, I assume that borrowing constraints impinge only on young families.

First, consider a case where a parent plans to transfer wealth to his child. Clearly the parent will time the transfer so as to alleviate any borrowing constraints that his child may face.

Suppose, conversely, that a child intends to give support to her parents. In this case the child, when young and liquidity constrained, can threaten to reduce the size of her eventual wealth transfer unless her parents grant her a loan. In other words, the child is willing to promise higher than market rates of interest on a loan extended by her parents. Parents would do well, in this case, to extend such a loan.

In all cases where intergenerational transfers are operative, therefore, parents have an incentive to give assistance, whether it be a loan or a wealth transfer, to children who are constrained in the credit market.

3 The Importance of Consumption Behavior for the Effects of Government Fiscal Policies

This chapter begins by demonstrating the pivotal roles played by liquidity constraints and intergenerational transfers for the effects of government fiscal policies on economic growth and aggregate demand. The fiscal policies analyzed are (1) long-run government debt policy, (2) the introduction of an unfunded social security system, and (3) short-run government debt policy.

Section 3.3 surveys recent empirical findings concerning liquidity constraints, intergenerational transfers, and the effects of government fiscal policies. It is observed that these findings are mixed and inconclusive. Methodological problems are cited as possible explanations.

Finally, Section 3.4 briefly contrasts the methodology employed in the current study with that utilized in previous studies.

3.1 Long-Run Fiscal Policy and Growth

In this subsection we consider the effects on the economy's long-run capital intensity of (1) the continual issuance of government debt so as to maintain a constant ratio of debt to labor income, and (2) the implementation of an unfunded social security system. We analyze these policies in the context of a simple one-sector overlapping generations growth model (Samuelson, 1958; Diamond, 1965), which is briefly described below.

3.1.1 A Simple Growth Model

Consider an economy producing one good and composed of individuals who live two periods, working in the first and being retired in the second. Individuals supply one unit of labor in the first period, earn a wage, w, pay taxes, t, on labor earnings, and consume $c_1(w - t,r)$ and $c_2(w - t,r)$, where r is the real net return on savings, in periods 1 and 2, respectively. (Wages, consumption, savings, and capital all are measured in units of product.) The consumption vector $[c_1(w - t,r), c_2(w - t,r)]$ maximizes a monotonically increasing and strictly concave utility function subject to the budget constraint. This implies that $0 < \partial c_1(w - t,r)/\partial(w - t) < 1$. We assume that $\partial c_1(w - t,r)/\partial r < 0$.

Firms combine the labor services of the young generation with the savings (capital) of the old generation in order to generate output. This process is assumed to be governed by a constant return to scale production function so that gross output per laborer, y, depends solely on capital per laborer, k. Let this relationship be represented by $y = f(k)$. Factors receive their marginal products so that $1 + r = f'(k)$ and $w = f(k) - kf'(k)$.

The base-case scenario (which we describe here) is such that government expenditure per worker, g, is constant and there is no government debt so that $t = g$.

The steady-state equilibrium is such that k, and hence w, r, $c_1(w - g,r)$, and $c_2(w - g,r)$, remain constant over time. Per capita savings, therefore, is time-invariant and the steady-state value of k is implicitly defined by the relation $k = [w - g - c_1(w - g,r)]/(1 + n)$. (Recall that w and r depend only on k.) The factor $(1 + n)^{-1}$ enters because laborers work with capital made possible by the savings of the older generation, whose numbers are smaller by the factor $(1 + n)^{-1}$.

3.1.2 Government Debt and Capital Intensity

Suppose the government issues b units of debt per laborer in each period while maintaining the level of its real spending. The steady-state equilibrium condition for this case is

$$k = (1 + n)^{-1}(w - t - c_1 - b) = (1 + n)^{-1}(s_1 - b),$$

where s_1 is the per capita saving of workers, which includes the purchase of government bonds. It is apparent that the steady-state value of k changes, relative to the case of no government debt, by

$$\partial k = (1 + n)^{-1}(\partial s_1 - b). \tag{3.1}$$

We wish to determine the sign of ∂k. Our strategy will be to break down the total change in k into two parts: (1) that which would occur if factor prices remain unchanged (the partial equilibrium effect), and (2) that which occurs because factor prices change (the difference between the general equilibrium effect and the partial equilibrium effect).

First suppose factor prices are unchanged by the new debt policy. Each laborer at the time of the policy change will enjoy a tax reduction of amount b. Per capita taxes of subsequent generations of workers will change by $(1 + r)[b/(1 + n)] - b = b[(1 + r)/(1 + n) - 1]$, where $b(1 + r)/(1 + n)$ is the per capita cost of retiring the debt issued in the previous period. (Per capita is interpreted as "per worker.") It is apparent that steady-state taxes increase or decrease according to whether r is greater than or less than n. Hence the total steady-state per capita saving of the young generation (s_1), which includes the purchase of government bonds, will decrease or increase according to whether r is greater than or less than n. This is the wealth effect of a steady-state increase in government debt and is given by the first term on the right-hand side of (3.1). (Diamond, 1965, refers to this as the "tax effect" of an increase in government debt.)

Government debt also has the effect of substituting paper for real capital in the portfolios of old people. Total per capita savings of the young generation include the purchase of b government bonds. Individual savers regard government bonds as real savings but, from society's point of view, these savings are unproductive. The asset substitution effect of an increase in the steady-state debt, therefore, is to reduce the capital-labor ratio by $b/(1 + n)$. This is the second term on the right-hand side of (3.1).

If $r > n$ then the wealth and asset substitution effects both work to reduce k. If $r < n$, conversely, then the wealth effect increases k and the asset substitution effect decreases k. But in this case the asset substitution effect dominates and the total effect is to reduce k. To see this, note that an upper bound to the wealth effect corresponds to the case where the entire reduction in taxes is saved, so that total per capita savings increase by $\partial s_1 = b[1 - (1 + r)/(1 + n)]$ and the associated change in k is $[b/(1 + n)][1 - (1 + r)/(1 + n)]$. Adding this to the asset substitution effect gives the total change in k, $-b(1 + r)/[(1 + n)^2]$, which clearly is negative.

These results may seem paradoxical when viewing them in terms of consumption. Suppose, for example, that $r = n$ so that taxes are unaffected by the issuance of debt. According to the above discussion, the partial equilibrium effect of an increase in government debt is to leave steady-state consumption at each age unaffected and to reduce capital intensity by $b/(1 + n)$. But, if steady-state consumption at each age is unaffected, aren't real savings (income – consumption – government spending) also unaffected? The paradox is resolved once it is realized that total per capita income is reduced by $(1 + r)$ times the reduction in capital intensity, or $b(1 + r)/(1 + n)$. Hence, when $r = n$, per capita income minus per capita consumption falls by b, which is in agreement with our earlier finding.

We conclude that the effect of increasing the steady-state debt, holding factor prices constant, is to reduce real savings and, hence, k. This decrease in k will increase the return to savings and decrease the wage. This likely will increase total savings, thereby dampening the partial equilibrium reduction in capital intensity.

3.1.3 An Unfunded Social Security System and Capital Intensity

Suppose a social security system is implemented where the government levies a social security tax of b per young person and immediately uses the proceeds to pay $b(1 + n)$ to each old person. The steady-state equilibrium condition in this case is

$$k = (1 + n)^{-1}(w - t - c_1 - b) = (1 + n)^{-1}(s_1 - b),$$

where t denotes ordinary taxes, b denotes social security taxes, and s_1, per capita savings of the young generation, is defined to include social security taxes. The change in k, relative to the case of no social security system, is given by (3.1).

First consider the partial equilibrium change in k. Then the change in the present value of an individual's net receipts is $-b + b(1 + n)/(1 + r) = b[(1 + n)/(1 + r) - 1]$, which is greater than or less than zero according to whether r is less than or greater than n. It follows that total per capita savings of workers (s_1), which are defined to include social security taxes, are increased or decreased according to whether r is greater than or less than n. This is the wealth effect of implementing an unfunded social security system and is given by the first term on the right-hand side of (3.1).

As with the case of government debt, there is also an asset substitution effect. Workers view their social security taxes, b, as if they are real savings. The asset substitution effect therefore reduces k by $b/(1 + n)$. This is the second term on the right-hand side of (3.1).

If $r < n$ then the wealth and asset substitution effects both work to reduce k. If $r > n$, then the wealth effect increases k and the asset substitution effect decreases k. But, as with the case of government debt, the asset substitution effect dominates and the total effect is to reduce k. To see this, note that an upper bound to the wealth effect corresponds to the case where consumption falls by the entire decrease in the present value of lifetime net receipts so that total per capita savings of workers increase by $\partial s_1 = b[1 - (1 + n)/(1 + r)]$ and the associated change in k is $b\{[1/(1 + n)] - [1/(1 + r)]\}$. Adding this to the asset substitution effect gives the total change in k, $-b/(1 + r)$, which is clearly negative.

We conclude that the partial equilibrium effect of an unfunded social security system is to reduce capital intensity. As with the case of government debt, changes in factor prices are likely to stimulate savings, thereby dampening the partial equilibrium reduction in capital intensity.

An important consideration that has been ignored thus far, and which cannot be analyzed in a two-period model, is the possibility that the age at retirement is affected by the social security system. Feldstein (1974) argues that the social security earnings test probably reduces the age at retirement and therefore causes agents to save more during their working years to provide for a longer retirement period.[1] This retirement effect potentially reverses our previous conclusion that the partial equilibrium effect of an unfunded social security system is to reduce capital intensity. We abstract from the retirement effect in the discussion that follows.

3.1.4 The Role of Intergenerational Transfers

Suppose, to simplify the exposition, that $r = n$. For this case we have established that (1) the partial equilibrium effect of introducing b units of government debt per worker is to leave consumption unaffected and to reduce capital intensity by $b/(1 + n)$, and (2) the partial equilibrium effect of introducing social security taxes of amount b per worker, and distributing the proceeds concurrently among members of the old generation, also is to leave consumption unaffected and to reduce capital intensity by $b/(1 + n)$. This case, where $r = n$, reveals yet another paradox. How is capital intensity reduced by these policies if steady-state consumption in unaffected? The answer is apparent once it is recognized that each of these policies, when initially implemented, is particularly beneficial to one generation. In the case of debt, each worker enjoys a reduction in taxes of amount b. In the case of social security, each retired person receives a gift of amount $b(1 + n)$. In each case, it is the fortunate generation that receives a windfall that eats the capital stock. This observation is important because it makes apparent the fact that the real effects of an increase in government debt, as well as the introduction of an unfunded social security system, are entirely due to the induced intergenerational transfers.

Let us pursue the case of government debt still further. Suppose that the young generation at the time of the policy change passes its windfall on to the next generation, say generation 1. Then generation 1 pays taxes to liquidate the debt it now holds. Hence its taxes are effectively reduced by the full amount of the new debt issue, which is b per worker, so that they are in the exact same position as were their parents. If, in turn, generation 1 passes on its windfall to its children, and all subsequent generations do the same, then the existence of the government debt has no real effects. Clearly a similar set of private intergenerational transfers completely offsets transfers induced by an unfunded social security system.

But is it reasonable to expect that these transfers will take place? Barro (1974) has shown that they will take place if, in the initial and final equilibriums, families are linked to their ancestors and descendants by a continual chain of nonzero altruistically motivated transfers. The extended family may be viewed as one agent in this case and any government policy that does not affect the consumption feasibility set for all generations combined will have no real effects. The reason, of course, is that the extended family has already chosen its most preferred consumption plan from among the feasible set (see section 2.3 of Chapter 2). Introducing government debt or an unfunded social security system does not affect the extended family's consumption feasibility set. Therefore, provided transfers are operative, these policies will have no real effects.

It is important to note that intergenerational transfers are operative in the Barro sense only if they are altruistically motivated. If transfers were selfishly motivated, say to influence the behavior of the beneficiaries as suggested by Bernheim, Schleifer, and Summers (1984), then such transfers would not offset government-induced intergenerational transfers. So long as transfers are selfishly motivated, therefore, government fiscal policies have the same qualitative effects as are implied by the standard life-cycle model.

3.1.5 The Role of Liquidity Constraints

In this subsection we suppose that intergenerational transfers are not operative and borrowing is not allowed.

Borrowing constraints cannot be binding in the model considered thus far. This is because there are only two periods and no income is earned in the second period. There are no future resources to borrow against.

Imagine breaking up the preretirement period into two periods, say periods 1A and 1B. Suppose that the initial steady-state equilibrium is such that income is lower at age 1A than at age 1B, and desired consumption at age 1A exceeds disposable income but, because borrowing is not allowed, consumption at age 1A is equal to disposable income. In this case any change in taxes levied on age 1A individuals will change their consumption one for one.

Policy-induced reductions in capital intensity, when liquidity constraints are and are not imposed, are difficult to compare. This is because the initial steady-state equilibrium is different in the two cases. In particular, the initial capital intensity is higher and the interest rate lower when liquidity constraints are imposed. This fact prevents us from making definitive statements in the discussion that follows.

THE CASE OF GOVERNMENT DEBT

It is likely that the partial equilibrium wealth effect of an increase in government debt is diminished in absolute value by the existence of liquidity constraints. If $r > n$ $(r < n)$, then the tax-induced reduction (increase) in total per capita savings of the young generation, which includes the purchase of government bonds, is probably made smaller. It follows that relative to the case where liquidity constraints are not binding, the partial equilibrium reduction in capital intensity is likely to be smaller or larger according to whether $r > n$ or $r < n$.

The effect of liquidity constraints on the general equilibrium change in capital intensity is more difficult to determine. Consider the realistic case where $r > n$. It is possible that the partial equilibrium conclusion for this case, that capital intensity is less affected in the presence of liquidity constraints, is reversed when considering the full general equilibrium change in capital intensity. This is because the interest elasticity of savings is made smaller by liquidity constraints. (Over some range, savings of liquidity-constrained individuals are totally unresponsive to the interest rate.) It follows that the general equilibrium capital intensity will be closer to the partial equilibrium capital intensity when borrowing is restricted than when it is not.

To see this more clearly, suppose $r > n$ and the postdebt general equilibrium interest rate is sufficiently high so that liquidity constraints are not binding. (We assume savings increase with the interest rate.) Then the only consequence of liquidity constraints is to make the predebt general equilibrium capital intensity higher. It follows that the *reduction* in capital intensity is greater when borrowing is restricted than when it is not.

THE CASE OF AN UNFUNDED SOCIAL SECURITY SYSTEM

Liquidity constraints have potentially important implications for the effect of an unfunded social security system on capital intensity. This is because a social security system requires that workers pay significantly higher taxes.

Consider the case where $r = n$. Then, holding w and r constant, social security decreases the net wage and increases disposable income in retirement while leaving the present value of lifetime income, as well as desired consumption at each age, unaffected. To the extent that workers are liquidity-constrained, however, social security taxes will cause consumption to decrease. This phenomenon has the effect of making the social security-induced, partial-equilibrium reduction in capital intensity smaller than it would be in the absence of liquidity constraints.

As with the case of government debt, the effect of liquidity constraints on the full general equilibrium reduction in capital intensity is less clear. Again the reason is that the interest elasticity of savings is made smaller by the existence of liquidity constraints.

In Chapter 11 we simulate the steady-state equilibrium of various stylized economies with and without unfunded social security systems. As expected, the results suggest that liquidity constraints dampen the social security-induced, partial-equilibrium reduction in capital intensity. But, perhaps surprisingly, the simulations suggest that liquidity constraints *magnify* the social security-induced, general-equilibrium reductions in capital intensity.

The simulations also indicate that a social security-induced decrease in the retirement age does *not* lead to a social security-induced increase in the steady-state capital stock.

3.2 Short-Run Fiscal Policy and Aggregate Demand

In this subsection we consider the effect of an aggregate demand of the government unexpectedly issuing debt, which is retired after a finite time interval, while maintaining its real expenditure. We will analyze this question with the aid of a simple life-cycle model similar to that introduced by Modigliani and Brumberg (1954).

Consider an economy composed of identical individuals who live three periods, working and receiving a gross wage w in the first two periods and being retired in the third. For simplicity we assume that (1) the population is stagnant and there is one individual of each age, (2) the interest rate is always zero, and (3) the gross wage is unchanging. These assumptions do not affect our qualitative results.

Following Modigliani and Brumberg we also assume that each individual plans to consume $2w/3$ in each period of his life. These plans are made on the presumption that no taxes will ever be paid.

In period 0, however, the government unexpectedly issues $2b$ one-period bonds, distributes the proceeds equally among workers, and announces that the debt will be retired by levying taxes of b per laborer in the following period. It is assumed that individuals revise their consumption plans in response to this change so as to maintain a constant level of consumption over the remainder of their lifetimes.

The individuals affected by the policy change are the workers at the time of the change, say P_1 and P_2, as well as the newborn in the following period, say P_0. P_1: is age 1 in period 0, receives b in period 0, and pays b in period 1. Her consumption plan, therefore, is unaffected by the policy change. P_2: is age 2 in period 0, also receives b in period 0, but pays no additional taxes in period 1 due to the fact that he is retired. His consumption, therefore, increases by $b/2$ in each of the periods 0 and 1. P_0 gains nothing in period 0 (she is not yet born) and pays taxes of b in period 1. Hence her consumption falls by $b/3$ in each of the periods 1, 2, and 3. Total consumption changes, therefore, by $b/2$, $b/6$, $-b/3$, and $-b/3$ in periods 0, 1, 2, and 3, respectively.

It is apparent that consumption is affected by the short-term issue of debt only to the extent that resources are transferred between generations. As is argued in Section 3.1.4, these debt-induced transfers will be entirely offset by private transfers if private intergenerational transfers are operative in the initial and final equilibriums. Government debt policy, given its expenditure policy, has no effect on consumption in this case.

The marginal propensity to consume the subsidy (tax reduction) in period 0 is only $1/4$. This is because only half the tax reduction is a windfall (P_1 pays additional taxes in period 1) and, of this half, only half is consumed in period 0.

The marginal propensity to consume the tax reduction would be even smaller in a more realistic model with more than three periods. This is because in a multiperiod model, (1) a smaller proportion of those individuals enjoying a tax reduction escape higher future taxes, and (2) those individuals who do receive a windfall allocate the windfall to more than two periods of consumption.

Past experience seems to indicate that tax policy has much larger short-run effects on consumption than is suggested by this example. One reason may be that capital markets are imperfect so that borrowing is restricted. Consider, for example, the above model with borrowing restrictions. Suppose that age 1 income is much smaller than age 2 income so that age 1 consumption is equal to disposable income and age 2 disposable income is equally divided between age 2 and age 3 consumption. We will continue to assume that the subsidy in period 0 as well as the tax increase in period 1 are equally divided among workers. In this case, (1) P_1 consumes her entire tax reduction in period 0 and reduces her consumption by $b/2$ in each of the periods 1 and 2, (2) P_2, as before, increases his consumption by $b/2$ in each of the periods 0 and 1, and (3) P_0 decreases her consumption by b in period 1, thereby leaving her consumption unchanged in periods 2 and 3. The total change in consumption, therefore, is $3b/2$, $-b$, $-b/2$ in periods 0, 1, and 2, respectively. Hence the increase in consumption in period 0, as a portion of the tax reduction, is tripled to $3/4$ by the existence of liquidity constraints.

This model is only illustrative. Again, the assumption of three-period lifetimes may be misleading. Also the assumption that age 1 laborers, who have a relatively low wage, pay the same taxes as age 2 laborers is likely to overstate the importance of liquidity constraints.

In Chapter 10, however, I present realistic simulations for the population of families used to estimate our empirical model. The results indicate that a one-year tax has approximately three to five times as great an effect on aggregate consumption when liquidity constraints are imposed than when they are not.

3.3 Previous Empirical Studies

Liquidity constraints and intergenerational transfers, as well as the effects of fiscal policies for which they play a role, have been the subject of numerous empirical studies. This section contains a brief and selective review of the recent contributions to this literature.

3.3.1 Liquidity Constraints

THE TIME-SERIES EVIDENCE

Modern empirical analyses of consumption were begun by Hall (1978). Hall observes that if intertemporal utility is additive, the within-period utility function is $U(C_t)$, and agents are unconstrained in the credit market, then the first-order conditions for expected utility maximization imply that

$$U'(C_t) = [(1 + \rho)/(1 + R)]U'(C_{t-1}) + \epsilon_t \tag{3.2}$$

where C denotes real consumption expenditures, ρ is the pure rate of time preference, R is the real rate of interest (assumed constant), and ϵ_t is a disturbance term whose expectation, conditional on information available at time $t - 1$, is zero. Note that any predictor of disposable income in period t that depends on information in period $t - 1$, say $\hat{Y}_t$, is independent of ϵ_t.

The consumption of liquidity-constrained agents, conversely, depends on the time profile of their net noninterest income. Those with one-year horizons consume their disposable income so that ϵ_t in (3.2) is correlated with $\hat{Y}_t$. Note that Y_t generally includes an unexpected component and will be correlated with ϵ_t even for life-cycle consumers.

A natural test of whether some consumers are liquidity constrained and have one-period horizons is to estimate (3.2) with $\hat{Y}_t$ included as an explanatory variable. If the coefficient on $\hat{Y}_t$ is negative and significant, the hypothesis that some agents have one-period horizons cannot be rejected. It is important to note, however, that (3.2) is consistent with the consumption behavior of agents that are not currently liquidity constrained but expect to be liquidity constrained at a future date. In other words, the test just proposed cannot be used to distinguish full-fledged life-cycle consumers from consumers with short multiperiod horizons (see Section 2.2 of Chapter 2).

Hall implements a more general test of the life-cycle model using aggregate quarterly U.S time-series data. He assumes that these data are consistent with expected utility maximization of a representative consumer with within-period utility function $(1/\gamma)C^\gamma$. In this case, (3.2) implies that

$$C_t^{\gamma-1} = \alpha C_{t-1}^{\gamma-1} + \mathbf{X}'\boldsymbol{\beta} + \epsilon_t \qquad (3.3)$$

where $\alpha = (1 + \rho)/(1 + R)$, $\mathbf{X}$ is a data vector including variables observable at time $t - 1$, and $\boldsymbol{\beta}$ is a parameter vector, conformable with $\mathbf{X}$, that is zero under the assumptions of the model. Hall considers three sets of variables for $\mathbf{X}$: (1) consumption lagged at least two periods, (2) lagged values of disposable income, and (3) lagged values of the market value of corporate stock. Since aggregate disposable income is well explained by its own lagged values, the second set of explanatory variables incorporates the possibility that the forecast of current disposable income, conditional on its own lagged values, enters (3.3) with a negative coefficient.

Hall begins by estimating (3.3) with $\boldsymbol{\beta}$ set to zero for three values of γ: $\gamma = -4$, $\gamma = 0$, and $\gamma = 2$. The last value of γ is inadmissible but Hall justifies it by a first-order approximation that indicates that consumption is approximately a random walk with trend. (For the random walk specification, a constant term is included and α has a different interpretation.) He finds that the fit of the equation is insensitive to the assumed value of γ. He also observes that the estimated residuals show no signs of autocorrelation for the random walk specification.

Hall then turns to testing the $\boldsymbol{\beta} = \mathbf{0}$ restriction using the three sets of explanatory variables listed above. In so doing he employs the random walk specification. He finds that (1) C_{t-2}, C_{t-3}, C_{t-4} are jointly insignificant; (2) four, as well as twelve, lagged values of disposable income are jointly insignificant; and (3) the lagged change in the value of corporate stock is significant. Hall conjectures that this last result is consistent with the life-cycle model and a short delay in the response of consumption to unexpected changes in wealth.

Flavin (1981) estimates the Hall model with revised data and finds that eight lagged values of income are jointly significant determinants of aggregate consumption. It would be incorrect, however, to attribute this finding to liquidity constraints. Other possibilities are that intertemporal utility is not additive, the within-period utility function is misspecified, and real interest rates vary and are stochastic.

As is argued above, testing whether a predictor of disposable income enters (3.3) with a significantly negative coefficient is a fair test of the life-cycle model vis-à-vis the hypothesis that some agents have one-period horizons. Hayashi (1982) performs such a test. He includes current disposable income as a separate term in his consumption equation and estimates it with instrumental variables.[2] Since his instruments are all observable at time $t - 1$, this amounts to including a predictor of current disposable income, conditional on the instruments, in his specification. He finds that predicted disposable income is an extremely insignificant determinant of nondurables expenditure plus the service flow of durables. He finds that predicted disposable income is a highly significant determinant of total expenditure, however.

These studies have been extended by Hansen and Singleton (1982) and Mankiw, Rotemberg, and Summers (1985). Hansen and Singleton allow the real interest rate to be stochastic. Mankiw et al. also allow the within-period preferences to be nonseparable in goods and leisure consumption. Each study rejects its version of the life-cycle model.

Each of these latter two studies utilize a powerful new estimation technique and specification test developed by Hansen and Singleton (1982). This specification test, if implemented appropriately, can be used to test the life-cycle model vis-à-vis the liquidity constraints hypothesis. I argue, however, that the tests of Hansen and Singleton (henceforth HS) and Mankiw et al., while valid tests of their respective versions of the life-cycle model vis-à-vis all alternatives, do not necessarily reflect the prevalence of liquidity constraints. I demonstrate this in the context of the HS study.

HS assume that the within-period utility function is $(1/\gamma)C^\gamma$ so that a first-order condition for expected utility maximization is

$$_{t-1}E[(1 + R_t)C_t^{\gamma-1}] = (1 + \rho)C_{t-1}^{\gamma-1} \qquad (3.4)$$

where $_{t-1}E$ denotes the expectation conditional on information available at time $t - 1$. The natural extension of the Hall procedure is to assume various values of γ and regress $(1 + R_t)C_t^{\gamma-1}$ on $C_{t-1}^{\gamma-1}$ and other variables observable at time $t - 1$. HS employ a more general procedure. Rearranging (3.4) gives

$$_{t-1}E\{[(1 + R_t)/(1 + \rho)](C_t/C_{t-1})^{\gamma-1}\} - 1 = 0 \qquad (3.5)$$

which implies that

$$h_t(\gamma,\rho) \equiv [(1 + R_t)/(1 + \rho)](C_t/C_{t-1})^{\gamma-1} - 1$$

has a zero mean conditional on any information available to the agent in period $t - 1$. Let Z be a $T \times q$ data matrix, $q \geqslant 2$, where Z_{ij} is observable at time $i - 1$. Then, according to (3.5),

$$_{t-1}E[\mathbf{g}(\gamma,\rho)] \equiv {}_{t-1}E[T^{-1}\mathbf{h}'(\gamma,\rho)Z] = \mathbf{0}_q$$

where $\mathbf{h}'(\gamma,\rho) = [h_1(\gamma,\rho),h_2(\gamma,\rho), \ldots ,h_T(\gamma,\rho)]$. HS suggest choosing γ and ρ so as to make $\mathbf{g}(\gamma,\rho)$ "close" to the zero vector. In particular, they obtain consistent estimates of γ and ρ by minimizing the scalar-valued function

$$J(\gamma,\rho) \equiv \mathbf{g}'(\gamma,\rho) \, W\mathbf{g}(\gamma,\rho)$$

where W is symmetric positive definite $q \times q$ weighting matrix chosen so as to minimize the asymptotic covariance matrix of the estimator. Note that $J(\gamma,\rho)$ is increasing in q, the number of variables (instruments) included in Z. Hansen (1982) shows that (3.5) implies that $J(\gamma,\rho) \cdot T$ is asymptotically distributed as a chi-square random variable with $q - 2$ degrees of freedom. (Recall that two parameters are estimated.) Since γ and ρ are identified with two instruments, the value of $J(\gamma,\rho) \cdot T$ for $q > 2$ can be used to test the overidentifying restrictions. An improbably high value of $J(\gamma,\rho) \cdot T$ casts doubt on the assumptions implicit in (3.5).

It is useful to determine how the Hall test of the life-cycle model compares with the HS procedure. For the case considered by Hall we have

$$h_t(\alpha) = C_t^{\gamma-1} - \alpha C_{t-1}^{\gamma-1}$$

where it is assumed that γ is known. It is easily shown that the HS estimator of α, when the errors are homoscedastic and the weighting matrix is chosen optimally, reduces to the two-stage least-squares estimator. Provided the instruments include $C_{t-1}^{\gamma-1}$, this implies that the HS estimator of α is the Hall least-squares estimator of α.

One would expect that the Hall F-test of whether additional explanatory variables observed at time $t - 1$ have zero coefficients in the regression of $C_t^{\gamma-1}$ on $C_{t-1}^{\gamma-1}$, and the HS test of the overidentifying restrictions due to including these same variables in their instrument list, are related. In fact, it can be shown that

$$S^{HS} = S^H(q-1)/[1 + S^H(q-1)/(T-1)] \simeq S^H(q-1) \qquad (3.6)$$

where S^{HS} is the HS chi-square test statistic, S^H is the Hall F-test statistic, and $q-1$ is the number of additional explanatory variables (overidentifying restrictions). The approximate equality in (3.6) assumes q is small relative to T. $S^H(q-1)$ is asymptotically distributed as a chi-square random variable with $q-1$ degrees of freedom. Hence, for large T, the Hall and HS test statistics give nearly identical results.

It is apparent, therefore, that the HS specification test is a fair test of the life-cycle model vis-à-vis the liquidity-constraints hypothesis only if $_{t-1}E[Y_t]$ is the only overidentifying instrument used. Since HS and Mankiw et al. (1985) do not include anything resembling $_{t-1}E[Y_t]$ in their respective instrument lists, their tests do not necessarily reflect on the prevalence of liquidity constraints.

Summers (1982) uses an alternative methodology to test the liquidity-constraints hypothesis in a model similar to that of HS. He assumes that liquidity-constrained individuals consume their entire labor income (presumably their net worth is zero) and that they earn the portion λ of aggregate labor income, YL. His model is exactly like the HS model except that $C_i - \lambda YL_i$ substitutes for C_i, $i = t-1, t$. Summers' estimate of λ is very sensitive to the measure employed for the interest rate and in no case is significantly different than zero. It appears, therefore, that HS's rejection of their model's overidentifying restrictions cannot be explained by the existence of liquidity-constrained individuals.

THE CROSS-SECTION EVIDENCE

Hall and Mishkin (1982) (henceforth HM) use data for a panel of U.S. families to measure the prevalence of liquidity constraints. They employ a unique methodology that requires them to make the following assumptions.

(1) Deterministic income change is a linear function of a constant, the age of the household head *(AGE)*, AGE^2, the change in the number of children in the household, the change in the number of adults in the household, and time. The parameters of this function are constant across families, and the econometrician is able to measure them without error.

(2) Families can, without error, decompose nondeterministic income change into a permanent component and a transitory component that follows a second-order moving average process with known parameters.

(3) The stochastic properties of nondeterministic income change are common to all families.

(4) Preferences are such that certainty-equivalence holds and families consume in accordance with the present value of expected future noninterest income.

(5) Preferences are such that a marginal increment to a family's lifetime resources causes the expected change in consumption to be the same at each future date.

These assumptions place restrictions on the joint distribution of changes in food consumption and income that identify the parameters of HM's model. (HM's data do not contain a reliable measure of total consumption.) Their initial estimates suggest that food consumption is excessively sensitive to transitory income. They also observe that the change in food consumption is negatively correlated with nondeterministic income change lagged one year. Their life-cycle model indicates that this correlation should be zero. This negative correlation is consistent with the hypothesis that some families are liquidity constrained and consume their entire disposable income. HM therefore estimate a model that allows the portion μ of families to consume their entire disposable income. Again, life-cycle consumers are not distinguished from consumers with short multiperiod horizons. The estimates of this augmented model indicate that it is 95% certain that more than 9.2% of families in the sample consume in accordance with their disposable income.[3] Also, the augmented model yields a more reasonable estimate of the life-cycle propensity to consume transitory income.

It is argued in Appendix C that the HM estimate of μ, say $\hat{\mu}$, is much less certain than its standard error would suggest. It is demonstrated that allowing for error in the measurement of nondeterministic income change biases the parameter estimates. The simple model given in Appendix C suggests that $\hat{\mu}$ is upward biased but this inference may not be valid for HM's more elaborate model.

Bernanke (1984) uses panel data and the HM methodology to fit a continuous stock adjustment model for automobile expenditures. His estimates indicate that it is 95% certain that less than 1.8% of his sample is liquidity constrained. This finding is not surprising in light of the discussion of Section 2.2.4 of Chapter 2. It was argued there that the desire to buy a durable leads to a short multiperiod horizon. As is pointed out above, the HM methodology treats short multiperiod horizons as being consistent with the life-cycle model.

Hayashi (1984) improves on the HM methodology to estimate the prevalence of liquidity constraints in a panel of Japanese families. His data are particularly well suited for this purpose. They include expenditures on seven mutually exclusive and exhaustive commodity groups, and one-quarter-ahead expectations of income and expenditures for each commodity group. Hence, unlike HM and Bernanke, Hayashi has a relatively error-free measure and expected income change.

Hayashi's preliminary analysis of the data reveals that (1) expenditure change tends to be negativ ly correlated with lagged income change, (2) expenditure change for each commodity group displays significant negative first-order autocorrelation, and (3) some forecast errors have a significant *sample* correlation across families with information available at the time of the forecast.

The first two findings are consistent with the findings of HM and the hypothesis that some families are liquidity constrained. Hayashi notes that these findings may also be explained by commodity durability. To see this, suppose that a family's current income is unexpectedly high. Then current expenditures rise and, because this expenditure yields future services, future expenditures tend to be depressed.

The third finding, which concerns forecast errors, appears to refute the rational expectations hypothesis. Hayashi points out, however, that rational expectations leads to no predictions concerning the correlation of forecast errors with other variables in a cross-section of families. This calls into question the HM and Bernanke estimation procedure, which assumes that forecast errors are uncorrelated across families with information available at the time of the forecast.

Hayashi formulates an optimizing model that allows for the possibility that commodities are durable and that some fraction of families are liquidity constrained and consume their entire disposable income. Since data are available for expected income and expenditure change, he is able to estimate the model without imposing the false rational expectations orthogonality conditions or making assumptions regarding the stochastic properties of income change. The estimates indicate that it is 95% certain that more than 12.6% of the sample is liquidity constrained. Furthermore, many commodity groups show significant durability.

Hall and Mishkin (1982), Bernanke (1984), and Hayashi (1984) each employ a hybrid consumption model. That is, their models are a combination of a life-cycle specification and a liquidity-constraints specification. Hence, when fitting such a model to cross-section data, the specification is incorrect for all families. This implies that these models include an error term with a binomial distribution. This error results in biased parameter estimates if, as is likely, the probability of being liquidity constrained is dependent on the explanatory variables. For example, the estimates of each of these three studies are biased if the mean and variance of expected income change are different for constrained and unconstrained families. (Appendix C argues this point in the context of the Hall and Mishkin study.)

Hayashi (1985) uses an innovative technique to study the effect of liquidity constraints in a cross section of families. He finds that a reduced-form consumption function fit for families whose predicted consumption is less than 85% of their disposable income plus 17% of their financial assets (the restricted sample) is significantly different than the same reduced-form specification estimated for his entire sample. He also finds that the consumption function fit for the restricted sample, which he interprets as the life-cycle reduced-form consumption function, tends to overpredict the consumption of families excluded from the restricted sample. Hayashi estimates that total consumption in the sample (population sampled) would be about 2.8% (5.8%) higher if all families consumed according to the estimated reduced-form life-cycle model.

An alternative interpretation of these results is that tastes (the parameters) are randomly distributed across families in the sample and are correlated with net worth. (See, for example, Crockett, 1964, and Crockett and Friend, 1967.) This implies that Hayashi's restricted sample, which overrepresents high-wealth families, tends to include families with an unusual tendency to postpone consumption. This view is given support by the fact that Hayashi's results are quite sensitive to the sample selection criterion. When the restricted sample includes families whose predicted consumption is less than 85% of disposable income, so that the sample selection criterion is more conservative and not so closely tied to net worth, Hayashi estimates that total consumption in the sample would be 0.002% *smaller* if all families consumed according to the estimated "life-cycle" model. This finding suggests that random tastes, which are correlated with net worth, are at least partially responsible for the apparent behavioral differences between Hayashi's preferred restricted sample and the entire sample.[4]

SUMMARY

Most of the time-series evidence does not necessarily reflect the importance of liquidity constraints. The exceptions are Hayashi (1982) and Summers (1982). Hayashi finds that liquidity constraints are unimportant for the consumption of nondurables plus the service flow of durables. Summers' findings suggest that Hansen and Singleton's (1982) rejection of the life-cycle model can not be explained by the existence of liquidity-constrained individuals.

The cross-section evidence suggests that liquidity constraints are important. The exception is Bernanke (1984), who finds that liquidity constraints have little effect on automobile expenditures. But as is argued above, Bernanke's methodology is inappropriate for detecting the influence of liquidity constraints on durables expenditure.

I wish to draw attention to two basic drawbacks to the methodology employed in the studies reviewed here. First, these studies do not differentiate between a life-cycle consumer from a consumer with a short multiperiod horizon. This potentially biases their conclusions considerably. My findings reported in Chapter 7 indicate that short multiperiod horizons are more common than one-period horizons. Second, previous cross-section studies employ hybrid models where, *if* the probability of being liquidity constrained is independent of the explanatory variables, a parameter measures the proportion of families in the sample that have one-period horizons. This parameter yields little information regarding the importance of liquidity constraints for aggregate consumption. Furthermore, since a hybrid model does not identify liquidity-constrained families, it is impossible to implement independent checks of such a model's specification. If liquidity-constrained families were identified, conversely, it would be possible to check that their observable characteristics are consistent with the liquidity constraints classification. We will return to these points in Chapter 7.

3.3.2 Intergenerational Transfers

This subsection reviews empirical evidence relating directly and indirectly to the prevalence of operative intergenerational transfers. The direct evidence surveyed concerns the prevalence and size of bequests, whether bequests are planned, the prevalence and size of gifts received by retired individuals, and whether the life-cycle model is consistent with (1) the wealth distribution, (2) the size of the capital stock, (3) the amount of aggregate annual savings, and (4) the rate that individuals dissave during retirement. The indirect evidence concerns the relationship of consumption to the government's debt policy and the existence of an unfunded social security system.

Much of the evidence presented below concerns only the issue of whether planned intergenerational transfers are common. As is pointed out in Section 3.1.4, operative transfers must also be altruistically motivated. Since the evidence suggests that planned transfers are uncommon, the issue of motivation is discussed only briefly.

DIRECT EVIDENCE

The current evidence suggests that about 50% of individuals never receive an inheritance, and large bequests are a rarity. In a 1959 survey,

73% of individuals between the ages of 55 and 64 reported never having received an inheritance. Less than 2% of individuals in this age group had received inheritances in excess of $25,000, which is about six times the average annual labor earnings in 1959 (Blinder, 1976). Tomes (1981, 1982) analyzes a random sample of estates probated in the Cleveland, Ohio, area in 1964–65 and finds that the average gross estate was only $12,000. There was a surviving spouse in about two-thirds of the cases, and children of decedents received only about one-third of the total sample bequests. In fact, 41.5% of decedents' children received no inheritance. Bloomquist (1979) analyzes data from a 1968 Swedish survey and finds that about 60% of individuals never receive an inheritance.

Although large bequests are unusual, it appears that they are quantitatively important. Kotlikoff and Summers (1981), in an extremely careful study, estimate that no more than 20% of the U.S. capital stock is explained by life-cycle savings. They attribute the residual to planned and unplanned bequests. This result is consistent with White (1978) who finds that aggregate savings in the United States are too large to be explained by the life-cycle consumption model. Further supporting evidence is given by Atkinson (1971) and Oulton (1976). They conclude that the life-cycle model cannot explain the large share of wealth held by top wealth-holders in Britain. Atkinson finds that the distribution of wealth among the lower 95% of the wealth distribution, however, can be explained by a reasonable life-cycle model that assumes complete equality of labor earnings within age cohorts. That is, age, population growth, and productivity growth can explain the observed variance in wealth among families in the lower 95% of the British wealth distribution.

The issue of primary concern is whether private intergeneration transfers are operative at the margin. The fact that material transfers at death tend to be small does not preclude the possibility that they are planned and altruistically motivated. Projector and Weiss (1966, Table A30) give evidence that planned bequests are uncommon in the United States. Only 4% of respondents in their survey, which overrepresents wealthy families, reported that they are saving to leave an estate or to help their children establish households. This figure is virtually constant across age groups. Tomes (1981), however, finds that a child's inheritance is negatively related to the average income of the decedent's children and that relatively affluent children tend to receive a smaller inheritance than their siblings. He interprets this as evidence that bequests, despite their small size, tend to be planned so as to help equalize consumption across generations. It should be noted, however, that this evidence is also consistent with completely selfish behavior on the part of each generation. There are at least two possibilities. First, affluent children may selfishly provide insurance to their parents against the possibility of their living relatively long lives and being caught short of resources (see Kotlikoff and Spivak, 1981). This ability to share risk results in parents holding a smaller precautionary asset reserve than they would otherwise. A second possibility is that parents of affluent children plan less conservatively than their children would like, knowing that their children will support them if necessary.

Another set of evidence relating to planned bequests concerns the wealth-age relationship. Mirer (1979) employs a linear regression of wealth on age and a constant for a sample of 8,248 families whose head is at least 65 years of age and retired. For the whole sample, he estimates that wealth falls only $142 per year. When segmenting the sample into groups according to education, which are more homogeneous with respect to lifetime earnings, he estimates that wealth actually increases after retirement. King and Dicks-Mireaux (1982) use Canadian survey data on 12,734 households to estimate a more elaborate net-worth specification that controls for lifetime income. They estimate that net worth increases until age 71 and then falls at about a 1% annual rate. The parameter that determines the timing and rate of decumulation, however, is not estimated very precisely. Their estimated rate of decumulation is in rough agreement with the simulation results of Davies (1981), which indicate that the optimal annual rate of asset decumulation between the ages of 65 and 85, when lifetimes are uncertain, is between 2% and 3%.

It is possible that bequests are largely unplanned but intergenerational transfers are operative and tend to take the form of gifts. A likely possibility, given that children tend to be more affluent than their parents and also receive substantial material transfers when young, is that retired parents tend to receive assistance from their children. The evidence, however, indicates that gifts from children to retired parents are of negligible importance. Bixby (1970), for example, analyzes a 1968 survey and finds that gifts were received by 3% of aged retired people. These gifts tended to be small, averaging 1% of the recipient's retirement income.

The evidence summarized above suggests that intergenerational transfers are planned by only a small minority of families, most of whom are extremely wealthy. Moreover, intergenerational transfers may be inoperative even for these families. Bernheim, Schleifer, and Summers (1984) present convincing evidence that a significant share of planned transfers are selfishly motivated.

These findings suggest that the social security system and government debt policy have significant effects on saving. This is especially true in the case of social security since social security wealth is concentrated among low-income and middle-income individuals.

GOVERNMENT DEBT AND SAVING

Kochin (1974) uses annual aggregate U.S. time-series data to estimate a consumption function including either the federal deficit or the full-employment federal deficit as an explanatory variable. He finds that each dollar of government debt (full-employment debt) decreases aggregate consumption by $0.22 ($0.12). Each of these estimates is significant at the 2.5% level.

Kormendi (1983) also investigates the debt issue with annual U.S. time-series data. He finds that government spending, and not taxes, is the relevant explanatory variable in the consumption function. This, of course, indicates that each dollar of debt is equivalent to a dollar of taxes in its effect on aggregate consumption.

Each of these studies fails to take account of the national income identity, $Y = C + I + G$, in their respective specifications. Suppose, for example, that income is independent of the governments debt/tax policy. Then an increase in government spending, holding taxes constant, must decrease the sum of consumption and investment regardless of whether individuals view new debt as equivalent to taxation. If individuals do not take future taxes into account, either due to myopia or the expectation of escaping future taxation, consumption is decreased by the deficit-induced increase in interest rates. Kochin and Kormendi do not include the interest rate in their respective specifications. Their results, therefore, are of limited value of determining the effect of government debt/tax policy on aggregate consumption.

SOCIAL SECURITY AND SAVINGS

The Time-Series Evidence All studies of social security that utilize time-series data have related aggregate U.S. consumption to a measure of aggregate social security wealth. To understand these studies it is useful to construct an aggregate consumption function that is consistent with a reasonable specification for individual consumption. Suppose a family's consumption at age i is

$$C_i = b_i[WN(O,T) - SSW(O,L) + \lambda SSW(O,T)], \qquad (3.7)$$
$$i = 0,1, \ldots ,T,$$

where L is the age of retirement, T is the certain age of death, $WN(O,T)$ is the present value, at economic age zero, of lifetime net noninterest income, $-SSW(O,L)$ is the present value at economic age zero of lifetime social security taxes, $SSW(O,T)$ is the present value at economic age zero of net lifetime social security benefits (taxes are negative benefits), and λ is a zero/one variable indicating whether or not social security has an effect on consumption. Note that social security taxes, but not benefits, are incorporated into $WN(O,T)$.

The scalars b_i, $i = 0,1, \ldots ,T$ satisfy the lifetime budget constraint. That is,

$$\sum_{i=0}^{T} (1 + R)^{-i}b_i = 1$$

where R is the real rate of interest and is assumed constant. Note that (3.7) implies that $C_{k+1}/C_k = b_{k+1}/b_k, k = 0,1, \ldots ,T$, and is consistent with the Yaari (1964) model (see Section 2.1 of Chapter 2).

Since (3.7) is linear in $WN(O,T)$, $SSW(O,L)$, and $SSW(O,T)$, with coefficients depending only on age, we have that

$$C_i = b_i[WN_i(O,T) - SSW_i(O,L) + \lambda SSW_i(O,T)], \qquad i = 0,1, \ldots ,T$$

where variables with an i subscript are understood to be aggregated over all individuals aged i. Summing over cohorts gives the aggregate consumption function

$$\sum C_i = \sum b_i WN_i(O,T) + \lambda \sum b_i(1 + R)^{-i}SSW_i(i,T) \qquad (3.8)$$
$$+ \sum b_i[\lambda SSW_i(O,i - 1) - SSW_i(O,L)]$$

where $SSW(i,T)$ is the present value at age i of net social security payments received between the ages of i and T.

All the time-series studies of social security have utilized specifications of the form:

$$C_i = C^* + \beta \sum SSW_i(i,T) \qquad (3.9)$$

where C^* controls for $\Sigma b_i WN_i(O,T)$ and is linear in such variables as disposable income, wealth, and retained earnings. The second term in (3.9) is appropriate, according to (3.8), only if individual consumption, and hence the b's, grow at the rate of interest. Granting this assumption, the specification (3.9) is still defective due to the omission of the third term in (3.8). This causes the OLS parameter estimates of (3.9) to be biased and sensitive to the joint distribution of $\Sigma b_i SSW_i(O,L)$, $\Sigma SSW_i(i,T)$, and $\Sigma b_i SSW_i(0,i - 1)$ over time. This suggests that the estimates of (3.9) are sensitive to the sample period.

Simulations performed by Auerbach and Kotlikoff (1983a) verify these conclusions. They estimate (3.9) with simulated aggregate data that are consistent with the life-cycle model. The estimated coefficient on $\Sigma SSW_i(i,T)$ is extremely sensitive to the sample period and is often the wrong sign.

Given these considerations, it is not surprising that estimates of (3.9) have yielded inconclusive results. Feldstein (1974) estimates a significantly positive coefficient on $\Sigma SSW_i(i,T)$ provided the years 1929–1940 are included in the sample. Barro (1978) shows that these results are sensitive to the specification for C^*. Leimer and Lesnoy (1982) correct an error in the social security wealth series and find that corrected variable is less significant in Feldstein's original specification (see also Feldstein, 1982). In fact, the estimated social security wealth coefficient is negative when excluding the prewar years from the sample.

The Cross-Section Evidence All the cross-section studies of social security here reviewed relate a family's net worth to a measure of social security wealth. To interpret these studies we continue to utilize the prototype consumption model given in (3.7). This model implies that net worth at age k is

$$A_k = A_k^* + \beta_1(1 + R)^{k-1}SSW(0,T) + \beta_2(1 + R)^{k-1}SSW(0,k - 1) \quad (3.10)$$

where A_k^* is net worth at age k if there were no social security system, $\beta_1 = -\lambda \Sigma_{i=0}^{k-1} (1 + R)^{-i}b_i$ is age-dependent, β_2 is one, and λ is the zero/one variable indicating whether or not social security has an effect on consumption. The second term in (3.10) is due to the social security-induced changes in consumption and the third term is due to social security-induced changes in net receipts. This specification assumes that all intergenerational transfers take place in the future.[5]

The only studies that utilize proper specification for the effect of social security on net worth are Kurz (1985) and Kotlikoff (1979b). Neither study, however, is able to statistically distinguish between the hypothesis $\beta_1 = 0$ and β_1 is in accord with the life-cycle model and the age distribution of the respective samples.[6] (Kurz allows β_1 to vary with age and Kotlikoff restricts his sample to families whose head is between the ages of 45 and 59.)

Feldstein and Pellechio (1979) and Feldstein (1983) estimate specifications of the form

$$A_k = A_k^* + \alpha SSW(k,T) \quad (3.11)$$

The prototype model (3.10) can be expressed as

$$A_k = A_k^* + \beta_1 SSW(k,T) + (\beta_1 + \beta_2)(1 + R)^{k-1}SSW(0,k - 1). \quad (3.12)$$

These two studies leave the third term of (3.12) out of their respective specifications. Retired families are not included in the sample of either

CONSUMPTION BEHAVIOR

study so that $(1 + R)^{k-1}SSW(0,k - 1)$ is minus the accumulated value of past social security taxes which is negatively correlated with $SSW(k,t)$. It follows since $\beta_1 + \beta_2 > 0$ that these studies obtain an estimate of α that is a downward-biased estimate of β_1. Even if this bias is ignored, the estimate of α for each study is too imprecise to distinguish between the life-cycle model and the alternative.

Blinder, Gordon, and Wise (1983) employ a tightly parameterized version of the life-cycle model for net worth with a free parameter measuring the impact of social security wealth on net worth. They fail to include social security taxes, past or future, in their measure of social security wealth. This biases their results in favor of the life-cycle model. Even so, they are unable to statistically distinguish between the life-cycle model and the alternative.

King and Dicks-Mireaux (1982) (henceforth KD) claim to have demonstrated that social security has a significant positive impact on consumption. Their specification for net worth is seriously flawed, however. They (1) fail to consider social security taxes, (2) assume the relationship between net worth and social security wealth is double-log-linear, and (3) include the entire age spectrum in their sample but fail to allow the coefficient on their social security wealth variable to depend on age. The last two assumptions are particularly disturbing. Consider, for example, a family whose social security wealth is 1% of total lifetime resources. The estimates of KD imply that doubling social security wealth to 2% of lifetime resources would lead to a 20% reduction in net worth at every age! It is my view, in light of these considerations, that KD's social security wealth variable is simply proxying for variables left out of the A^* portion of their specification.

Summary The time-series evidence regarding social security and consumption is extremely weak. This is not surprising given that multicollinearity is so pervasive in aggregate time-series data. This problem is compounded by the failure of these studies to control for past social security taxes.

Previous cross-section studies are also unable to distinguish between the life-cycle model and the alternative. Three reasons are apparent. First, all but two of the studies reviewed here are misspecified with respect to social security's effect on net worth. Second, net worth is extremely difficult to explain. The R^2 statistics are Kurz, 0.34; Kotlikoff, 0.33; Feldstein and Pellechio, 0.16; Feldstein, 0.03, and King and Dicks-Mireaux, 0.46. (Blinder et al. do not report a meaningful measure of fit.) It is difficult to isolate social security's effect on net worth when the variance of the underlying disturbance is so high. The third reason for the inconclusive results is that social security benefits and taxes are nonlinear functions of labor income so that the social security wealth variables in these studies are correlated with the components of A^*. This multicollinearity results in imprecise estimates of social security's impact on net worth. This explains why social security is estimated to have a smaller and less significant effect on net worth when A^* is allowed to be nonlinear in labor income. (See Feldstein and Pellechio, 1979, and Feldstein, 1983.)

3.4 Summary and Conclusion

Liquidity constraints and intergenerational transfers are of fundamental importance to the effects of government fiscal policies on long-run growth and aggregate demand. Unfortunately, our current understanding of these phenomena is quite limited.

This study seeks to shed further light on these important issues. In so doing I utilize a new methodology that enhances the significance of my results considerably. The unique features of this methodology, and their advantages, are listed below.

(1) Cross-section data are used to estimate a structural consumption model that distinguishes between life-cycle consumers and consumers with short multiperiod horizons.

(2) The estimated model identifies liquidity-constrained families. Hence, it is possible to access the importance of liquidity constraints for aggregate consumption and implement independent checks of the model's specification.

(3) In Chapter 8 the model's specification for social security is consistent with the life-cycle model as well as the alternative model where private intergenerational transfers offset social security induced intergenerational transfers.

(4) The model incorporates the lifetime budget constraint so that social security's effect on consumption cannot be attributed to ordinary human wealth. Multicollinearity, therefore, is less problematic than it has been for earlier cross-section studies of social security.

4 An Estimable Consumption Model with Liquidity Constraints

This chapter presents an estimable consumption model that incorporates liquidity constraints. The model is a direct derivative of the model presented in Section 2.2 of Chapter 2.

Our ultimate objective is to estimate this model with data for families. As is pointed out in Chapter 2, uncertain lifetimes pose an insurmountable obstacle to obtaining a closed-form solution to the optimal consumption plan when the agent is a multiple-person family. Section 4.1 proceeds, therefore, on the assumption that lifetimes are certain. Here the family's consumption plan is expressed as a function of (1) its net worth, (2) the time path of its net noninterest income, (3) the time path of its "effective" family size, and (4) the time path of its minimal allowable level of net worth.

The model is adapted to the case of uncertain lifetimes in Section 4.2. Section 4.3 specifies the time paths of the effective family size and the minimal allowable level of net worth as parametric functions of the family's observable characteristics. The consumption plan derived in Section 4.1 then may be expressed as a function of observable variables and six parameters. Section 4.4 contains an analysis of the effect of each of these six parameters on a family's optimal consumption plan. Finally, Section 4.5 discusses the potential biases which may result from our simplifying assumptions concerning uncertainty. This section draws heavily on Appendix D, which surveys the pertinent literature on consumption under uncertainty.

4.1 The Model with Certain Lifetimes

The model of Chapter 2, as well as the model of this chapter, assumes an intertemporal utility function of the form

$$V[\mathbf{C}(t,T)] = \sum_{i=t}^{T} \alpha(i,t)U(i,C_i), \tag{4.1}$$

where t is the current period, T is the terminal date, $\alpha(i,t)$ is the subjective discount factor on utility experienced in period i, $\mathbf{C}(t,T) = (C_t, C_{t+1}, \ldots, C_T)$ gives consumption in each period of the agent's remaining lifetime, and $U(i,C_i)$ is the within-period utility function for period i. It is common in the literature to assume an intertemporal utility function of this form. Among its noteworthy features, discussed extensively in Appendix A, are (1) utility derived from the consumption of goods (the term "goods", in what follows, excludes leisure) in each period depends on *one* index of total expenditure, and (2) labor supply, and hence leisure consumption, affects goods consumption only through the lifetime budget constraint.

The first feature of (4.1) is valid if preferences for goods in each period are homothetic or if relative goods prices are expected to remain constant over time. The latter assumption seems to be reasonable.

The second feature of (4.1) implies that the marginal utility of goods consumption in each period is independent of leisure consumption or that leisure consumption is relatively constant over time. The evidence suggests that leisure consumption is relatively constant prior to retirement for primary workers.[1] This implies that the within-period utility function for goods consumption is well approximated by (4.1) except that the function may change form at retirement when leisure consumption increases (see Appendix A). As will be seen in Section 4.2, allowance is made for the within-period utility function to shift at the time the family head reaches age 65.

The within-period utility function we utilize in our empirical model is

$$U(i,C_i) = (1/\gamma)FS_i(C_i/FS_i)^\gamma = (1/\gamma)FS_i^{1-\gamma}C_i^\gamma, \tag{4.2}$$
$$\gamma < 1, \gamma \neq 0; i = t, t+1, \ldots, T,$$

where FS_i is the "effective" family size in period i and is specified in Section 4.2. Equation (4.2) is the standard isoelastic utility function modified to allow for a changing family size. It was established in Section 2.1.3 of Chapter 2 that the within-period utility function must be of the isoelastic form for the implied optimal consumption plan to satisfy the proportionality hypothesis.

The subjective discount factors are assumed to take the standard form

$$\alpha(i,t) = (1 + \rho)^{t-i}, \qquad i = t, t+1, \ldots, T, \tag{4.3}$$

where ρ is interpreted as the pure rate of time preference and is unchanging over time. It is recalled that this form for the subjective discount factors insures dynamic consistency (see Section 2.1.2 of Chapter 2).

Combining (4.1), (4.2), and (4.3) gives the family's intertemporal utility function:

$$V[\mathbf{C}(t,T)] = (1/\gamma) \sum_{i=t}^{T} (1 + \rho)^{t-i} FS_i^{1-\gamma} C_i^{\gamma}.$$

Invoking Proposition 2.1 of Chapter 2 and assuming the family's horizon extends to period s, $s \geq t$, the first phase of the family's consumption plan, $\mathbf{C}^u(t,s)$, maximizes

$$V[\mathbf{C}(t,s)] = (1/\gamma) \sum_{i=t}^{s} (1 + \rho)^{t-i} FS_i^{1-\gamma} C_i^{\gamma}, \tag{4.4}$$

subject to

$$A_{s+1} \equiv (1 + R)^{s-t+1} \left[A_t + \sum_{i=t}^{s} (1 + R)^{t-i}(YL_i - C_i) \right] = B_{s+1}, \tag{4.5}$$

where for period i YL_i is net noninterest income, A_i is net worth, and B_i is the minimal allowable level of net worth. Note that it is assumed that agents *expect* the real net rate of return, R, to remain constant over time.

As functions of $\mathbf{C}(t,s)$, the objective function (4.4) is concave, and the constraint (4.5) is convex. It follows that $\mathbf{C}^u(t,s)$ exists and is the solution to the Kuhn-Tucker necessary conditions. Deriving and solving these conditions is straightforward and gives the solution

$$C_j^u(t,s) = b(j,s)[W(j,s) - (1 + R)^{j-s-1}B_{s+1}], \tag{4.6}$$
$$j = t, t+1, \ldots, s,$$

where

$$b(j,s) = \left\{ 1 + \sum_{i=j+1}^{s} [\beta_1^{i-j}(FS_i/FS_j)] \right\}^{-1}, \quad \text{for } j = t, t+1, \ldots, s-1,$$
$$= 1, \quad \text{for } j = s.$$
$$\beta_1 = [(1 + R)^{\gamma}/(1 + \rho)]^{1/(1-\gamma)},$$

$$W(j,s) = A_j + \sum_{i=j}^{s} (1 + R)^{j-i} YL_i.$$

Setting j equal to t in (4.6) gives the optimal level of current consumption for an arbitrary cutoff date s:

$$C_t^u(t,s) = b(t,s)[W(t,s) - (1 + R)^{t-s-1}B_{s+1}]. \tag{4.7}$$

Finally, invoking Proposition 2.3 of Chapter 2, the optimal amount of current consumption is

$$C_t^* = C_t^u(t,v), \tag{4.8}$$

where

$$v = [\text{Max } s | C_t^u(t,s) \leqslant C_t^u(t,k), \quad t \leqslant k, s \leqslant T].$$

In words, Equation (4.7) may be used to determine which value of s in the range $[t,T]$ minimizes $C_t^u(t,s)$. The value of s so found is v, the first cutoff date. Substituting v for s in Equation (4.6) gives the first phase of the optimal consumption plan. Likewise, substituting v for s in Equation (4.7) gives the optimal level of current consumption.

The intuition for the solution is most easily understood by multiplying and dividing $b(t,v)$, given in (4.6) with v substituted for s, by the current effective family size, FS_t:

$$b(t,v) = FS_t \Big/ \left(FS_t + \sum_{i=t+1}^{v} \beta_1^{i-t} FS_i \right), \quad v > t. \tag{4.9}$$

The denominator of (4.9) is the discounted sum of effective family members that must be provided for over the interval $[t,v]$. Hence (4.9) indicates that the family consumes a share of available resources during the interval $[t,v]$ that is equal to the portion of discounted effective family members over the interval $[t,v]$ that are currently in the household. The discount factor, β_1, is a parameter to be estimated.

4.2 Adaptation of the Model to the Case of Uncertain Lifetimes

Uncertainty about the longevity of life gives rise to two distinct complications: (1) given a consumption plan, intertemporal utility is stochastic; and (2) future earned noninterest income is contingent on the survival of the earner and is therefore uncertain. Each of these complications renders the solution for the optimal consumption plan unexpressible in a closed form when the family consists of more than one individual. We discuss these complications, and our remedy for them, below.

INCOME UNCERTAINTY

It is not possible to obtain a closed-form solution for the optimal consumption plan when future labor income is uncertain. (Labor-income uncertainty is discussed in Section 4.5.) It is assumed, therefore, that net labor income in each future period is fully insured at a fair price against the possibility that an earner might die *and* other members are alive.[2] In other words, a fair life insurance premium is deducted from net noninterest income in each future period. The resulting stream of net receipts is certain to be realized provided at least one family member is alive and, therefore, all relevant income uncertainty is eliminated. Note that the family has no incentive to insure future earned income against the possibility that no family members are alive given the assumption that net worth can never be negative and creditors are assured repayment of any outstanding loans.

This assumption is not meant to reflect the real world.[3] Instead it should be viewed as an approximation that amounts to discounting future labor earnings more heavily the less likely it is that they will be realized.

Also, the reader should not infer a close relationship between this model and the model developed by Yaari (1965), which assumes the existence of perfect insurance and annuities markets. A detailed comparison of our model with Yaari's model is contained in Section 4.5. For now it is noted that Yaari's model is such that the agent purchases fair life insurance exactly covering his debt in each period.

UNCERTAIN FUTURE FAMILY COMPOSITION

When lifetimes are uncertain, consumption in each period is contingent on family composition and all available information that is pertinent to the probability distribution of family composition in future periods. The appropriate method of solving the family's problem, therefore, is dynamic programming. Unfortunately this involves taking mathematical expectations of complex functions of family composition, which are generally impossible to express in a closed form.

Since a rigorous solution to our problem is not possible, it is assumed that the family behaves as if expected family composition in each future period will be realized with certainty. This implies that Equation (4.8), which gives the optimal amount of *current* consumption, continues to be valid with the simple modifications that FS_i is replaced by its mathematical expectation at time t and the date T is interpreted as the maximal, rather than actual, terminal date.

Note that this assumption implies that uncertain lifetimes present no risk to the family. This approximation will be relatively less accurate for older families since, for them, the variance of future effective family size is particularly high. It is established in Section 4.5 that the utility function we employ has the property that saving increases in response to increased variance of future income or, similarly, future needs. Our consumption function, therefore, is likely to overestimate the consumption of older families, a possibility that will be kept in mind when interpreting the empirical results.

It is important to understand that the expectation of family composition in future periods will be revised each period to reflect new information. If, for example, current family composition is the only variable affecting the probability distribution of future family composition, the family's consumption plan is contingent on family composition, as well as net worth, in each period. It is not possible, therefore, to project the time profile of the family's consumption without knowing the time path of family composition. In other words, a counterpart to the deterministic plan, given by Equation (4.6) with s replaced by v, does not exist, even under our assumption of certainty equivalence.

4.3 The Detailed Econometric Specification

Our consumption model is estimable once the time profiles of the expected effective family size and the minimal level of net worth are specified as parametric functions of the family's observable characteristics. This is done in Sections 4.3.1 and 4.3.2, respectively. Section 4.3.3 contains a complete specification of the model.

4.3.1 Expected Effective Family Size

Expected effective family size is assumed to take the form

$$_tE(FS_i) = {}_tE(AD_i)\{d(i,65) + [1 - d(i,65)]\beta_2\} \qquad (4.10)$$
$$+ {}_tE(AO_i)\beta_3 + {}_tE(CH_i)\beta_4,$$
$$i = t, t+1, \ldots, T,$$

where i is the family head's age; T is the maximal attainable age; $_tE$ denotes the mathematical expectation at time (age) t; $d(i,65)$ is one if i is less than 65 and is zero otherwise; AD_i (core adults) is two if, in period i, the family is headed by a married couple and is one otherwise; AO_i (other adults) is the number of adults, other than the family head and spouse, in the household during period i; and CH_i is the number of children in the household during period i. The parameter β_2 is a proportionality factor converting an adult older than 64 into an equivalent younger adult for consumption purposes. Its value reflects age-dependent taste changes as well as the complementarity or substitutability of goods and leisure. (On this latter point, see Appendix A and the discussion in Section 4.1.)[4] The parameters β_3 and β_4 have similar interpretations: They convert other adults and children, respectively, into equivalent young adults for consumption purposes.

Our method of estimating the expected effective family size for each future period is described below.

OTHER ADULTS AND CHILDREN

Our sample is restricted so that any adults in the household other than core adults are likely to be children over age eighteen. These adults are assumed to leave the family at the end of the current period so that

$$_tE(AO_i) = 0, \qquad i = t+1, t+2, \ldots ,T. \qquad (4.11)$$

The data include the number of children under age nineteen for each family but only give the ages of the youngest and the oldest. The age distribution of children is approximated by assuming that half the children have ages equal to the youngest and half have ages equal to the oldest. Children are assumed to leave the family when they reach age nineteen so that children leave the household at, at most, two distinct future dates. In addition, it is assumed that children live to age nineteen with certainty and no additional children are expected in the future. It follows from these assumptions that

$$_tE(CH_i) = 0.5CH_t[d(i, t+19-AGO) \qquad (4.12)$$
$$+ \; d(i, t+19-AGY)],$$
$$i = t, t+1, \ldots ,T,$$

where $d(i,j)$ is one for i less than j and is zero otherwise, AGO is the current age of the oldest child, and AGY is the current age of the youngest child.

HEAD AND SPOUSE (CORE ADULTS)

Households headed by a single adult under age 65 are eliminated from the sample because their future circumstances are difficult to predict. Single individuals at least 65 years old are assumed to expect to stay single, and married couples are assumed to expect to stay married. Therefore, only the death of one or both core adults affects the expected number of future core adults. Mortality data for the U.S. population is used to estimate the expected number of core adults in each future year as a function of the current age and sex of each core adult. The details of this estimation are given in Chapter 5.

4.3.2 The Minimal Levels of Net Worth

The essence of liquidity constraints is conveyed, I think, in a restriction of the following type: The borrower must have tangible collateral that: (1) has a value, less the transactions costs associated with its liquidation, at least as great as his outstanding debt, and (2) is not likely to be quickly liquidated and consumed. This restriction implies that extremely liquid assets are not acceptable as collateral so that the market value of the agent's nonliquid assets, less the transactions cost of selling them, must exceed his debt. This is equivalent to requiring that the agent's net worth be at least as great as the sum of his liquid asset holdings and the transactions costs of selling his nonliquid assets. Each of these components is discussed below.

LIQUID ASSET HOLDINGS

One of the commodities making up the consumption aggregate in each period is liquidity services. (See Appendix A for a discussion of the consumption aggregate.) It is assumed that within-period preferences are such that the expenditure elasticity of the demand for liquid assets is approximately constant and equal to one.[5] In this case the demand for liquid assets in period i is given by

$$M_i = \beta_5 C_i^u(t,v), \qquad i = t, t+1, \ldots, v, \qquad (4.13)$$

where for period i, M_i is real liquid asset holdings and β_5 is a function of relative goods prices. It is assumed that relative goods prices are expected to remain constant over time. Hence β_5 may be treated as a parameter.

EQUITY IN CONSUMER DURABLES

It is assumed that only the sale of real assets involve significant transaction costs. The only real assets whose values are included in our data are homes and automobiles. (We exclude the self-employed from our sample so that business assets need not be considered.) The required equity in these assets is assumed to be given by

$$WHA_i^+ = \text{Min}\{[WHA_t + EHA(t,i)], \beta_6 VHA_t\}, \qquad (4.14)$$
$$i = t, t+1, \ldots, T,$$

where WHA_i^+ is the required equity in home(s) and automobile(s) in period i, WHA_t is the actual current equity in home(s) and automobile(s), VHA_t is the current value of home(s) and automobile(s), and $EHA(t,i)$ is a monotonically increasing function of i.

Equation (4.14) states that equity in home(s) and automobile(s) must be accumulated according to the schedule $EHA(t,i)$ until the family owns the portion β_6 of these assets. The schedule $EHA(t,i)$ is chosen so as to be consistent with standard mortgage contracts and is specified in Chapter 5.[6]

The minimal level of net worth in each period, given by the sum of liquid asset holdings (4.13), and the minimal level of equity in home(s) and automobile(s), (4.14), is

$$B_i = \beta_5 C_t^u(t,v) + \text{Min}\{[WHA_t + EHA(t,i)], \beta_6 VHA_t\}, \qquad (4.15)$$
$$i = t, t+1, \ldots, v.$$

Note that $C_t^u(t,v)$ is used as a proxy for $C_i^u(t,v)$ for greater simplicity.

4.3.3 The Fully Specified Econometric Model

Equations (4.10), (4.11), (4.12), and (4.15) specify the time profiles of the expected effective family size and the minimal level of net worth as parametric functions of the family's observable characteristics. Substituting these expressions into Equation (4.7) gives *current* consumption for an arbitrary cutoff date s:

$$C_t^u(t,s) = \{b(t,s)\beta_7 / [1 + \beta_5(1+R)^{t-s-1}b(t,s)]\} \qquad (4.16)$$
$$\cdot [W(t,s) - (1+R)^{t-s-1}\text{Min}\{[WHA_t + EHA(t,s)], \beta_6 VHA_t\}],$$

where

$$W(t,s) = A_t + \sum_{i=t}^{s} (1+R)^{t-i} YL_i^+,$$

$$b(t,s) = \left[1 + \frac{AD_t ZD(t,s) + \beta_4 CH_t ZC(t,s)}{AD_t + \beta_3 AO_t + \beta_4 CH_t} \right]^{-1},$$

$$ZD(t,s) = \sum_{i=t+1}^{s} \beta_1^{i-t}\{[_t E(AD_i)/AD_t][d(i,65) + [1 - d(i,65)]\beta_2]\},$$
$$\text{for } s = t+1, t+2, \ldots, T,$$
$$= 0, \quad \text{for } s = t,$$

$$ZC(t,s) = 0.5 \left(\sum_{i=t+1}^{a} \beta_1^{i-t} + \sum_{i=t+1}^{b} \beta_1^{i-t} \right),$$
$$\text{for } s = t+1, t+2, \ldots, T,$$
$$= 0, \quad \text{for } s = t,$$

$$a = \text{Min}(s, t+19 - AGO),$$

$$b = \text{Min}(s, t+19 - AGY),$$

and YL_i^+ is noninterest income in period i net of taxes and a fair life insurance premium. Finally, s is made endogenous by the condition given in (4.8):

$$C_t^* = C_t^u(t,v), \qquad (4.17)$$

where

$$v = [\text{Max } s|C_t^u(t,s) \leqslant C_t^u(t,k), \qquad t \leqslant k, s \leqslant T].$$

The proportionality factor, β_7, is appended to the model so we may estimate it and test whether it equals one, as the theoretical model predicts.

At first glance, the model appears overwhelmingly complex. But as is demonstrated in the next section, the central idea of the model is quite simple and intuitive.

4.4 Comparative Dynamics

The model contains seven parameters, of which one, β_7, is appended to the theoretical consumption model. In this section we study how each of these parameters influences the "expected" consumption profile.

4.4.1 The Consumption Growth Rate

It is easy to lose sight of the model's appealing simplicity when viewing the detailed econometric specification given in (4.17) and (4.16). It is most revealing to analyze the model in its less detailed form given in (4.8) and (4.7). Provided v, the first cutoff date, is greater than t, these equations indicate that the proportionate change in consumption between periods t and $t + 1$ is

$$C_{t+1}^* / C_t^* = \frac{\beta_1(1 + R)(FS_{t+1}/FS_t) \sum\limits_{i=t+1}^{v} \beta_1^{i-t}{}_t E(FS_i/FS_t)}{\sum\limits_{i=t+1}^{v} \beta_1^{i-t}{}_{t+1} E(FS_i/FS_t)} \qquad (4.18)$$

In deriving (4.18) it is assumed that the cutoff date, v, does not change between periods t and $t + 1$. This is a reasonable assumption so long as FS_{t+1} is close to its expected value at time t.

Equation (4.18) is made complicated by the possibility that expectations are revised between periods t and $t + 1$. An approximation to the expected proportionate change in consumption is given by (4.18) with ${}_{t+1}E(FS_i)$ replaced by ${}_t E[{}_{t+1}E(FS_i)] = {}_t E(FS_i)$, $i = t + 1, t + 2, \ldots, v$:

$$_t E(C_{t+1}^*/C_t^*) \simeq \beta_1(1 + R)_t E(FS_{t+1})/FS_t. \qquad (4.19)$$

Note that the parameters β_5, β_6, and β_7, which we refer to as the resource parameters, do not enter (4.19). The resource parameters determine the portion of full wealth arising within the interval $[t,v]$ that the family eventually consumes during the same interval. For example, if $\beta_5 = 0.1$, $\beta_6 = \beta_7 = 1$, and $v = T$, then the family consumes all its lifetime resources except for 10% of a typical year's consumption (liquid asset holdings) and the value of its home(s) and automobile(s). These parameters have the same proportionate effect on consumption in periods t and $t + 1$.

The remaining parameters, β_1, β_2, β_3, and β_4, enter (4.19) directly or indirectly as components of the effective family size. Since these parameters affect the timing of consumption, and not the present value of lifetime consumption, we refer to them as the allocation parameters.

The expected consumption growth rate yields important insights into the determinants of the entire expected consumption profile. The higher is the consumption growth rate between periods t and $t + 1$, holding the consumption growth rate in other periods constant, the smaller is consumption in every period prior to period $t + 1$ and the larger is consumption in every period subsequent to period t. Our objective, therefore, is to study how the allocation parameters influence the expected consumption growth rate.

It is instructive to review the logic underlying (4.19) before proceeding. Substituting for β_1 from (4.6) and bringing the effective family size terms to the left-hand side of the equation, it is apparent that the consumption growth rate per expected effective family member is

$$\beta_1(1 + R) = [(1 + R)/(1 + \rho)]^{1/(1-\gamma)},$$

which is precisely the gross growth rate of consumption for the Yaari model presented in Section 2.1.3 of Chapter 2. It was explained there that a high interest rate encourages late consumption by making it relatively cheaper than early consumption.[7] Similarly, a high pure rate of time preference makes early consumption relatively more appealing than late consumption. The net impact of these two factors is given by their ratio raised to the power $1/(1 - \gamma)$ which, it is recalled, is the elasticity of intertemporal substitution. The higher is $1/(1 - \gamma)$, the more responsive is the family to relative prices when planning its consumption.

Turning to our analysis of the expected consumption growth rate, we note that an immediate implication of (4.19) is:

Proposition 4.1: The expected consumption growth rate is an increasing function of β_1 in every period.

Next consider the expected proportionate change in the effective family size. Assuming that the family does not include other adults, $_tE(FS_{t+1})/FS_t$ is given by

$$\frac{_tE(AD_{t+1})\{d(t+1,65)+[1-d(t+1,65)]\beta_2\}+_tE(CH_{t+1})\beta_4}{AD_t\{d(t,65)+[1-d(t,65)]\beta_2\}+CH_t\beta_4}. \quad (4.20)$$

Other adults are assumed to leave the household after the current period, so they are not considered here. We note, however, that the current consumption of families that include other adults increases with β_3.

Equations (4.19) and (4.20) have the following implications.

Proposition 4.2: When newborns join the family, consumption is expected to rise abruptly and, when childen leave the family, consumption is expected to fall abruptly. These changes are more dramatic the larger is β_4.

Proposition 4.3: The larger is β_4, the greater is the expected consumption growth rate while children are in the household.

Proposition 4.4: The effect of β_2 is to shift the expected consumption profile up or down when the family head reaches age 65. A β_2 greater than one shifts the expected profile up and a β_2 less than one shifts it down; the magnitude of these shifts depending on the magnitude of β_2.

Propositions 4.2 and 4.4 are easily verified by inspecting (4.20). Proposition 4.3 is less obvious and may be verified by differentiating (4.20) with respect to β_4 and letting $_tE(CH_{t+1}) = CH_t$. The intuition for Proposition 4.3, however, is clear: The survival of children is assumed certain so that the effective family size is expected to shrink proportionately less the more weight that is put on children in determining the effective family size.

One should use caution when applying these results to a cross section of families. For example, Proposition 4.1 implies that a higher value of β_1 decreases the consumption of young families but increases the consumption of old families. In a cross section, where full wealth is fixed, it appears as if everyone's current consumption is reduced by an increase in β_1 regardless of age. The fallacy, of course, is that a higher value of β_1 implies that older families will have higher full wealth than they would have otherwise and, despite the fact that a high β_1 decreases the propensity to consume out of full wealth at all ages less than T, the consumption of older families still increases. Another example is the fact that the weight on retirement consumption appears to have no effect on the consumption of childless retired families in a cross section (β_2 cancels out for these families). Again the fallacy is that the current full wealth of retired families is dependent on the value of β_2. An implication of this observation is that β_2 is statistically identified only by data for families whose head is younger than 65.

4.4.2 The Family's Horizon

Given the time profile of the family's net noninterest receipts, the family's horizon is shorter the more it desires early consumption relative to later consumption. It is immediately apparent from Proposition 4.1 that a higher value of β_1, other things equal, tends to lengthen the family's horizon. Similarly, a higher value of β_2 increases the relative importance of old-age consumption and also tends to lengthen the family's horizon.

The effect of β_4 on the family's horizon is less clear. Consider, for example, a young couple with a rising income profile who, if not anticipating children, has a one-period horizon. The same couple, if anticipating children with significant "needs," may be induced to save so as to be more able to provide for their children. In this case a sufficiently high value of β_4 lengthens the family's horizon. Suppose, conversely, that a young couple has a flat income profile and, if not anticipating children, has a horizon that extends into retirement. This couple, if anticipating children and if β_4 is sufficiently large, are likely to have a horizon that extends to a time when their children become independent (see Section 2.2.4 of Chapter 2). A sufficiently large value of β_4 therefore, shortens this family's horizon.

4.5 Uncertainty

The empirical model abstracts entirely from the problem of risk associated with uncertain lifetimes and uncertain labor income. In addition, the model does not allow for the inclusion of risky assets in the agent's portfolio.

This section analyzes our simplifying assumptions regarding uncertainty. Our primary purpose is to determine how our assumptions might bias the empirical results. The shortcomings of alternative approaches to incorporating uncertainty into a structural consumption model also are pointed out.

4.5.1 Lifetime Uncertainty

Our method of incorporating lifetime uncertainty into the model, and its drawbacks, are discussed in Section 4.2.

An alternative approach to lifetime uncertainty, which assumes the existence of perfect insurance and annuities markets, is given in Yaari

(1965). It is argued here that (1) the Yaari model cannot be utilized to model the consumption of multiple-person families, and (2) for the case where the agent is one individual, our model has much more realistic implications for the effect of lifetime uncertainty on consumption than does the Yaari model.

Yaari's agent purchases fair life insurance covering his debt in each period and holds all his assets in the form of fair annuities. The implicit interest rate on loans, therefore, is the same as that earned on annuities. Furthermore, the nature of the agent's assets and liabilities is such that he cannot die with negative net worth. The only restriction on the agent's consumption plan, therefore, is that is assure solvency after the maximal attainable age, if the agent should live that long.

The Yaari model does not generalize to a multiple-person family (in Yaari's terms, an agent with a bequest motive). Clearly an agent with dependents for whom she cares will insure her life for more than her outstanding debt.

Consider our model for the case where the agent is one individual. In this case no life insurance is purchased (see Section 4.2) and the proportionate change in consumption between periods t and $t + 1$, contingent on the agent living beyond period t, is[8]

$$C_{t+1}^* / C_t^* = \beta_1(1 + R)PR(t + 1|t), \qquad (4.21)$$

where $PR(i|j)$, $i \geq j$, is the probability the agent lives to period i given survival to period j. Equation (4.21) is Equation (4.18) with the substitutions $FS_{t+1} = FS_t = 1$, and $_tE(FS_i) = PR(i|t) = PR(i|t + 1)PR(t + 1|t)$, $i = t + 1, t + 2, \ldots, T$. Equation (4.21) assumes, of course, that liquidity constraints are not binding in period t.

The comparable Yaari model, which employs the same intertemporal utility function, implies that the proportionate change in consumption is

$$C_{t+1}^* / C_t^* = \beta_1(1 + R),$$

which is precisely the consumption growth rate for the case of certain lifetimes (see Section 2.1.3 of Chapter 2). This result obtains because a fair annuity yields a higher rate of return the lower is the conditional probability of living. Hence the agent receives an ever-increasing rate of return as he ages and this exactly offsets the higher effective rates of time preference that result from an uncertain lifetime.

Our model, in contrast, implies that consumption falls, relative to the case of a certain lifetime, as the agent ages. This is because the agent's assets consist entirely of ordinary bonds. The agent's desire to consume early is kept in check, however, by the imposition of inequality constraints on her net worth.[9]

In summary, the empirical application of the Yaari model is untenable for two reasons. First, it cannot be applied in the case of a multiple-person family. Second, the assumption of perfect annuities markets, which in fact do not exist, leads to the unrealistic conclusion that lifetime uncertainty has no effect on the agent's plans concerning the amount consumed when young relative to the amount consumed when old.

4.5.2 Labor Income Uncertainty

It is not possible to obtain a closed-form solution to our consumption model when future labor income is stochastic. In fact I am unaware of any pertinent results in the literature that concern the effect of income uncertainty in a multiperiod consumption model.[10] Comparative static results derived in the context of two-period models, however, do exist and are surveyed in Appendix D. The relevant finding, which concerns the case where the intertemporal utility function is additive and the within-period utility function is of the form $(1/\gamma)C^\gamma$, is that first-period consumption is smaller when second-period labor income is uncertain than when it is certain to equal its mean. This result, of course, holds for all admissible values of γ.

It is shown in Appendix D that this result extends to a multiperiod horizon. That is, current consumption is lower when labor income in each future period is stochastic than when it is certain to equal its mean.[11] This finding suggests that our empirical model, which assumes certainty equivalence, will tend to overestimate the consumption of working families. This potential bias will be kept in mind when evaluating the empirical results.

4.5.3 Rate-of-Return Uncertainty

Our model is intractable for the case where the agent includes risky assets in her portfolio. This is because the agent must, in each period, evaluate the risks of becoming liquidity constrained in each future period when deciding the appropriate amount of current consumption.

Hakansson (1970) presents a model identical to ours in all important respects except: (1) borrowing is unrestricted provided the agent is solvent at death, and (2) an arbitrary number of risky assets are available in addition to one riskless asset. An important assumption, on which the model's tractability depends, is that the joint distribution of asset returns in each future period is known in the initial period.

The Hakansson model provides a useful benchmark and it is analyzed extensively in Appendix D. The important results are summarized below.

(1) The Hakansson model yields a consumption plan that is remarkably similar to ours when liquidity constraints are not imposed. The only difference is that β_1, defined in (4.6), is given a slightly different interpretation. Also, human wealth is defined the same in the Hakansson model as in ours, that is labor income is discounted by the risk-free rates of return.

(2) The demand for risky assets in each period is proportional to full wealth, the proportions depending only on the joint distribution of asset returns.

(3) Increased capital risk[12] decreases (increases) the propensity to consume full wealth in each period if γ is less (greater) than zero.

(4) The coefficient of relative risk aversion is $1 - \gamma$. Hence the within-period utility function displays constant relative risk aversion and, as already noted, portfolio shares are independent of full wealth.

The Hakansson findings lead us to conclude that our model's failure to allow for risky assets is unlikely to seriously bias the empirical results. Capital risk, when a risk-free asset is available, would appear to affect the composition of the agent's portfolio more than it does the qualitative nature of his consumption plan. This conjecture is substantiated for the case where liquidity constraints are not imposed. As is noted above, the inclusion of risky assets in the agent's portfolio does not change the qualitative nature of the optimal consumption plan in this case.

One may argue that it is more important to model portfolio choice accurately than to oversimplify on that dimension of the problem so that liquidity constraints can be more easily modeled. This argument is seriously flawed, however, since the existing models of portfolio choice depend heavily on the existence of perfect capital markets. As is noted above, the Hakansson model has the property that the share of full wealth invested in risky assets is independent of the size and composition of full wealth. This implies that the agent must borrow heavily in the early years of life when most of her full wealth is in the form of future earnings. It is apparent, therefore, that portfolio choice cannot be accurately modeled without taking liquidity constraints into account.

We conclude that a consumption model that acknowledges liquidity constraints, but abstracts from the problem of portfolio choice, can be no less accurate than a consumption model that allows for risky assets but ignores liquidity constraints. In fact, the model proposed herein is arguably a first step toward a more acceptable model of portfolio choice.

5 The Data and Variable Definitions

We estimate the parameters of our model with data collected in two surveys conducted by the Federal Reserve Board of Governors in 1963 and 1964. The first, the *Survey of Financial Characteristics of Consumers* (Projector and Weiss, 1966), surveyed 2,557 U.S. households to obtain information pertaining to income received in 1962 as well as wealth, broken down into its various components, held as of December 31, 1962. The 1964 *Survey of Changes in Financial Characteristics of Consumers* (Projector, 1968) reinterviewed 2,164 of the original households to obtain 1963 income as well as the changes in the holdings of the various assets and liabilities. The present study uses 798 of the 2,164 reinterview observations. The eliminated observations fall into two categories: those that are likely to contain inaccurate information, and those that do not include sufficient information to construct one or more variables called for by the model. The sample selection criteria are explained in Section 5.2.

High-income individuals are purposely overrepresented in the Federal Reserve Board survey to facilitate the study of their consumption and investment behavior. A true random sample large enough to permit inferences to be made for this important group of families would be prohibitively large and expensive. Table 5.1 compares the distribution of gross 1963 income for: our sample of 798 families, the Projector sample of 2,164 families, and the entire population in 1963. Our sample includes a larger proportion of families in the middle income range than does the Projector sample. This is because families whose head is self-employed, or young and single, are eliminated from our sample. Our sample still overrepresents high-income families, as can be seen by comparing the income distribution for our sample with that for the entire population in 1963.

Table 5.1. Percentage distribution of income for families and unrelated individuals

Income ($1,000s)	Our sample	Projector and Weiss sample	Total 1963 population
≤3	14.4	15.4	27.5
3–5	11.5	12.6	17.5
5–10	46.5	29.7	38.4
10–15	14.9	16.4	12.1
15–25	6.5	9.0	3.7
25–50	4.0	7.8	} 0.9
>50	2.1	9.0	

Sources: Projector and Weiss, 1966; U.S. Department of Commerce, Census Bureau, 1963; author's own data.

The remainder of this chapter is organized into two sections. Section 5.1 gives a detailed account of the data construction, and Section 5.2 explains the sample selection criteria.

5.1 Variable Definitions

The model calls for data on the family's current composition, income net of taxes, consumption, and net worth, as well as the family's current expectations of future family composition, net-of-tax labor income, retirement income, and minimal home and automobile equity. A substantial amount of estimation is necessary to construct these variables. Among the estimated quantities are (1) current federal, state, and local taxes; (2) current consumption of durables and liquidity services; (3) future labor income net of income taxes; (4) future social security tax contributions; (5) future retirement income; and (6) future minimal home and automobile equity.

I believe my estimates are as accurate as possible although, in some cases, there may be reasonable alternative estimation procedures. It is important to note, however, that the estimation techniques employed were developed prior to the analysis of the data and were *not* subsequently altered.

The data construction may be divided into four categories that pertain to (1) family composition; (2) consumption; (3) full wealth; and (4) the minimum allowable level of net worth. Each of these categories is discussed below.

CONSUMPTION BEHAVIOR

5.1.1 Family Composition

The method for projecting the number of future children and other adults is explained in Section 4.3 of Chapter 4. Here I explain the method for estimating the expected number of core adults in each future period.

It is assumed that as of the current period t, the expected number of core adults in a future period, i, relative to the number of core adults alive currently, can be approximated by a second-degree polynomial in $(i - t)$:

$$_tE(AD_i)/AD_t = 1 + \alpha_1(i - t) + \alpha_2(i - t)^2, \qquad (5.1)$$
$$i = t, t + 1, \ldots, T.$$

The parameters α_1 and α_2 are fitted for *each* family in the sample as follows.

(1) The quantity $_tE(AD_i)$ is estimated with mortality data for the 1963 U.S. population as the sum of the conditional probability that the family head and the spouse (if any) will be alive in period i given their current respective ages. Dividing this estimate by AD_t gives the left-hand side of (5.1) for each i.

(2) Equation (5.1) is forced to fit perfectly at two dates: (1) when the oldest core adult is age 100 and (2) when the oldest core adult is halfway to age 100. These two restrictions are sufficient to determine α_1 and α_2. Note that Equation (5.1) necessarily fits perfectly in the current period.

(3) The estimates of α_1 and α_2 are checked to be sure that the estimated value of $_tE(AD_i)/AD_t$ monotonically declines in i over the relevant range. If not, the midway date when the equation is forced to fit perfectly is moved in the appropriate direction to yield the desired pattern.

The actual and fitted family mortality probability paths have been compared for a number of observations and the fitted values are quite accurate.

It is important to note that α_1 and α_2 are different for each family in the sample and can be thought of as part of the data set. They are not parameters that are free to vary in order to improve the fit of the consumption function.

Utilizing (5.1), the discounted number of expected core adults over the interval $[t,s]$, which is denoted $AD_tZD(t,s)$ in Equation (4.16) of

Chapter 4, can be expressed as

$$AD_t ZD(t,s) = AD_t \sum_{i=t+1}^{s} \{\beta_1^{i-t}[d(i,65) + [1 - d(i,65)]\beta_2][1 + \alpha_1(i - t)$$
$$+ \alpha_2(i - t)^2]\}.$$

The advantage of the approximation (5.1) is that it greatly simplifies evaluating the consumption function and its derivatives so that the computations involved in estimating the model are reasonable.

5.1.2 Consumption

The family's current consumption is defined as:

$$C = YG + GIFT - TAX - SSTAX - SAVING + DURCON$$
$$+ LIQCON,$$

where for the current period, C is consumption; YG is gross income exclusive of realized and unrealized capital gains; $GIFT$ is the value of net cash gifts received; TAX is an estimate of federal and state income taxes paid; $SSTAX$ is an estimate of social security taxes paid; $SAVING$ is net cash investment in all assets; $DURCON$ is an estimate of the consumption of durables services, and $LIQCON$ is an estimate of the consumption of liquidity services.

It might appear that the exclusion of capital gains (both realized and unrealized) from gross income presents a problem. This exclusion is appropriate, however, since realized capital gains are included as a negative component of $SAVING$ and unrealized capital gains are excluded from $SAVING$. So, for example, if a family's stock holdings appreciate in value from \$100 to \$200 and the family sells \$100 worth of stock, saving in stock is counted as $-\$100$ despite the fact that true saving in stock is zero. If, conversely, the family does not sell any stock, saving in stock is counted as zero despite the fact that true saving is $+\$100$. It is apparent, therefore, that the exclusion of capital gains from gross income is balanced by the peculiar definition of $SAVING$ to yield the correct measure of consumption.

It is unfortunate that the data do not include expenditure on durables other than homes and automobiles. Our measure of consumption, therefore, is contaminated by investment in other household durables. This problem is partially remedied by excluding any increment to consumer installment debt in 1963 from our measure of $SAVING$. The presumption is that there is a new consumer durable not included in wealth that offsets the additional debt. Also, consumer installment debt is excluded from the measure of net worth for the same reason.

The data do not contain information pertaining to tax liabilities or to the consumption of durables and liquidity services. Our methods for estimating these quantities are explained below.

FEDERAL INCOME TAXES

Current federal income taxes are estimated as follows.

(1) Adjusted gross income (AGI) is computed as gross income minus (a) interest income from state and local bonds; (b) retirement income; and (c) half of long-term realized capital gains.

(2) Deductions are the maximum of estimated itemized deductions and the standard deduction. Itemized deductions are estimated as the sum of (a) gifts made to organizations; (b) 6% of home and automobile debt (interest payments); and (c) the value of home(s) multiplied by the average property tax rate for the family's region of residence. The standard deduction is given by the lesser of $1,000 and 10% of AGI.

(3) Taxable income is computed as AGI minus deductions minus exemptions, which are $600 per family member.

(4) If the family is headed by a married couple, let $X = 2$; otherwise, let $X = 1$. Then taxable income is divided by X, the 1963 tax schedule (Tax Foundation Inc., 1964) is applied to this amount, and the result is multiplied by X to obtain total taxes paid.

The average property tax rates used in this calculation, for each of the four regions of residence given in the data, are Northeast 1.7%; North Central, 1.2%; South, 0.8%; and West, 1.2%.[1]

STATE INCOME TAXES

State income taxes are more difficult to estimate since the effective rates vary from state to state, yet the data include the region rather than the state of residence. Thirty-five states levied income taxes in 1963. The rates were generally mildly progressive, starting at 1% and topping out at 5–7% of the tax base. Federal taxes were deductible in most cases, as was some fixed amount depending on family composition.

The effective tax rates generally were quite small and did not vary much among states. The average effective tax rate as a percent of AGI for the United States was 1.2%. By region, rates varied from 0.6% in the southwest to 1.6% in the mideastern states. The highest effective rate was 3.2% in Oregon.

These small rates suggest that our treatment of state income taxes is not that crucial. This is fortunate since we have little to go by other than average regional rates. The estimated average effective state income tax rates for the four regions specified in the data are Northeast, 1.55%; North Central, 0.90%; South, 1.00%; and West, 1.10%.[2]

SOCIAL SECURITY TAXES

In 1963 social security taxes were 3.4% of the first $4,800 of labor income for individuals who were covered by the program and who were not self-employed. Households headed by a self-employed individual are eliminated from the sample so that their taxes need not be considered.

DURABLES CONSUMPTION

The rental price of a durable is given by the sum of: (1) the real net rate of return multiplied by the value of the durable; (2) the economic depreciation of the durable; and (3) any property taxes paid on the value of the durable.

These considerations lead to the following specification for durables consumption:

$$DURCON = 0.03WHA + 0.1VA + PTR \cdot VH,$$

where, for the current period, WHA is equity in home(s) and automobile(s); VA is the value of automobile(s); VH is the value of home(s); and PTR is the estimated property tax rate. This specification assumes the real net rate of return is 3%; the real price of housing increases so as to exactly offset physical depreciation; and the value of automobiles declines at a 10% annual rate. Again, average regional property tax rates are utilized to estimate the family's property tax rate. Note that the portion of the rental price of durables corresponding to the debt portion of the value of durables is included in explicit expenditures and is not included in $DURCON$.

CONSUMPTION OF LIQUIDITY SERVICES

It is assumed that liquidity services are provided exclusively by demand and time deposits. The opportunity cost of holding these assets is

$$LIQCON = (0.03 + \pi^e)\text{Demand Deposits}$$
$$+ \{0.03 - [0.035(1 - MTR) - \pi^e]\}\text{Time Deposits},$$

where, for the current period, π^e is the expected annual inflation rate and MTR is the combined federal and state marginal income tax rate. The real net rate of return on nonliquid assets is, again, assumed to be 3% and, in 1963, the nominal rate of return on demand and time deposits was 0% and 3.5%, respectively. Marginal tax rates are estimated in the process of estimating federal and state tax liabilities. The expected inflation rate is estimated at 2%, the average annual rate of inflation between 1953 and 1963.

5.1.3 Full Wealth

Full wealth for the interval $[t,s]$ is defined as

$$W(t,s) = A_t + YD_t + YC_t \sum_{i=1}^{a} (1 + R)^{-i} + \sum_{i=t+1}^{s} (1 + R)^{t-i} YL_i^+, \quad (5.2)$$

where $a = \text{Min}(19 - AGO, s - t)$; AGO is the current age of the oldest child; A_t is the family's current net worth; YD_t is the family's current disposable income net of realized capital gains; YC_t is the current net income of children; and YL_i^+ is an estimate of labor income earned by core adults, net of taxes and a fair life insurance premium, in period i. The real net rate of return, R, is assumed to be 0.03.

The contribution of children to full wealth is contained in disposable income, which includes their current earnings, and the third term, which is the discounted value of their future earnings net of tax assuming they stay at their current level until the oldest child reaches age nineteen.

Labor income earned by a married couple in a future period i, net of taxes and a life insurance premium, is defined as

$$YL_i^+ = (YLM_i + YLW_i + YR_i - TAX_i) \qquad (5.3)$$
$$- RM_i(YLM_i + YRM_i - TM_i)$$
$$- RW_i(YLW_i + YRW_i - TW_i),$$

where the terms on the right-hand side are defined as follows.

YLM_i (YLW_i)   Labor income of male (female) partner in period i conditional on survival.

TAX_i Income and social security taxes paid in period i conditional on both partners surviving.

YR_i Total retirement income in period i conditional on both partners surviving.

YRM_i (YRW_i)   Increment to total retirement income in period i due to the male (female) partner surviving given that the female (male) partner survives.

TM_i (TW_i)   Increment to total tax paid in period i due to the male (female) partner surviving given that the female (male) partner survives.

RM_i (RW_i)   Probability that only the female (male) partner survives to period i conditional on family composition in period t, and at least one family member being alive in period i.

For families headed by a single adult, the quantities corresponding to the nonexistent partners are set to zero. Hence, for single males, $RM_i = 0$, $YRM_i = YR_i$, and $TM_i = TAX_i$. Similarly, for single females, $RW_i = 0$, $YRW_i = YR_i$, and $TW_i = TAX_i$.

The definition (5.3) is made complicated by the need to adjust for uncertain future labor income due to an uncertain time of death. Recall that this factor is only important for multiple-person families, who are assumed to purchase life insurance against the possibility that one or more earners die and leave behind surviving family members (see Section 4.2 of Chapter 4). Since income received subsequent to the death of all family members is irrelevant, the family does not insure such income.

A quick check of the definition can be made by considering a family headed by a single adult who, for example, is male. Then $YLW_i = YRW_i = TW_i = 0$, $RM_i = 0$, $TM_i = TAX_i$, and $YRM_i = YR_i$ so that full wealth, as defined by (5.2) and (5.3), reduces to current resources plus the simple discounted value of future net receipts conditional on survival:

$$W(t,s) = A_t + YD_t + YC_t \sum_{i=1}^{a} (1 + R)^{-i}$$

$$+ \sum_{i=t+1}^{s} (YLM_i + YRM_i - TAX_i)(1 + R)^{t-i}.$$

This household treats all future receipts that are contingent on survival as if they are certain. This is as the model requires, provided that the probability of death is negligible prior to the time the youngest child departs the household. This condition is likely to be satisfied since all single household heads in the sample are at least age 65 and are unlikely to have children.

Now consider the case of a married couple. The terms on the right-hand side of (5.3) are interpreted as follows.

$YLM_i + YLW_i + YR_i - TAX_i$	Net receipts in period i if both the husband and the wife are alive and no insurance is purchased.
$YLM_i + YRM_i - TM_i$	Husband's marginal contribution to net receipts in period i, conditional on the survival of both partners.

$RM_i(YLM_i + RM_i - TM_i)$ Insurance premium covering the husband's marginal contribution to net receipts against the possibility that he dies on or before period i and his wife lives to period i; paid only if one or both partners live to period i.

The corresponding terms for the female partner have analogous definitions.

It is clear that the insurance is fair as of time t and that (5.3) gives the family's net receipts in period i conditional on at least one partner living. It is assumed that the probability that both partners die while children are dependent is sufficiently small to ignore.

Each of the components of full wealth are defined below.

NET WORTH

Current net worth is defined as of December 31, 1962, and includes all financial assets, business property (book value), and homes and automobiles. The survey did not turn up reliable life insurance valuations. This component of wealth, therefore, is eliminated from the Projector and Weiss (1966) study. Since life insurance premiums are subtracted from projected future income, we include the apparently inaccurate life insurance valuations in net worth on the grounds that the empirical results would probably be more seriously biased by their exclusion than by their inclusion.

As was mentioned above, data on the value of consumer durables other than homes and automobiles are not available. Consumer installment debt, therefore, is not included as a negative element of net worth on the supposition that consumer durables exist which offset the debt.

DISPOSABLE INCOME

Current "disposable income," denoted YD_t, includes realized labor and capital income of all family members minus (1) capital gains; (2) an estimate of state and federal income taxes; and (3) an estimate of social security taxes. It is not technically correct to include capital income in disposable income as this amounts to counting income on A_t in the current period twice and corresponds to a model where current consumption depends on end-of-period wealth. I feel this drawback is overshadowed by the advantage of capturing any unusual current returns to capital in the measure of full wealth. Capital gains are excluded, however, since they may have accumulated for more than one year, in which case they are already included in A_t.

THE LABOR INCOME PROFILE

Data on the average wage by age, sex, and education for the 1963 U.S. population are used to generate an expected labor income profile up to the age of retirement for each core adult in the sample. This estimation assumes that (1) annual hours worked remain constant until retirement so that an individual's labor income path tracks his wage path, and (2) the ratio of an individual's wage to the wage of the average person in her age-sex-education category is expected to remain constant at its 1963 level in each future period. The average person of a given sex-education category, in turn, is assumed to follow an age-wage path equal to the 1963 cross-section profile for the same sex-education category scaled up by an annual secular growth rate of 2%.

The 1963 wage profiles employed in this estimation are tabulated in Table 5.2. The table gives the average 1963 age-wage profile by sex and education. These wage profiles end at age 65. A flat wage profile is assumed after age 65. The estimated retirement age is discussed in the next subsection.

Current labor income is computed as the average of labor income earned in 1962 and 1963. So few observations on income leave room for significant measurement error. To minimize this error we eliminate from the sample (1) all observations for which the family head is

Table 5.2. Hourly earnings for four age groups, as a portion of their level at ages 55–64, by sex and education

Education (years)	Age			
	25–34	35–44	45–54	55–64
		Men		
0–8	0.68	0.85	0.98	1.00
9–11	0.52	0.83	0.97	1.00
12–12	0.53	0.79	0.95	1.00
13–15	0.34	0.70	0.92	1.00
>15	0.34	0.59	0.86	1.00
		Women		
0–8	0.72	0.82	0.87	1.00
9–11	0.69	0.90	0.98	1.00
12–12	0.85	0.94	0.96	1.00
13–15	0.61	0.90	0.93	1.00
>15	0.69	0.80	0.90	1.00

Note: Only columns of a given row are comparable.
Source: Gallop and Jorgenson (1980).

younger than 65 in 1963 and worked part time, or less than ten months, in either year; (2) all observations for which the family head is younger than 66 in 1963 and worked part time, or less than ten months, in 1962; and (3) all observations for which the family head is self-employed. The latter group is eliminated because there is substantial evidence that the self-employed systematically under-report their income. In fact, a large portion of self-employed individuals report saving in excess of their income.

Income earned by other adults is included in current disposable income and is not expected to persist since other adults are assumed to leave the family after the current period. Income of other family members, in families who have no other adults, is attributed to the oldest child. This income is assumed to persist at its current level until the oldest child reaches age nineteen.

RETIREMENT INCOME

All observations for which the head is working full time and is not covered by social security are eliminated from the sample. All other households whose heads work full time are assumed to expect no pensions other than social security.

The following procedure is used to estimate retirement income for each family in the sample.

(1) Compute the retirement age of the family head as follows. If the family head is currently not working (must be at least age 65), set the retirement age equal to his current age. Otherwise use Table 5.3 to assign a retirement age conditional on his current age, say t. The table

Table 5.3. Assigned retirement ages of working individuals

Current age (t)	Assigned retirement age
≤ 61	65
62	66
63	67
64–65	68
66–67	70
68	71
69	72
70–71	74
72–74	75
>74	$t+1$

gives the age where 50% of those currently age t and working are expected to retire based on data on the frequency of retirement by age among household heads in the sample.

(2) For families headed by a married couple, determine the retirement age of the spouse as follows. Let h be the wife's age when the husband retires and let w be the wife's retirement age. Then: (a) If $62 \leqslant h \leqslant 65$ then set $w = h$; (b) If $h < 62$ then set $w = 62$; and (c) If $h > 65$ then set $w = \text{Max}$ (65, spouse's current age $+$ 1).

(3) Compute each core adult's position in the labor income distribution for men of the same age. Assign them monthly social security benefits equal to the amount received by a new social security recipient who falls at the same point in the distribution of social security benefits for new awardees, scaled up at the annual rate of 2% until the estimated age of retirement.

(4) If the wife's benefits, as computed above, are less than half the husband's benefits, then set the wife's benefits equal to half the husband's benefits at the date that either he or she retires, whichever is later.

(5) If the wife retires prior to age 65, reduce her benefits by α% for each month prior to age 65 that she retires. Define α as $5/9$ if the wife collects on the basis of her own earnings. Otherwise, set $\alpha = 25/36$.

It is assumed that *real* social security benefits remain constant after an individual begins collecting.[3]

FUTURE INCOME TAXES

It is assumed that the average federal income tax rate for a family in an arbitrary period i may be represented parametrically as follows:

$$TAX_i/YT_i = \delta_1 + \delta_2 AGI_i + \delta_3 AGI_i^2,$$

$$AGI_i = YL_i - 600FAMS_i + \delta_4(A_i - VHA_i),$$

where, for period i; TAX_i are total federal income taxes paid; YT_i is gross income; AGI_i is adjusted gross income; YL_i is gross labor income; $FAMS_i$ is family size; A_i is net worth; and VHA_i is the value of the home(s) and automobile(s). Combining these equations gives

$$TAX_i/YT_i = \delta_1 + \delta_2[YL_i - 600FAMS_i + \delta_4(A_i - VHA_i)] \quad (5.4)$$
$$+ \delta_3[YL_i - 600FAMS_i + \delta_4(A_i - VHA_i)]^2,$$
$$i = t+1, t+2, \ldots, T).$$

Our estimates of the 1963 federal tax liabilities for families in the sample are used to construct the dependent variable in (5.4). Using nonlinear least squares, the following parameter estimates are obtained:

$$\hat{\delta}_1 = 0.06 \qquad (23.5)$$

$$\hat{\delta}_2 = 0.10 \times 10^{-5} \qquad (29.5)$$

$$\hat{\delta}_3 = -0.53 \times 10^{-10} \quad (12.1)$$

$$\hat{\delta}_4 = 0.012 \qquad (1.9)$$

Student's t statistics, testing the hypothesis that the respective parameters are zero, are given in parentheses.

When applying Equation (5.4) to future periods, it is assumed that net worth and the value of the home(s) and automobile(s) remain constant at their 1963 levels.

The total income tax rate is found by adding the state tax rate (assumed constant) to the estimated federal tax rate given by (5.4).

FUTURE SOCIAL SECURITY TAXES

In 1963 the Social Security Administration projected the future social security tax rates and the maximum taxable labor income as follows:[4]

Date	Tax Rate	Maximum Taxable Income
1963	0.034	$4,800
1966	0.035	$6,600
1969	0.040	$6,600
1973+	0.045	$6,600

These projections are utilized to estimate social security tax liabilities for each future period as a function of earned income.

5.1.4 Minimal Home and Automobile Equity

The minimal allowable equity in home(s) and automobile(s) is given in Equation (4.14) of Chapter 4 as:

$$WHA_i^+ = \text{Min}\{[WHA_t + EHA(t,i)], \beta_6 VHA_t\}, \qquad i = t, t+1, \ldots, T,$$

where, for the current period, WHA_t is equity in home(s) and automobile(s), and VHA_t is the value of home(s) and automobile(s).

Here we specify the term $EHA(t,i)$, which gives the accumulated equity between periods t and i. To do so, we assume: (1) a 4% real loan rate, and (2) that as long as payments on debt are compulsory (that is, $WHA_t + EHA(t,i) < \beta_6 VHA_t$), they are made for home(s) and automobile(s), respectively, in equal yearly payments such that, if continued for thirty years for homes and five years for automobiles, the debt will expire. In this way, we estimate the family's annual compulsory payments for its home(s) and automobile(s), respectively. Given these estimates, it is straightforward to determine the family's required equity in its home(s) and automobile(s) at each future date.

5.2 The Sample Selection Criteria

Our sample includes 798 of the original 2,164 observations contained in the Projector reinterview sample. The eliminated observations fall into four categories; observations for which (1) relevant data are missing; (2) the family's current situation is such that the values of important future variables are particularly uncertain; (3) the family's composition is uncertain; or (4) measurement errors are especially likely.

The following symbols are used in explaining our criteria for selecting the sample.

$AGEH$	Age of the family head in 1963
$AGEW$	Age of the wife (if any) in 1963
YLH	Labor income of the family head in 1963
YLW	Labor income of the wife (if any) in 1963
AD	Total number of adults in the family in 1963

Our criteria and rationale for eliminating observations are as follows:

(1) Missing data.
(2) $AGEH \leqslant 24$.
   Future labor income and family composition uncertain.
(3) Family head is self-employed.
   Current and future income uncertain.
(4) Family head is single and $AGEH < 65$.
   Future family composition and labor income uncertain.
(5) Family head is not working full time in 1963 and $AGEH \leqslant 65$ or family head is not working full time in 1962 and $AGEH \leqslant 66$.
   Future income uncertain.
(6) Family head is working full time and is not covered by social security.
   Future pension income uncertain.
(7) $62 \leqslant AGEH \leqslant 72$ and $1,200 \leqslant YLH \leqslant 1,700$.
   Computation of social security benefits is difficult because, for individual younger than 72, benefits are reduced one for two when earned income is in the range $1,200 to $1,700.
(8) $62 \leqslant AGEW \leqslant 72$ and $1,200 \leqslant YLW \leqslant 1,700$.
   See preceding criterion.

   (9) Net cash saving exceeds realized disposable income.
       Measurement error.
 (10) Business income exceeds 10% of labor income.
       Current and future income uncertain.
 (11) Value of business exceeds $1,000.
       Current and future income uncertain.
 (12) Other family members are receiving pensions.
       Current and future family composition uncertain.
 (13) $AGEH \geq 65$, head is married, and $AD > 2$ or $AGEH \geq 65$, head is single, and $AD > 1$.
       Current and future family composition uncertain.
 (14) $AGEH \geq 55$ and $AD > 4$.
       Current and future family composition uncertain.
 (15) Head is married, $AGEW \leq 34$, and $AD > 2$.
       Current and future family composition uncertain.
 (16) Disposable income is negative.
       Measurement error.

6 The Econometric Methodology

This chapter develops a methodology for estimating the parameters of the consumption model presented in Chapter 4, testing hypotheses concerning the parameter values, and testing the validity of the model's specification. Section 6.1 proposes a stochastic specification of the model for which nonlinear least squares is the appropriate estimation procedure. The algorithm for computing the least-squares estimator is sketched in Section 6.2. Section 6.3 presents procedures for testing hypotheses concerning the parameter values and the model's specification. Errors in variables and varying tastes, two problems that would invalidate the stochastic specification of Section 6.1, are the topics of Section 6.4.

6.1 The Stochastic Specification and the Estimation Procedure

Equations (4.17) and (4.16) of Chapter 4 give the optimal level of current consumption as an implicit function of the parameter vector $\beta = (\beta_1, \beta_2, \ldots, \beta_7)$ and an all-inclusive data vector $\mathbf{X}$. Letting the subscript i index the family (observation), the equation to be estimated may be written as

$$C_i^* = f(\beta, \mathbf{X}_i), \qquad i = 1, 2, \ldots, N, \tag{6.1}$$

where $f(\beta, \mathbf{X}_i)$ is the consumption function implied by Equations (4.17) and (4.16) of Chapter 4, and N is the number of families in the sample. Since data are available only for one year's consumption, the time period is understood to be the current period.

It is assumed that (6.1) is accurate up to an additive normal error term, which is independent of the data vector, with mean zero and standard deviation proportional to a normalization factor $ZNORM$. Under this assumption the actual consumption of the N families in the sample satisfy the following regression equation:

$$C_i/ZNORM_i = f(\boldsymbol{\beta},\mathbf{X}_i)/ZNORM_i + \epsilon_i, \qquad i = 1,2, \ldots ,N, \quad (6.2)$$

where

$$[(\epsilon_i|\mathbf{X}_i), i = 1,2, \ldots ,N] \sim \text{i.i.d. } N(0,\sigma^2), \tag{6.3}$$

and C_i is the actual current consumption of the ith family.

The normalization factor is assumed to take the form

$$
\begin{aligned}
ZNORM_i &= CCAP_i^\delta \\
&\equiv \{\text{Max}[(A_i + YD_i - WHA_i), YD_i]\}^\delta, \qquad \delta > 0, \\
i &= 1,2, \ldots ,N,
\end{aligned}
\tag{6.4}
$$

where δ is a parameter to be estimated and, for the ith family: A_i is net worth, YD_i is disposable income, and WHA_i is equity in home(s) and automobile(s). That is, the variance of the error term is an increasing function of the family's capacity to consume as measured by $CCAP_i$, the family's consumable resources.

A two-stage procedure, originally due to Glezser (1969), is used to estimate the model. In the first stage δ is set to unity and model is estimated by nonlinear least squares. The estimated residuals, $\mathbf{e}$, are then employed to run the regression

$$\log|e_i| = \log(\sigma) + (\delta - 1)\log(CCAP_i), \quad i = 1,2, \ldots ,N, \quad (6.5)$$

to obtain an estimate of δ which, with the aid of Equation (6.4), is used to estimate $ZNORM_i$, $i = 1,2, \ldots ,N$. In the second stage the model is reestimated using the revised values of $ZNORM$. Although this procedure could be repeated until convergence, only one iteration is employed since the parameter estimates and their standard errors are insensitive to the initial adjustment in δ.

Under assumption (6.3) the first-stage estimate of $\boldsymbol{\beta}$ is consistent.[1] It follows that the first-stage residuals are consistent estimates of the true disturbances so that regression (6.5) yields a consistent estimate of δ.[2] Hence the asymptotic properties of our estimator for $\boldsymbol{\beta}$ are unaffected by the fact that δ is unknown and must be estimated (Chow, 1983, pp. 220–231). In particular our estimator of $\boldsymbol{\beta}$ has the asymptotic properties of the maximum likelihood estimator. That is, it is consistent, efficient, and asymptotically normal.

6.2 The Estimation Algorithm

The method of scoring is used to obtain the least-squares parameter vector, say $\hat{\beta}$. This estimation procedure is described below.

(1) The model is linearized around an initial guess of $\hat{\beta}$, say $\beta_0 = (\beta_{01}, \beta_{02}, \ldots, \beta_{0k})$, as follows:

$$D_i \equiv C_i - f(\beta_0, \mathbf{X}_i) = \sum_{j=1}^{k} \left[\frac{\partial f}{\partial \beta_j} (\beta_0, \mathbf{X}_i) \right] (\beta_j - \beta_{j0}),$$

$$\equiv \sum_{j=1}^{k} Z_{ij} \Delta_j \equiv \mathbf{Z}_i' \Delta, \qquad i = 1, 2, \ldots, N.$$

Ordinary least-squares is applied to this linearized model to obtain $\hat{\Delta}$. Note that the normalization factor has been omitted from the estimated model for notational convenience.[3]

(2) Let $SSR(\beta)$ be the sum of squared residuals as a function of β. If $SSR(\beta_0 + \Delta) < SSR(\beta_0)$ then β_1, the revised estimate of β, is set equal to $\beta_0 + \Delta$. Otherwise a λ, $0 < \lambda < 1$, is found such that $SSR(\beta_0 + \lambda\Delta) < SSR(\beta_0)$ and β_1 is set equal to $\beta_0 + \lambda\Delta$. Such a λ necessarily exists.

(3) Steps 1 and 2 are repeated, using the revised estimate of β, to obtain yet another revised estimate of β. This procedure is repeated until at some iteration $j + 1$,

$$CON \equiv \text{Max}\{[\Delta_i, (\Delta_i/\beta_{ji})]\}, \qquad i = 1, 2, \ldots, k\} \leq CONMAX,$$

where β_{ji} is the estimate of β_i on the jth iteration, and CONMAX is the convergence criterion. Note that CON is zero at a local peak of the likelihood function.

(4) The asymptotic variance-covariance matrix of $\hat{\beta}$ is estimated as

$$V(\hat{\beta}) = [SSR(\hat{\beta})/(N - k)] \left[\sum_{i=1}^{N} \mathbf{Z}_i \mathbf{Z}_i' \right]^{-1}, \tag{6.6}$$

where $\mathbf{Z}_i$, $i = 1, 2, \ldots, N$, are evaluated at $\hat{\beta}$ (Chow, 1983, pp. 220–231).[4]

THE DERIVATIVES

The optimal level of current consumption for the ith family, $f(\beta, \mathbf{X}_i)$, can be written as

$$f(\beta, \mathbf{X}_i) = g[\beta, \mathbf{X}_i, v_i^*(\beta, \mathbf{X}_i)],$$

where $v_i^*(\beta, \mathbf{X}_i)$ is the ith family's first cutoff date, and the function g is Equation (4.16) of Chapter 4 with $v_i^*(\beta, \mathbf{X}_i)$ replacing s. Note that the cutoff date v_i^* is an implicit function of β and $\mathbf{X}_i$.

Analytic derivatives are employed in our least-squares algorithm. They may be expressed as

$$\frac{\partial f(\beta, \mathbf{X}_i)}{\partial \beta_j} = \frac{\partial g}{\partial \beta_j} + \frac{\partial g}{\partial v_i^*} \frac{\partial v_i^*}{\partial \beta_j} \qquad i = 1, 2, \ldots, N; \qquad (6.7)$$

$$j = 1, 2, \ldots, k.$$

The first term is easily calculated since $g(\beta, \mathbf{X}_i, v_i^*)$ is expressed in a closed form. A closed form for $v_i^*(\beta, \mathbf{X}_i)$ does not exist, however. Fortunately this is not a problem since v_i^* is discreet and $\partial v_i^*/\partial \beta_j$ is nonzero on a set of measure zero. It is appropriate, therefore, to disregard the second term in (6.7).

Note that $\partial g/\partial \beta_j$ depends on v_i^*. Hence, at each iteration, the cutoff date for each observation must be computed before the derivatives can be computed.

THE CONVERGENCE CRITERION AND THE
VARIANCE-COVARIANCE MATRIX

The model is quite well behaved. Two or three iterations are usually sufficient to get "near" the peak of the likelihood function from reasonable starting values. (Given our estimate of δ, our estimator for β is the maximum likelihood estimator.)

The discrete nature of v_i^*, however, makes the derivatives discontinuous on a set of measure zero.[5] This implies that the surface of the likelihood function includes ridges. In some cases these ridges make convergence difficult. Our convergence criterion *(CONMAX)* is 0.02. For most estimations, however, the value of *CON* achieved is less than 0.01.

As already noted, the model is well behaved and it is not difficult to get near the peak of the likelihood function. The major advantage of obtaining tight convergence, therefore, is that it allows for consistent estimates of the variance-covariance matrix. Since the variance-covariance matrix depends on the local properties of the likelihood function, small changes in the estimated parameter vector could potentially have a relatively large impact on the estimated variance-covariance matrix. Not a single case has been discovered, however, where the estimated variance-covariance matrix is sensitive to the value of the parameter vector in the neighborhood of the maximum likelihood estimate.

Nevertheless, the dependence of the estimated variance-covariance matrix on the local properties of the likelihood function is bothersome. We verify all important statistical inferences that utilize the estimated variance-covariance matrix, therefore, with likelihood ratio statistics.

The likelihood ratio statistic, of course, is not dependent on the local properties of the likelihood function. (The likelihood ratio test statistic is discussed in the next section.)

6.3 Statistical Inference

Our sample includes 798 families. The distribution of our estimator for β, therefore, is well approximated by its asymptotic analogue, which is normal with mean β and variance-covariance matrix (6.6).

THE LIKELIHOOD RATIO TEST

We shall have occasion to test hypotheses of the form

$$H_0: M\beta = \mathbf{c}, \tag{6.8}$$

where M is a q by k matrix of constants with rank q, $\mathbf{c}$ is a vector of q constants, and β is a vector of k parameters. It is easily seen that (6.8) constitutes q independent linear constraints on the parameter vector.

Let β^* be the unrestricted maximum likelihood estimator of β and let β_0 be the maximum likelihood estimator of β when (6.8) is imposed. Finally, let $L(\beta)$ be the value of the likelihood function as a function of the parameter vector. Then, under the null hypothesis (6.8),

$$\lambda = -2\log[L(\beta_0)/L(\beta^*)] \tag{6.9}$$

is asymptotically distributed as a chi-square random variable with q degrees of freedom (Theil, 1971, pp. 396–397).

When the true errors satisfy (6.3), expression (6.9) is equivalent to

$$\lambda = N\log[SSR(\beta_0)/SSR(\beta^*)], \tag{6.10}$$

where $SSR(\beta)$ is the sum of squared residuals as a function of the parameter vector, β, and N is the number of observations.

Our estimator for β is asymptotically equivalent to the maximum likelihood estimator. It is appropriate, therefore, to use the statistic (6.10) to test hypotheses of the form (6.8).

TESTS OF THE MODEL'S SPECIFICATION

Our estimator for β is consistent. It follows that the estimated error terms are consistent estimators of the true disturbance terms and, under assumption (6.3), are asymptotically distributed as independently and identically distributed normal random variables. Furthermore, they are asymptotically independent of the variables on the right-hand side of the regression equation. This implies that the estimated residuals may be grouped according to family characteristics, and each group will have the properties of a random sample.[6] In particular, the groups so selected should share a common mean and variance. This implication of the model is easily tested. Such tests are implicit tests of the model's specification.

We are primarily concerned with testing for the consistency of our parameter estimates. We therefore focus our attention on testing for the equality of group residual means. For this purpose we construct the test statistic

$$(\bar{e}_i - \bar{e}_j)/\{VAR[(1/N_i) + (1/N_j)]\}^{1/2},$$

where VAR is the sample variance of all N estimated residuals, and for the kth group, $\bar{e}_k$ is the sample mean of the estimated residuals and N_k is the number of observations. This statistic is asymptotically distributed as a standard normal variable under the assumptions of the model. This fact will be utilized extensively to test the model's specification.

6.4 Errors in Variables and Varying Tastes

The stochastic specification of Section 6.1 assumes that the disturbances in the regression equation (6.2) are independent of the right-hand-side variables. This assumption is not appropriate if there are errors in measuring the right-hand-side variables or if tastes (β) vary over families in the sample. These problems have plagued previous empirical studies of consumption. It is argued below, however, that our parameter estimates are relatively insensitive to these potential problems.

6.4.1 Errors in Variables

The problem of estimating the consumption function is the classic textbook example of the econometric problem of errors in variables. Friedman (1957) and Modigliani and Brumberg (1954) show that the estimated coefficient on measured income in the standard consumption function, which is linear and includes a constant as well as measured income, will give a downward-biased estimate of the effect of "permanent" income on consumption. This is because measured income is an imperfect measure of permanent income.

Our problem is similar. We include the appropriate concept of resources, full wealth, in our consumption function, but it is invariably measured with error. To investigate how this affects the consistency of the least-squares parameter estimates, it is helpful to give a more detailed representation of Equation (6.2):

$$C_i/ZNORM_i = g(\boldsymbol{\beta},\mathbf{X}_i)h(\boldsymbol{\beta},\mathbf{X}_i)/ZNORM_i + \epsilon_i, \tag{6.11}$$
$$i = 1,2, \ldots ,N,$$

where

$$g(\boldsymbol{\beta},\mathbf{X}_i) = b(t_i,v_i^*)\beta_7/[1 + \beta_5(1 + R)^{t_i-v_i^*-1}b(t_i,v_i^*)],$$
$$h(\boldsymbol{\beta},\mathbf{X}_i) = W(t_i,v_i^*) - (1 + R)^{t_i -v_i^*-1}$$
$$\cdot \text{Min}\{[WHA_i + EHA(t_i,v_i^*)], \beta_6 VHA_i\},$$
$$v_i^* = v_i(\boldsymbol{\beta},\mathbf{X}_i).$$

The decomposition of $f(\boldsymbol{\beta},\mathbf{X}_i)$ given in Equation (6.11) follows from Equations (4.17) and (4.16) of Chapter 4. Symbol definitions are given there. Note that the function g given in (6.11) is unrelated to the function g given in the last section.

If full wealth is measured with error, then

$$W_i(t_i,v_i^*) = W_i^m(t_i,v_i^*) + W_i^e(t_i,v_i^*),$$

where, for family i, $W_i(t_i,v_i^*)$ is actual full wealth, $W_i^m(t_i,v_i^*)$ is measured full wealth, and $W_i^e(t_i,v_i^*)$ is the error in measurement of full wealth. The estimated equation, which uses measured full wealth as a proxy for actual full wealth, may be written as

$$C_i/ZNORM_i = g(\boldsymbol{\beta},\mathbf{X}_i)[h(\boldsymbol{\beta},\mathbf{X}_i) - W_i^e(t_i,v_i^*)]/ZNORM_i + \mu_i,$$
$$i = 1,2, \ldots ,N,$$

where

$$\mu_i = \epsilon_i + g(\boldsymbol{\beta},\mathbf{X}_i)W_i^e(t_i,v_i^*)/ZNORM_i.$$

The estimated specification includes the term $-g(\boldsymbol{\beta},\mathbf{X}_i)W_i^e(t_i,v_i^*)/ZNORM_i$, which is correlated with the disturbance term. Hence, *if ZNORM is uncorrelated with the error in measured full wealth*, measured full wealth is negatively correlated with the disturbance term. Least squares, in this case, attempts to reduce the importance of measured full wealth in the estimated equation, thereby giving biased parameter estimates.

This problem is not nearly so serious for our model as it has been for the models of consumption considered by Friedman and by Modigliani and Brumberg. This is true for four reasons. First, we attempt to measure the appropriate concept of resources and, provided the life-cycle model is correct, there are no conceptual errors of measurement. Second, the sample includes only families whose head, if not retired, is employed by others and has worked full time for two consecutive years, so that measured income is likely to reflect normal earnings. Third, the theoretical specification constrains the coefficient on full wealth to be one, a coefficient that would be downward biased by measurement error *if* the estimated relation is not normalized and includes a constant term. Any attempt by least-squares to reduce the importance of measured full wealth in the estimated equation therefore must be indirect. Fourth, the absence of a constant term in the specification significantly reduces any bias which would otherwise be present. In fact, when the consumption function has no constant term and is normalized, it is possible that the bias is such that measured full wealth is given *too much* weight in the estimated consumption function. This last possibility is a consequence of the fact that $ZNORM$ is positively correlated with the error in measuring full wealth. (Recall that current disposable income is a component of full wealth.)

These last points are not well known and are worth further elaboration. They are most easily explained in the context of the model analyzed by Friedman (1957), which is linear and includes measured income and a constant as explanatory variables. In this model, the proportional downward bias in the least-squares income coefficient is equal to the proportion of the variance of measured income that is due to measurement error. (Friedman considers conceptual errors of measurement and labels this error transitory income.) With no constant term included, the proportional downward least-squares bias is equal to the proportion of the sum of squares of income that is due to measurement error. Clearly the bias in the former case dwarfs that in the latter case.

The intuition for this result is as follows. With a constant term present, least squares can adjust the estimated coefficients from their true values so that the fit of both high-income and low-income observations improves. When there is no constant term in the regression, however, least squares adjusts the income coefficient to accommodate measurement error so as to trade off the fit of the low-income observations with exceptionally large average propensities to consume *(APC)* against that of high-income observations with exceptionally low *APCs*. The high-income observations win out because a small downward bias in the income coefficient reduces the size of their residuals a great deal while increasing the residuals of the low-income observations very little. The necessity of a tradeoff, however, reduces the absolute magnitude of the least-squares bias.

This tradeoff is illustrated in Figure 6.1. The figure is drawn under the assumption that measured income is uniformly distributed between 0 and Y_2 and that its mean is $\overline{Y}$. Line OF is the true relation between

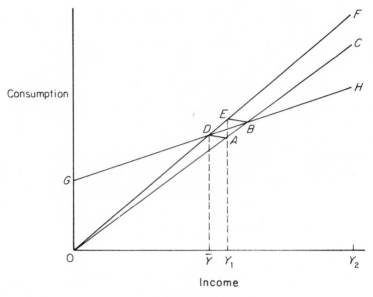

Figure 6.1

consumption and income. The observations are assumed to fall on the line GH due to the inaccurate measurement of income.

If the estimated slope coefficient is downward biased, then the estimated relation is a line like OC. Relative to the true relation, the residuals increase for families with income less than Y_1 and decrease for families with higher incomes. The sum of the absolute deviations changes, relative to the true relation, by area OAD minus area $BCFE$, which appears to be negative as drawn. It is intuitively clear from the figure why this should be so. The fact that the criterion for choosing the line OC is to minimize the sum of squared deviations reinforces this conclusion. This is true since least-squares gives relatively more weight to large absolute deviations and: (1) for those observations where the absolute deviation of the estimated relation is enlarged relative to that of the true relation, the change is smaller the larger is the deviation associated with the true relation; and (2) for those observations where the absolute deviation of the estimated relation is made smaller relative to that of the true relation, the improvement is greater the larger is the deviation associated with the true relation.

This discussion suggests that normalizing the consumption equation by measured income, or some increasing function of measured income, may reverse the roles of high-income and low-income observations in the above analysis and reverse the direction of the bias. This is in fact what happens.

Consider the Friedman model normalized by measured income and with no constant term:

$$C_i/Y_i^m = k(Y_i^p/Y_i^m) + e_i/Y_i^m, \qquad i = 1,2, \ldots ,N. \qquad (6.12)$$

For the ith observation, C_i is measured consumption, Y_i^m is measured income, Y_i^p is permanent income, and e_i is the disturbance term. The parameter k is the propensity to consume permanent income. Following Friedman it is assumed that

$$Y_i^m = Y_i^p + u_i,$$

$$E(u_i) = E(e_i) = 0,$$

$$E(e_iu_j) = E(e_iY_j^p) = E(u_iY_j^p) = 0, \quad \text{all } i \text{ and } j,$$

and

$$E(e_ie_j) = E(u_iu_j) = 0, \quad \text{all } i \neq j.$$

The expectation operator is denoted E. Under these assumptions (6.12) can be written as

$$C_i/Y_i^m = k - k*u_i' + e_i', \qquad i = 1,2, \ldots ,N,$$

where

$$u_i' = u_i/Y_i^m$$

$$e_i' = e_i/Y_i^m$$

$$E(e_i'u_j') = 0, \quad \text{all } i \text{ and } j.$$

The least-squares estimate of k, say $\hat{k}$, has expected value

$$E(\hat{k}) = k - k(\text{mean of } u').$$

The mean of u' is clearly negative, so $\hat{k}$ is upward biased.

To summarize, we believe measurement error is not a serious problem in our model for the following reasons.

(1) The sample is restricted so that measured income is likely to reflect normal earnings, so that measurement error in full wealth is minimized.

(2) Measurement error in full wealth can only have an indirect effect on the parameter estimates since the coefficient on full wealth is constrained to be one.

(3) The absence of a constant term in the specification reduces the magnitude of any bias in the parameter estimates which would otherwise be present.

(4) The estimated consumption function is normalized so that the direction of any bias in the parameter estimates due to measurement error is uncertain. Given that the direction of bias may be reversed, we conjecture that its absolute magnitude is reduced.

6.4.2 Varying Tastes: A Random Parameter Model

It is not realistic to suppose that all families share the same tastes. A more plausible assumption is that families share the same preference function but that the parameters of the function vary over families. In this case the ith family's parameter vector may be expressed as

$$\boldsymbol{\beta}_i = (\beta_{i1}, \beta_{i2}, \ldots, \beta_{i7}) = \boldsymbol{\beta} + \mathbf{d}_i, \qquad i = 1, 2, \ldots, N,$$

where $\boldsymbol{\beta}$ is the mean parameter vector and $\mathbf{d}_i$ is the deviation of the ith family's parameter vector from the mean.

The estimated model (6.2) becomes

$$C_i/ZNORM_i = f(\boldsymbol{\beta}, \mathbf{X}_i)/ZNORM_i + \mu_i, \qquad i = 1, 2, \ldots, N, \quad (6.13)$$

where

$$\mu_i = \epsilon_i + [f(\boldsymbol{\beta}_i, \mathbf{X}_i) - f(\boldsymbol{\beta}, \mathbf{X}_i)]/ZNORM_i.$$

If $\mathbf{d}_i$ is independent of the data vector $\mathbf{X}_i$, then μ_i is independent of the right-hand side variables in (6.13) and the least-squares estimator of the mean parameter vector, $\boldsymbol{\beta}$, is consistent.

It is probable, however, that $\mathbf{d}_i$ is not independent of $\mathbf{X}_i$. For example, an unusually strong preference for late consumption over early consumption (that is, $\beta_{1i} > \beta_1$) would reflect itself in an unusually high level of full wealth given the family's other characteristics. This would cause μ_i to be correlated with normalized full wealth. This correlation is necessarily negative if $ZNORM$ is uncorrelated with $\mathbf{d}_i$. Least-squares, in this case, will attempt to reduce the importance of full wealth in the estimated consumption function, thereby giving biased parameter estimates.

This has proved a formidable problem in past efforts to use cross-section data to estimate a linear consumption function that includes net worth as an explanatory variable. It is generally agreed that the phenomenon of varying tastes is responsible for the typically low explanatory power of net worth in these studies. (See, for example, Crockett, 1964, and Crockett and Friend, 1967.)

Varying tastes are not nearly so problematic for our model as they have been for earlier estimated models, however. The reasons are the same as in the case of errors in variables. First, the coefficient of full wealth is constrained to be one and any bias due to varying tastes must be indirect. Second, the estimated equation is normalized. Since *ZNORM* is positively correlated with the taste for late consumption it is not obvious that normalized full wealth is correlated with μ. (Note that the portion of μ due to random tastes is normalized.)

6.4.3 The Liquidity-Constraints Classification

It was pointed out in Chapter 3 (Section 3.3.1) that a major problem with the important recent studies of liquidity constraints, namely Hall and Mishkin (1982) and Hayashi (1984), is that they make questionable assumptions concerning the characteristics of liquidity-constrained families. Hayashi, for example, assumes that the unconditional mean and variance of expected income change are the same for constrained and unconstrained families. Likewise, Hall and Mishkin assume that constrained and unconstrained families share the same conditional expectation for deterministic income change.

Our study is guilty of making similar assumptions. The shape of each family's labor income profile is assumed to depend only on age, sex, and education. In addition, it is assumed that preferences (or average preferences) are the same for constrained and unconstrained families. (Hall and Mishkin also assume identical preferences; Hayashi does not make this assumption.)

It is plausible that, given age, sex, and education, liquidity-constrained families expect a more rapidly rising labor income profile than do unconstrained families. Hence there is a tendency to understate (overstate) the future resources of constrained (unconstrained) families. It would appear, therefore, that our model will classify constrained families as unconstrained just as frequently as it classifies unconstrained families as constrained. But the tendency to misclassify families as constrained is checked by the fact that unconstrained families tend to have accumulated a stock of consumable wealth. There is no such check on the misclassification of constrained families. We conclude that the failure to allow the income profile to depend on the liquidity-constraints classification leads our model to understate the prevalence of liquidity constraints.

It is also plausible that liquidity-constrained families tend to have a higher pure rate of time preference than do unconstrained families. Hence our model will understate (overstate) the desired consumption of constrained (unconstrained) families. As in the previous case, this causes the model to misclassify families in both directions. Again, the tendency to misclassify unconstrained families is checked by the fact that unconstrained families tend to have accumulated a stock of consumable wealth. We conclude that the failure to allow preferences to depend on the liquidity constraints classification again causes our model to understate the prevalence of liquidity constraints.

The estimates reported in the next chapter indicate that liquidity constraints are quite important. This conclusion is robust with respect to the potential biases discussed in this subsection.

6.4.4 Conclusion

We conclude that the presence of measurement error and varying tastes reduces the explanatory power of our consumption model but does not seriously bias the parameter estimates. One implication of this observation is that there might exist other models that fit the data better than our model precisely because their parameter estimates are sensitive to measurement error and varying tastes. Such models will appear superior on the criterion of fit but will yield little information about the preference structure that underlies the behavior of the families in the sample.

7 The Estimated Consumption Function and Its Interpretation

In this chapter we utilize the cross-section data described in Chapter 5 and the econometric methods of Chapter 6 to estimate and analyze the consumption model presented in Chapter 4.

Section 7.1 refines the model of Chapter 4 to take into account the apparent dependency of tastes on the level of education attained by the family head. The parameter estimates of this "preferred" model are then scrutinized.

Section 7.2 concerns the importance of liquidity constraints and includes (1) an analysis of the estimated cutoff dates (horizons), (2) a presentation of independent evidence indicating that the preferred model correctly identifies liquidity-constrained families, and (3) a comparison of the preferred model with a model that does not impose liquidity constraints on young families.

An analysis of the preferred model's fit is presented in Section 7.3. This section includes (1) a comparison of the preferred model with a standard linear model, (2) an analysis of the normalization factor's influence on the parameter estimates, and (3) a breakdown of the preferred model's goodness of fit for subsamples sharing common family characteristics. These last two topics reflect the validity of the preferred model's specification.

Finally, Section 7.4 gives a brief summary.

7.1 The Preferred Model

This section begins with a presentation of parameter estimates for various versions of the model. It is discovered that the family head's level of education influences consumption in a way that the model of Chapter 4

100

is incapable of explaining. In particular a family tends to save more, relative to the model's prediction, the higher is the family head's level of education. Two possible explanations are considered: either future labor income is less certain the higher is its expected rate of growth, or families with higher levels of education are less myopic. We conclude that the second explanation is definitely valid but that the data do not reveal whether the first explanation is also valid. Our preferred model, therefore, incorporates only the second explanation.

Section 7.1.2 takes a closer look at the parameter estimates of the preferred model.

7.1.1 The Role of Education

Table 7.1 gives parameter estimates for five versions of the model. Recall that the parameters have the following interpretations:

β_1 $[1/(1 + R)]$ times the growth rate of consumption per effective young adult.

β_2 A conversion factor converting core adults older than 65 into equivalent young core adults.

β_3 A conversion factor converting other adults into equivalent young core adults.

β_4 A conversion factor converting children into equivalent young core adults.

β_5 The demand for liquid assets as a portion of a typical year's consumption.

β_6 The portion of the value of the family's home(s) and automobile(s) that the family does not plan to consume.

β_7 A proportionality factor that the theoretical model predicts to be one.

There are five additional parameters listed in Table 7.1 that are not included in the discussion of Chapter 4. Letting ED represent the level of education attained by the family head in years, these parameters are defined as follows:

$ED1(X)$ The value of parameter X for families with   (7.1) $ED \leqslant 8$.

$ED2(X)$ The value of parameter X for families with $9 \leqslant ED \leqslant 11$.

$ED3(X)$ The value of parameter X for families with $ED = 12$.

Table 7.1. Parameter estimates: the role of education

Parameter	Model 1[a]	Model 2[b]	Model 3[c] $X = \beta_2$	Model 4[d] $X = \beta_1$	Model 5[e] $X = \beta_1$
β_1	1.0067	1.0052	1.0070	—	—
	(0.0016)	(0.0016)	(0.0015)		
β_2	0.4995	0.5140	—	0.5346	0.5485
	(0.0375)	(0.0378)		(0.0408)	(0.0416)
$ED1(X)$	—	—	0.4749	0.9660	0.9967
			(0.0223)	(0.0027)	(0.0027)
$ED2(X)$	—	—	0.4990	1.0018	1.0019
			(0.0358)	(0.0024)	(0.0024)
$ED3(X)$	—	—	0.5170	1.0067	1.0059
			(0.0478)	(0.0018)	(0.0018)
$ED4(X)$	—	—	0.5251	1.0097	1.0065
			(0.0550)	(0.0021)	(0.0021)
$ED5(X)$	—	—	0.5491	1.0104	1.0043
			(0.0511)	(0.0020)	(0.0021)
β_3	0.4352	0.4155	0.4420	0.4190	0.3948
	(0.0704)	(0.0681)	(0.0666)	(0.0689)	(0.0664)
β_4	0.3051	0.2908	0.3160	0.2963	0.2832
	(0.0507)	(0.0490)	(0.0518)	(0.0493)	(0.0484)
β_5	0.0270	0.0045	0.0300	−0.0123	−0.0168
	(0.0301)	(0.0302)	(0.0298)	(0.0301)	(0.0293)
β_6	0.7552	0.7604	0.7501	0.7993	0.7812
	(0.0604)	(0.0603)	(0.0660)	(0.0458)	(0.0483)
β_7	1.0000*	1.0000*	1.0000*	1.0000*	1.0000*
$SSR \times 10^{-2}$	3.6171	3.5204	3.5940	3.4632	3.4408
R^2	0.6358	0.6455	0.6381	0.6513	0.6535

Note: Asymptotic standard errors are in parentheses. An asterisk indicates that the parameter is constrained to equal the value shown. The sample includes 798 families.

a. Original Chapter 4 specification.
b. All income profiles shaped like that of a high-school graduate.
c. β_2 varies with the family head's level of education.
d. β_1 varies with the family head's level of education.
e. Combination of models 2 and 4.

$ED4(X)$ The value of parameter X for families with $13 \leqslant ED \leqslant 15$.

$ED5(X)$ The value of parameter X for families with $ED \geqslant 16$.

These parameters are applicable to models 3, 4, and 5 of Table 7.1. For model 3, X is β_2, and for models 4 and 5, X is β_1.

The parameter estimates for the original model presented in Chapter 4 (model 1) are listed in column 1 of Table 7.1. Note that β_7 is constrained to equal one as the theoretical model requires. All of the parameter estimates are reasonable and are estimated precisely. Only β_5 is not significantly different than zero. The estimates indicate that: (1) consumption per effective young core adult grows at about the rate of interest; (2) a core adult older than 65 is equivalent, for consumption purposes, to 0.4995 young core adult; (3) an other adult is equivalent, for consumption purposes, to 0.4352 young core adult; (4) a child is equivalent, for consumption purposes, to 0.3051 young core adult; (5) the family demands an amount of liquid assets equal to 2.7% of a typical year's consumption; and (6) the family does not intend to consume 75.52% of the value of its home(s) and automobile(s).

Part I of Table 7.2 gives the mean of the estimated residuals, by education group, for each of the five models whose estimates are given in Table 7.1. The education groups, it is recalled, are defined in (7.1).

Column 1 of the table shows that the group means monotonically decline with the level of education for model 1. Model 1 tends to under-

Table 7.2. Residual means for groups stratified by education and a test for the equality of the group means

Group or group pair	N^a	Model 1	Model 2	Model 3	Model 4	Model 5
I. Group residual means
ED1	186	0.2528	0.2100	0.2338	0.0960	0.0928
ED2	141	0.0550	0.0188	0.0510	−0.0354	−0.0331
ED3	216	−0.0075	−0.0343	0.0042	0.0359	0.0325
ED4	93	−0.0882	−0.0564	−0.0705	0.0444	0.0205
ED5	162	−0.1522	−0.0512	−0.1147	−0.0174	−0.0365
II. Test statistics exceeding 1.96 in absolute value
(1,2)	—	2.6	2.6	2.4	—	—
(1,3)	—	3.8	3.7	3.4	—	—
(1,4)	—	4.0	3.1	3.6	—	—
(1,5)	—	5.6	3.6	4.8	—	—
(2,5)	—	2.7	—	2.1	—	—
(3,5)	—	2.1	—	—	—	—

a. Number of observations in the respective groups.

estimate the consumption of low-education families and tends to over-estimate the consumption of families with high levels of education.

Part II of the table indicates that several pairs of the group residual means are significantly different. For each group pair of each model, statistics have been computed that are asymptotically standard normal random variables under the null hypothesis that the respective group residual means are equal. The table reports the absolute value of this statistic for all cases where it exceeds 1.96, an event that occurs with a frequency of 5% under the null hypothesis. (See Section 6.3 of Chapter 6 for an explanation of these statistics.)

One possible explanation for the residual pattern shown in Table 7.2 is that those families with high levels of education and who, if young, expect a rapidly rising labor-income profile, are relatively less certain of their future earnings than those families expecting a flatter income profile. Nagatani (1972) suggests that these families discount expected future income more heavily than families with relatively safe income streams, thereby lowering their consumption levels relative to the predictions of our model. A more rigorous analysis, presented in Appendix D and discussed in Section 4.5.2 of Chapter 4, confirms this conclusion. The model would, if this hypothesis is correct, also underestimate the consumption of families with low levels of education because least squares copes with the misspecification by choosing a middle ground between low-education and high-education families in estimating the parameters.

To test this possibility, the model is reestimated under the assumption that all families have a certainty-equivalent labor-income profile *shaped* the same as the expected labor income profile of families with a high-school education. The results are given in column 2 of Table 7.1. The parameter estimates are virtually the same as in column 1; the primary difference is that the consumption growth rate $[\beta_1(1 + R)]$ and the demand for liquid assets (β_5) are slightly lower. The fit of model 2 is substantially better than that of model 1. (The symbol SSR in the table denotes the sum of squared residuals.) A statistical test is not possible, however, since the models are not nested. The improvement in the fit of model 2 over model 1 seems to contradict Watts (1958) who finds that a family's propensity to consume current income tends to increase with the educational attainment of the primary earner. Our finding is consistent, however, with Ando and Modigliani (1960) who find that the elasticity of mean consumption with respect to mean income is less than one for groups classified by education.[1]

Model 2 also performs better than model 1 with respect to the group residual means. But, as Table 7.2 shows, the lowest education group still consumes significantly more than the model predicts. This is true in spite of the fact that they are attributed a more rapidly growing income profile than they can in fact expect.

These findings suggest that tastes may vary systematically with the level of education, a possibility that we now consider.

Taste differences would reflect themselves in the parameter values. The two obvious possibilities are that the weight on retirement consumption (β_2) increases with the level of education, and that the pure rate of time preference decreases with the level of education (that is, β_1 increases with the level of education; see Equation 4.6 of Chapter 4 for the definition of β_1). Each of these possibilities is considered below.

Column 3 of Table 7.1 gives the parameter estimates for the case where the weight on retirement consumption varies with education (model 3).[2] As expected, the estimated weight on retirement consumption increases monotonically with the level of education. The fit of model 3 is not significantly better than that of model 1. Since model 1 is model 3 with four linear restrictions on the parameters, these restrictions may be tested. The asymptotic chi-square test statistic testing the validity of model 1 is 5.1, which is less than the 25% critical value for a chi-square random variable with four degrees of freedom. Model 1, therefore, cannot be rejected in favor of model 3 with 75% confidence. (See Section 6.3 of Chapter 6 for a discussion of this test statistic.)

Not surprisingly, model 3 is not much of an improvement over model 1 with regard to its treatment of education. Table 7.2 indicates that several pairs of the group residual means for model 3 are significantly different.

Column 4 of Table 7.1 gives the parameter estimates for the model that allows β_1 to vary according to education (model 4). As expected, the estimated value of β_1 monotonically increases with the level of education. The fit of model 4 is significantly better than that of model 1. Again, since model 1 is model 4 with four linear restrictions on the parameters, these restrictions may be tested. The asymptotic chi-square test statistic is 34.7, far in excess of the 0.1% critical value, which is 18.5. Model 1 is rejected in favor of model 4, therefore, with more than 99.9% confidence.

Table 7.2 shows that the group residual means of model 4 do not reveal any specification error with respect to education.

We conclude that the rate of time preference definitely varies with education and that allowing for this dependence eliminates any evidence of misspecification in relation to education.

Given that model 2 results in a large improvement in fit over model 1, it is appropriate to consider the composite hypothesis that β_1 varies according to education and that all families have a certainty-equivalent labor-income profile shaped like that expected by families with a high-school education. The estimates of this model (model 5) are given in column 5 of Table 7.1. Model 5 results in similar parameter estimates and a slightly better fit than model 4. We conclude that the data cannot discriminate between models 4 and 5.

Given the ad hoc nature of model 5, model 4 is adopted as our preferred specification.

OTHER TESTS OF THE PREFERRED MODEL'S SPECIFICATION

Tests of the preferred model's specification, analogous to the tests of Table 7.2, have been performed for all important independent variables. These tests are reported in Section 7.3.3 and, with one exception, do not reveal any specification error. The one exception is net worth— the model is misspecified for *extremely* wealthy families. But, as is demonstrated in Section 7.3, the parameter estimates for the preferred model are very insensitive to whether wealthy families are included in the sample. We therefore proceed to analyze the properties of the preferred model.

7.1.2 The Parameter Estimates

Table 7.3 gives six versions of the preferred specification.

Inspection of Table 7.1 reveals that the estimated value of β_5 for the preferred specification (model 4) is insignificantly negative. Since a negative demand for liquid assets cannot be rationalized, the value of β_5 is constrained to be zero in column 1 of Table 7.3. The other parameter estimates and the fit are hardly affected. Henceforth, model 1 of Table 7.3 is referred to as the preferred model.

The preferred estimate of β_1 for each of the five education groups yields, information regarding the probable values of the elasticity of intertemporal substitution, $[1/(1 - \gamma)]$, and the pure rate of time preference, ρ, for each group. It follows from the definition of β_1, given in Equation (4.6) of Chapter 4, that

$$\gamma = 1 - \{\log[(1 + R)/(1 + \rho)]/\log[\beta_1(1 + R)]\},$$

where R is the real net rate of return. For given R and ρ, a 95% confidence interval for β_1 yields a 95% confidence interval for γ. Table 7.4 gives, for each education group and each of four values for ρ, 95% confidence intervals for γ assuming the real net rate of return is 3%. These confidence intervals suggest that the elasticity of intertemporal substitution, $[1/(1 - \gamma)]$, is significantly greater than has been pre-

Table 7.3. Parameter estimates — the preferred specification

Parameter	Model 1	Model 2	Model 3	Model 4	Model 5
$ED1(\beta_1)$	0.9963	1.0039	1.0045	0.9818	0.9977
	(0.0027)	(0.0021)	(0.0021)	(0.0030)	(0.0030)
$ED2(\beta_1)$	1.0018	1.0062	1.0065	0.9933	1.0030
	(0.0024)	(0.0021)	(0.0020)	(0.0023)	(0.0026)
$ED3(\beta_1)$	1.0069	1.0078	1.0086	0.9984	1.0077
	(0.0018)	(0.0017)	(0.0017)	(0.0016)	(0.0020)
$ED4(\beta_1)$	1.0099	1.0097	1.0106	1.0003	1.0112
	(0.0021)	(0.0020)	(0.0020)	(0.0021)	(0.0023)
$ED5(\beta_1)$	1.0103	1.0124	1.0128	1.0020	1.0115
	(0.0020)	(0.0020)	(0.0019)	(0.0018)	(0.0022)
β_2	0.5300	0.5193	0.5153	1.0000*	0.5380
	(0.0408)	(0.0365)	(0.0353)		(0.0410)
β_3	0.4160	0.4298	0.4308	0.7128	0.4158
	(0.0690)	(0.0698)	(0.0699)	(0.0838)	(0.0691)
β_4	0.2922	0.3011	0.3089	0.3216	0.2954
	(0.0497)	(0.0433)	(0.0432)	(0.0554)	(0.0488)
β_5	0.0000*	0.1079	0.0000*	0.0144	0.0000*
		(0.0424)		(0.0253)	
β_6	0.7947	0.0000*	0.0000*	0.9082	0.8238
	(0.0444)			(0.0500)	(0.0487)
β_7	1.0000*	1.0000*	1.0000*	1.0000*	1.0213
					(0.0191)
$SSR \times 10^{-2}$	3.4648	3.6801	3.7022	3.7463	3.4583
R^2	0.6511	0.6294	0.6272	0.6228	0.6518
$\chi^2\ STAT$ [a]	1.4985	48.1074	52.8422	62.3348	
	{5}	{1}	{1}	{1}	

Note: Asymptotic standard errors are in parentheses. An asterisk indicates that the parameter is constrained to equal the value shown. The sample includes 798 families.
a. The unrestricted model is given in braces.

Table 7.4. 95% confidence intervals for γ conditional on selected values of ρ

ρ	Education groups				
	ED1	ED2	ED3	ED4	ED5
0.000	−0.422−0.052	−0.114−0.182	0.102−0.260	0.161−0.322	0.175−0.325
0.010	0.044−0.371	0.261−0.458	0.405−0.509	0.443−0.550	0.453−0.552
0.020	0.524−0.687	0.632−0.730	0.704−0.756	0.723−0.776	0.728−0.777
0.029	0.953−0.969	0.963−0.973	0.971−0.976	0.972−0.978	0.973−0.978

viously estimated. For example, Friend and Blume (1975) use data on the portfolio composition of families in the Projector (1968) sample to estimate γ to be less than zero and, perhaps, as small as -1. In a more recent study Hall (1981) uses aggregate consumption data to estimate γ to be as small as -15. I believe that both of these estimates are extremely tenuous and am not inclined to reject our estimates in favor of theirs.[3] Unfortunately, the accuracy of our estimates is also suspect. This is because we have been unable to isolate the effect of the net rate of return on consumption.[4] Our estimates of γ would be much more reliable if the real net rate of return varied across the families in the sample.

The other parameter estimates of the preferred specification are quite reasonable. Perhaps the most controversial parameters are those relating to the portion of home(s) and automobile(s) that the family intends to acquire (β_6), the demand for liquid assets (β_5), and the weight on retirement consumption (β_2). The estimates and their asymptotic standard errors indicate that each of the hypotheses $\beta_6 = 0$ and $\beta_2 = 1$ is rejected with far greater than 99.9% confidence. Furthermore, it is 95% certain that $\beta_6 \geq 0.72$, and $\beta_2 \leq 0.60$. A 95% confidence interval for β_5 in model 4 of Table 7.1 is $-0.07 \leq \beta_5 \leq 0.05$, which includes reasonable values.

Since the asymptotic variance-covariance matrix can be misleading for a nonlinear model (see Section 6.2 of Chapter 6), the model is reestimated for the cases $\beta_6 = 0$, $\beta_5 = \beta_6 = 0$, and $\beta_2 = 1$, respectively. These estimations are reported in columns 2, 3, and 4 of Table 7.3, respectively. The asymptotic chi-square test statistics, reported in the row of the table labeled "$\chi^2 STAT$," indicate that each of these hypotheses may be rejected with at least 99.9% confidence.

Recall that our specification for the minimal allowable level of net worth requires that equity in home(s) and automobile(s) monotonically increase up to the limit given by β_6 times the current value of the family's home(s) and automobile(s):

$$\text{Minimum equity}_i = \text{Min}[WHA_t + EHA(t,i), \beta_6 VHA_t],$$
$$i = t, t+1, \ldots, T.$$

It is pointed out in Chapter 4 that this specification is unfortunate in that it does not allow the equity to peak and then decrease as the family ages. It turns out, however, that this possibility may be ruled out by the estimate of β_6. This is because the first cutoff date, v, is typically either the current period (56 observations), a date when a child leaves the home (63 observations), or when the family head is between the ages of 75 and 99 (648 observations). (The cutoff dates are discussed in the next section.) Since the estimate of β_6 is so high, it is apparent that β_6 has a marginal effect on consumption (that is, $WHA_t + EHA(t,v) > \beta_6 VHA_t$) mostly for families with cutoff dates in the latter group and $\beta_6 VHA_t$ therefore measures the desired home and automobile equity at those late dates. In other words, families apparently do not wish to decumulate equity in their home(s) and automobile(s) as they age.

It appears, therefore, that families intend to bequeath 79% of the value of their home(s) and automobile(s). It is argued in Chapter 8, however, that this asset accumulation is precautionary and hence is selfishly motivated. (Recall that the model does not allow for risk associated with uncertain lifetimes.)

The proportionality factor, β_7, is estimated in model 5 of Table 7.3. (The parameter β_5 is fixed at zero because its unconstrained estimate is insignificantly negative.) Recall that the theoretical model predicts this parameter to be one. The estimated value of β_7 is 1.0213, incredibly close to its theoretical value. This finding may be viewed as verification of the model's specification. Alternatively, if one is willing to maintain that β_7 is one, this is evidence that the normalization of the consumption function has eliminated the correlation between the true disturbance term and measured full wealth. (See Section 6.4 of Chapter 6.)

Recall that the normalization factor is defined in Equation (6.4) of Chapter 6 as

$$ZNORM = [\text{Max}(A_t - WHA_t + YD_t, YD_t)]^\delta.$$

The estimated value of δ is 0.85. (The estimation procedure is described in Section 6.1 of Chapter 6.) This value of δ has been used to construct $ZNORM$ for each of the estimations presented thus far. The sensitivity of the parameter estimates to δ is discussed in Section 7.3.2.

7.2 The Importance of Liquidity Constraints

This section analyzes the horizons estimated by the model and relates them to family characteristics. Estimates of an alternative model, which imposes constraints on the family's net worth only after the family head reaches age 65, also are presented.

7.2.1 The Horizons

Of the 798 families in the sample, 56 are estimated to have a one-year horizon, 63 are estimated to have a horizon that extends to a date when a child becomes independent (the oldest child in 55 cases and the youngest child in 8 cases), 648 are estimated to have a horizon that extends past the family head's 75th birthday, and the remaining 31 families in the sample tend to have a horizon that extends for only a few years. Table 7.5 cross-tabulates the sample according to the family head's current age and his or her age at the end of the family's horizon for three mutually exclusive groups: those with one-year horizons, those whose horizon extends to a time when a child becomes independent, and all others, respectively.

The results are in accord with our expectations. It was argued in Section 2.2.4 of Chapter 2 that the horizon is likely to (1) last for one period (the common perception of liquidity constraints), or (2) extend to a time when the family becomes smaller, or (3) extend to a time when the conditional probability of living becomes sufficiently small that the family would like to move noninterest income backward to years when the family is more likely to exist. All of the estimated horizons fall into one of these three horizon categories except for the 22 observations falling in the upper left 2 × 2 partition of Part III of Table 7.5. The discussion of Chapter 2 suggests at least two possible explanations for these observations: either the family has received some sort of windfall, or the family anticipates an unusual future expense. Given the young

Table 7.5. Numbers of observations by the horizon category, the family head's current age, and the family head's age at the end of the horizon

Head's age	Age of family head at end of horizon				
	25–30	31–45	46–60	61–75	76–92
I. Horizon = 1 year					
25–92	14	28	3	6	5
II. Horizon = number of years until child's independence					
25–30	0	8	0	0	0
31–45	0	30	13	0	0
46–60	0	0	6	2	0
61–75	0	0	0	2	1
76–92	0	0	0	0	1
III. Horizon = all others					
25–30	5	9	0	0	47
31–45	0	8	0	0	206
46–60	0	0	0	3	209
61–75	0	0	0	6	136
76–92	0	0	0	0	50

Table 7.6. The number of liquidity-constrained families

Horizon category	N^a	Percentage of sample	Percentage of population sampled
One year	56	6.89	9.64
When child independent	63	8.02	9.77
All others	679	85.09	80.59

a. Number of observations in each category.

ages of the family heads for these observations, it is likely that a number of these families are saving to purchase a consumer durable.[5]

Table 7.6 gives the proportion of families in the sample that are in each of the three horizon categories, and the corresponding figures for the population of families represented by the sample and each of the three horizon groups. (The latter figures are computed using sample weights that are included in the data.)[6] It is seen there that 14.9% of the sample, and 19.4% of the population sampled, are liquidity constrained (that is, fall into horizon categories I and II of Table 7.5). Note, however, that the sample excludes families whose heads are either self-employed or young and single.

It is difficult to ascertain the importance of liquidity constraints from the numbers of families who are liquidity constrained. More important is the proportion of total consumption undertaken by liquidity constrained families. Table 7.7 gives the proportion of total consumption undertaken by families in the sample that is undertaken by each of the three horizon groups, and the corresponding figures for the population of families represented by the sample and each of the three horizon groups. Our estimates indicate that 16.74% of consumption undertaken by families represented by the sample is undertaken by families

Table 7.7. The portion of consumption undertaken by liquidity-constrained families

Horizon category	Portion of consumption —	
	In sample (%)	In population sampled (%)
One year	3.07	6.81
When child independent	4.97	9.93
All others	91.96	83.26

falling into horizon categories I and II. Again, it should be kept in mind that the sample is not representative of the entire U.S. population.[7]

It is important to understand that the cutoff dates are not chosen to improve the model's fit but instead to insure that each family's consumption plan never violates the constraints on net worth. This criterion leads to a one-year horizon when currently available resources are small relative to total lifetime resources — which is most likely for low-wealth families. It is possible, however, that these families are not, in fact, consuming as large a portion of their resources as would be consistent with being liquidity constrained. Such a finding would cause us to doubt that the model is, in fact, identifying liquidity-constrained families.

To test this possibility, the following variable is constructed:

$$CR = C/(A + YD - WHA - SAVCON)$$

where, for the current period, C is consumption, A is net worth, YD is disposable income, WHA is equity in home(s) and automobile(s), and $SAVCON$ is the amount of saving in home(s) and automobile(s). This is a measure of the proportion of the available resources that are consumed and should be near one for families with one-year horizons. Table 7.8 cross-tabulates the sample according to the horizon category and the value of CR. It is seen there that all of the families that the model identifies as having one-year horizons consume more than 85% of their available resources. Nearly 93% consume more than 95% of their available resources. Likewise, more than 80% of the families whose horizons extend to the time that a child becomes independent consume more than 85% of their available resources. In contrast, less than 30% of those families in the third horizon category consume more than 85% of their resources. It would appear, therefore, that the vast majority of those families that are identified as being liquidity constrained consume an amount that is consistent with that hypothesis.

A further check on the model's specification of liquidity constraints is its fit for those families identified as liquidity constrained. The model

Table 7.8. Numbers of observations by the horizon category and the value of CR

Horizon category	Value of CR				
	0.00–0.50	0.50–0.85	0.85–0.90	0.90–0.95	>0.95
One year	0	0	4	4	48
When child independent	3	9	3	9	39
All others	286	194	26	46	127

does well on this score; it explains 66% and 47% of the *within-group* variance of consumption (unnormalized) for families in horizon groups I and II, respectively.

7.2.2 A Modified-Constraint Model

Here we compare the preferred specification with a model that does not impose constraints on the net worth of families prior to the time the family head reaches age 65. After age 65, the constraints on net worth are the same as those for the preferred model. This alternative model tends to attribute longer horizons to young families so that, relative to the preferred model, their full wealths tend to increase proportionately more than does the length of their horizons.

The parameter estimates for this modified-constraint model are presented in column 2 of Table 7.9. For the sake of comparison, the estimates for the preferred model are given in column 1 of the table.

The fit of the alternative model is slightly worse than that of the preferred model. Since the models are not nested, it is not possible to distinguish between them statistically.

The parameter estimates change so as to reduce the propensity to consume full wealth for young families (thereby countering the increase in their full wealths) while having little effect on this propensity for older preretirement families. To see this, note that the consumption growth rates are higher for the modified-constraint model (except for the 4th education group), which decreases the propensity to consume full wealth for families of all ages, but relatively more so the younger is the family. Countering this is the decrease in the weight on retirement consumption, which increases the propensity to consume full wealth of all preretirement families, but relatively more so the older is the family. On net, the propensity to consume full wealth is reduced for young families and is left relatively unchanged for older preretirement families.

A final comparison of these two models is given in Table 7.10. Here are presented the second moments of the residuals for each model, for each of the three horizon groups estimated by the preferred model. The preferred model fits better for all three horizon groups.

Our preferred specification is not overwhelmingly superior to the alternative model on the criterion of fit. The uniformity of this superiority demonstrated in Table 7.10, however, is supportive of the proposition that liquidity constraints have important effects on consumption behavior.

Note that the comparison of this section does not really constitute a test for the existence of liquidity contraints. The alternative model imposes liquidity constraints on families once the family head reaches age 65. There is not a plausible alternative model which does not involve liquidity constraints when the longevity of life is uncertain. The only alternative is the Yaari model (Yaari, 1965) which assumes the existence of perfect insurance and annuities markets. It is argued in Section 4.5.1 of Chapter 4 that this model cannot be generalized to multiple-person families and that it has unrealistic implications for the effect of lifetime uncertainty on an individual's consumption.

We conclude that even if one is willing to assume that young families are unconstrained in the credit market, our model remains useful for

Table 7.9. Parameter estimates: a modified-constraint model

Parameter	Model 1[a]	Model 2[b]
$ED1(\beta_1)$	0.9963	1.0025
	(0.0027)	(0.0020)
$ED2(\beta_1)$	1.0018	1.0057
	(0.0024)	(0.0019)
$ED3(\beta_1)$	1.0069	1.0079
	(0.0018)	(0.0016)
$ED4(\beta_1)$	1.0099	1.0092
	(0.0021)	(0.0020)
$ED5(\beta_1)$	1.0103	1.0120
	(0.0020)	(0.0019)
β_2	0.5300	0.4777
	(0.0408)	(0.0354)
β_3	0.4160	0.4336
	(0.0690)	(0.0663)
β_4	0.2922	0.2392
	(0.0497)	(0.0362)
β_5	0.0000*	0.0222
		(0.1233)
β_6	0.7947	0.7837
	(0.0444)	(0.0733)
β_7	1.0000*	1.0000*
$SSR \times 10^{-2}$	3.4648	3.5264
R^2	0.6511	0.6449

Note: Asymptotic standard errors are in parentheses. An asterisk indicates that the parameter is constrained to equal the value shown. The sample includes 798 families.

a. The preferred model.

b. Net worth is unconstrained prior to the family head's 65th birthday.

Table 7.10. Second moments of the residuals, for each horizon group, for the preferred and modified-constraint models

Horizon category	Model	
	Preferred	Modified-constraint
One year	0.619	0.626
When child independent	0.441	0.459
All others	0.418	0.425

properly modeling the effect of an uncertain lifetime on consumption behavior.[8]

7.3 The Model's Fit

The R^2 statistics given in Table 7.3 are unusually high for cross-section estimates and warrant a closer look.

This section begins with a comparison of the model's fit with that of a familiar linear model. This comparison reveals two reasons for the extraordinary fit of the preferred model: the data are apparently quite clean, and the normalization factor, ZNORM, gives relatively less weight to wealthy families, for whom the variance of consumption is greatest. Given this finding, we turn to an analysis of how the normalization factor affects the parameter estimates. Finally, the model's specification is tested by analyzing the preferred model's fit for subsamples sharing common family characteristics.

7.3.1 A Comparison with a Standard Linear Model

To provide a standard for comparison, we have employed ordinary least-squares to estimate the following standard linear consumption model:

$$C/ZNORM = [0.355 + 0.697YD - 0.038(A - WHA) \quad (7.2)$$
$$(0.169) \quad (0.046) \quad (0.027)$$
$$+ 0.040WHA + 1.17AGEH$$
$$(0.007) \quad (0.532)$$
$$+ 94.3FAMS]/ZNORM$$
$$(20.9)$$

$R^2 = 0.754$; standard errors are in parentheses. For the current period, C is consumption, YD is disposable income, A is net worth, WHA is equity in home(s) and automobile(s), *AGEH* is the age of the family head, *FAMS* is the family size, and *ZNORM* is the normalization factor. The fit of the linear model is better than that of the preferred model, which has an R^2 of 0.651.

The proportion of the variation of unnormalized consumption explained by the two models is: preferred model, $R^2 = -4.66$; linear model, $R^2 = 0.25$. This suggests that the preferred model performs worst, relative to the linear model, for wealthy families. This hypothesis is verified by Table 7.11, which gives the *within-group* R^2s of both models for a mutually exclusive and exhaustive set of net worth classifications. It is apparent that neither model performs well for wealthy families but that the preferred performs much worse. Both models tend to overestimate the consumption of wealthy families. For families with net worth less than \$250,000, which includes 94% of the sample, the models perform about equally well.

An alternative method of comparing the models is to tabulate their respective within-group R^2s for subsamples consisting of families with some maximal level of net worth. This is done in Table 7.12. Again the two models perform similarly for subsamples including families with net worth as high as \$250,000, and the linear model gives a substantially

Table 7.11. Within-group R^2, for unnormalized consumption, for mutually exclusive net-worth classifications

Net worth[a] (in \$1,000s)	N[b]	Model	
		Preferred	Linear
≤ 0	48	0.759	0.865
0–10	350	0.757	0.796
10–20	140	0.639	0.713
20–30	71	0.411	0.417
30–40	44	0.287	0.159
40–50	25	0.370	0.358
50–75	32	0.040	0.487
75–100	8	0.580	0.723
100–150	22	0.295	0.632
150–250	12	−0.146	−0.073
250–500	16	−1.486	0.406
500–1000	12	−6.398	0.071
>1000	18	−8.129	−0.170

a. Each category for net worth excludes the lower limit and includes the upper limit.
b. Number of observations in the respective categories.

Table 7.12. Within-group R^2, for unnormalized consumption, for nested net worth classifications

Net worth (in $1,000s) up to:	N[a]	Model	
		Preferred	Linear
100,000	798	−4.660	0.253
5,000	795	0.168	0.319
1,000	780	−0.118	0.672
750	776	−0.067	0.672
500	768	0.381	0.691
250	752	0.603	0.677
100	718	0.646	0.700
75	710	0.635	0.684
50	678	0.666	0.684
25	580	0.737	0.790
15	491	0.775	0.824
10	398	0.766	0.809
6	299	0.750	0.795
4	248	0.743	0.822
2	163	0.705	0.785

a. Number of observations in the respective categories.

better fit for subsamples including families with higher levels of net worth.

The preferred model's fit for extremely wealthy families is further discussed in Chapter 8.

It is discouraging that a model as simple as (7.2) does as well as our much more elaborate model. It is important to keep in mind, however, that our objective is to obtain an understanding of the determinants of consumption that extends beyond whatever peculiarities may be present in a particular sample. Our model is a structural model; the parameters, one hopes, remain stable for different times and different samples. The consumption equation (7.2), however, is not a structural model. There is no theory of choice underlying it, and it has proved notoriously unstable over time and across samples (see Friedman, 1957, chapter 4). To the extent that Equation (7.2) can be said to be a structural model, its income coefficient is sensitive to measurement error and its wealth coefficient is biased down by the negative correlation of wealth with the taste for early consumption (see Section 6.4 of Chapter 6). The existence of "bias" due to varying tastes is evidenced by the fact that the coefficients on the components of net worth are so low in (7.2).

(The term bias is used loosely here; bias is only meaningful in the context of a model with some underlying structure). In fact, the coefficient on net worth exclusive of the family's equity in its home(s) and automobile(s) is negative.

Further evidence of bias in the estimates of (7.2) is given by the fact that the estimates are very sensitive to the normalization factor. Below are presented the estimates of this model when δ, the exponent on the normalization factor, is one.

$$C/ZNORM^+ = [-58.06 + 0.803YD + 0.016(A - WHA)$$
$$(2.86) \quad (0.016) \quad (0.011)$$
$$+ \ 0.389WHA + 2.3AGEH + 90.2FAMS]/ZNORM^+$$
$$(0.057) \quad\quad (2.09) \quad\quad (21.1)$$

$R^2 = 0.823$; standard errors are in parentheses, where:

$$ZNORM^+ = ZNORM^{(1/0.85)}.$$

The parameter estimates are very different than those in (7.2). As is demonstrated in the next subsection, the estimates of our preferred specification are not sensitive to whether the normalization factor is $ZNORM$ or $ZNORM^+$.

We conclude that our preferred model is much more valuable for the purpose of understanding behavior than is model (7.2). The estimates of our model are precise, are consistent with a concave preference function, satisfy a plausible budget constraint, and conform with our prior notions as to what is reasonable. The parameters of Equation (7.2), conversely, are not structural parameters and have no behavioral implications.

7.3.2 The Normalization Factor

The findings of the last section indicate that extremely wealthy families tend to consume much less than the preferred model predicts, and the normalization factor utilized in the estimations disguises this fact.

These findings bring two questions to the forefront: (1) does the inclusion of wealthy families in the sample significantly affect the parameter estimates? and (2) does the normalization factor have a significant impact on the parameter estimates?

Models 1 and 3 of Table 7.13 shed light on the first issue. Model 3 restricts the sample to the 752 families with net worth less than $250,000. (The parameter β_5 is constrained to be zero for models 1, 2, and 3 of Table 7.13 because, for each model, its estimated value is insignificantly negative.) Model 1 is estimated with data for all 798

Table 7.13. Parameter estimates: the normalization factor

Parameter	Model 1[a]	Model 2[b]	Model 3[c]	Model 4[d]
$ED1(\beta_1)$	0.9963	0.9893	0.9968	1.0104
	(0.0027)	(0.0037)	(0.0027)	(0.0049)
$ED2(\beta_1)$	1.0018	1.0028	1.0019	1.0075
	(0.0024)	(0.0025)	(0.0025)	(0.0041)
$ED3(\beta_1)$	1.0069	1.0075	1.0067	1.0075
	(0.0018)	(0.0018)	(0.0018)	(0.0032)
$ED4(\beta_1)$	1.0099	1.0100	1.0098	1.0095
	(0.0021)	(0.0023)	(0.0022)	(0.0036)
$ED5(\beta_1)$	1.0103	1.0109	1.0102	1.0116
	(0.0020)	(0.0022)	(0.0021)	(0.0032)
β_2	0.5300	0.5126	0.5191	0.4568
	(0.0408)	(0.0444)	(0.0408)	(0.0361)
β_3	0.4160	0.4409	0.4026	0.4294
	(0.0690)	(0.0782)	(0.0682)	(0.0798)
β_4	0.2922	0.3086	0.2868	0.1966
	(0.0497)	(0.0565)	(0.0491)	(0.0612)
β_5	0.0000*	0.0000*	0.0000*	0.1030
				(0.0920)
β_6	0.7947	0.9297	0.7784	0.6167
	(0.0444)	(0.0340)	(0.0494)	(0.2611)
β_7	1.0000*	1.0000*	1.0000*	1.0000*
$SSR \times 10^{-2}$	3.4648	—	3.3471	—
R^2	0.6511	0.7130	0.5874	0.6137

Note: Asymptotic standard errors are in parentheses. An asterisk indicates that the parameter is constrained to equal the value shown.
  a. Full sample of 798 families, $\delta = 0.85$.
  b. Full sample of 798 families, $\delta = 1.00$.
  c. Restricted sample of 752 families, $\delta = 0.85$.
  d. Restricted sample of 752 families, $\delta = 0.00$.

families and is equivalent to model 1 of Table 7.3. The value of δ is 0.85 for both models. It is apparent that when δ is 0.85, the parameter estimates are insensitive to whether or not the 46 wealthiest families are included in the sample. (Each estimated parameter for model 1 is within 2% of its counterpart in model 3.) This is because the normalization factor gives wealthy families so little weight in the estimation of model 1.

All four of the estimated models given in Table 7.13 reflect on the sensitivity of the parameter estimates to δ. Model 2 gives the parameter estimates when $\delta = 1.0$ and the sample includes all 798 families. This model, it is recalled, is the preliminary estimation that yields the estimated value of δ. The parameter estimates are very similar to those of column 1; the primary difference is that the estimated value of β_6 is higher.

Column 4 gives the parameter estimates for the case where $\delta = 0.00$ (no normalization) and the sample is restricted to the 752 least wealthy families.[9] (When δ is zero and all 798 families are included in the sample, the 46 wealthiest families virtually determine the parameter estimates. In fact, one of these families is responsible for about half of the sum of squared residuals in this case.) Again, the parameter estimates are quite similar to those of the other models.

In conclusion, the inclusion of the 46 wealthiest families in the sample has little effect on the parameter estimates provided δ is at least 0.85, and the value of δ does not have a major impact on the parameter estimates except for the case where it is low *and* the 46 wealthiest families are included in the sample.

7.3.3 Other Specification Tests

This subsection tests for the possibility that the residuals of our preferred model (model 1 of Table 7.3) are related to family characteristics. The analysis is restricted to the 752 families with net worth less than $250,000. It already has been established that the consumption behavior of the 46 wealthiest families deviates significantly from the model's predictions.

Table 7.14 investigates the relationship of the residuals to net worth. The full sample of 752 families is divided into five mutually exclusive net worth classifications. The maximum net worth in each group is given in column 2 of the upper portion of the table. In the table, N is the number of families; R^2 is the within-group R^2, $\bar{e}$ is the mean residual, *BMED* is the portion of families whose residual is less than the overall median residual, *ZMED* is the absolute value of a standard normal variable under the null hypothesis that the group population value of *BMED*, for each group, is 0.5,[10] $\bar{C}$ is mean unnormalized consumption, *STDC* is the standard deviation of unnormalized consumption, RU^2 is the within-group R^2 for unnormalized consumption, and $\overline{eu}/\bar{C}$ is the mean of the denormalized residuals divided by $\bar{C}$. The ijth element of the *ZMEAN* matrix given in the lower portion of the table gives the absolute value of a standard normal variable under the null hypothesis that the mean residual for the ith group is equal to that of the jth group. (See Section 6.3 of Chapter 6 for a discussion of these statistics.)

The statistics of most interest, and that are discussed here, are $\bar{e}$, *BMED, ZMED,* and *ZMEAN.* The table indicates that (1) $\bar{e}$ tends to

Table 7.14. The relation of the residuals to net worth

Group	Max value ($1,000s)	N	R^2	$\bar{e}$	BMED	ZMED	$\bar{C}$ ($1,000s)	STDC ($1,000s)	RU^2	$\overline{eu}/\bar{C}$
1	1.975	159	−0.497	0.173	0.346	3.886	4.266	2.292	0.699	0.039
2	6.627	159	0.348	0.067	0.415	2.141	5.333	2.616	0.763	0.027
3	13.803	159	0.534	0.088	0.509	0.238	6.440	3.367	0.761	0.033
4	34.612	159	0.424	−0.038	0.616	2.934	7.815	3.588	0.396	−0.010
5	—	116	0.382	−0.060	0.655	3.342	13.022	9.940	0.385	−0.047

ZMEAN statistics

	Group				
Group	1	2	3	4	5
1	—	1.4	1.1	2.8	2.8
2		—	0.3	1.4	1.5
3			—	1.7	1.8
4				—	0.3

Table 7.15. The relation of the residuals to home and automobile equity

Group	Max value ($1,000s)	N	R^2	$\bar{e}$	BMED	ZMED	$\bar{C}$ ($1,000s)	STDC ($1,000s)	RU^2	$\overline{eu}/\bar{C}$
1	0.596	156	0.405	0.129	0.385	2.882	4.356	2.909	0.802	0.009
2	3.800	154	0.424	0.045	0.435	1.612	6.120	2.966	0.595	0.018
3	8.302	156	0.552	0.078	0.493	0.160	5.774	3.071	0.635	0.006
4	16.500	159	0.659	−0.023	0.597	2.458	7.375	3.464	0.389	−0.059
5	—	127	0.494	0.027	0.606	2.396	12.661	9.571	0.423	0.025

ZMEAN statistics

	Group				
Group	1	2	3	4	5
1	—	1.1	0.7	2.0	1.3
2		—	0.4	0.9	0.2
3			—	1.3	0.6
4				—	0.6

Table 7.16. The relation of the residuals to tenure class

Group	Max value	N	R^2	$\bar{e}$	BMED	ZMED	$\bar{C}$ ($1,000s)	STDC ($1,000s)	RU^2	$\overline{eu}/\bar{C}$
1	Renter	222	0.458	0.104	0.369	3.893	5.060	3.170	0.690	0.009
2	Owner	530	0.615	0.030	0.555	2.519	7.887	6.103	0.567	−0.002

ZMEAN statistics

	Group 1	2
Group 1	—	1.4

Table 7.17. The relation of the residuals to disposable income

Group	Max value ($1,000s)	N	R^2	$\bar{e}$	BMED	ZMED	$\bar{C}$ ($1,000s)	STDC ($1,000s)	RU^2	$\overline{eu}/\bar{C}$
1	4.000	157	0.565	0.145	0.446	1.357	2.336	1.417	0.360	−0.010
2	6.296	159	0.510	−0.063	0.547	1.190	4.845	1.378	−0.333	−0.059
3	8.208	160	0.517	0.047	0.506	0.158	6.814	2.538	0.143	0.004
4	11.335	158	0.559	0.068	0.487	0.318	8.862	4.432	−0.043	0.030
5	—	118	0.656	0.068	0.517	0.368	14.201	8.052	0.412	0.001

ZMEAN statistics

Group	1	2	3	4	5
1	—	2.8	1.3	1.0	0.9
2	—	—	1.5	1.7	1.6
3	—	—	—	0.3	0.3
4	—	—	—	—	0.0

Table 7.18. The relation of the residuals to the head's labor income

Group	Max value ($1,000s)	N	R^2	$\bar{e}$	BMED	ZMED	$\bar{C}$ ($1,000s)	STDC ($1,000s)	RU^2	$\overline{eu}/\bar{C}$
1	2.320	141	0.580	0.113	0.511	0.253	2.774	2.837	0.447	−0.117
2	5.750	161	0.302	0.142	0.422	1.970	5.393	4.538	0.247	0.105
3	7.443	156	0.548	0.008	0.493	0.160	6.339	2.204	0.326	0.004
4	10.820	156	0.570	−0.011	0.538	0.961	7.954	2.455	0.205	−0.016
5	—	138	0.602	0.004	0.543	1.021	13.146	7.950	0.445	−0.016

ZMEAN statistics

Group	1	2	3	4	5
1	—	0.4	1.4	1.6	1.4
2	—	—	1.8	2.0	1.8
3	—	—	—	0.2	0.0
4	—	—	—	—	0.2

Table 7.19. The relation of the residuals to the spouse's labor income

Group	Max value ($1,000s)	N	R^2	$\bar{e}$	BMED	ZMED	$\bar{C}$ ($1,000s)	STDC ($1,000s)	RU^2	$\overline{eu}/\bar{C}$
1	Single	79	0.744	−0.011	0.557	1.013	2.461	3.612	0.759	−0.174
2	0.000	393	0.522	0.059	0.509	0.353	7.735	6.619	0.548	0.009
3	2.000	146	0.468	0.001	0.507	0.165	6.067	2.960	0.750	−0.007
4	4.000	73	0.566	0.170	0.370	2.224	7.812	2.948	0.206	0.024
5	—	61	0.809	0.065	0.508	0.128	10.048	2.762	0.215	−0.002

ZMEAN statistics

Group	1	2	3	4	5
1	—	0.9	0.1	1.7	0.7
2		—	0.9	1.3	0.1
3			—	1.8	0.6
4				—	0.9

Table 7.20. The relation of the residuals to the head's age

Group	Max value (years)	N	R^2	$\bar{e}$	BMED	ZMED	$\bar{C}$ ($1,000s)	STDC ($1,000s)	RU^2	$\overline{eu}/\bar{C}$
1	30	83	0.041	−0.080	0.518	0.329	5.891	5.659	0.197	0.051
2	45	281	0.509	0.056	0.455	1.491	7.197	3.064	0.516	0.007
3	60	211	0.607	0.048	0.545	1.308	9.614	6.571	0.599	−0.004
4	75	127	0.603	0.141	0.480	0.444	4.731	6.237	0.639	0.017
5	—	50	0.513	0.033	0.580	1.131	3.252	4.410	0.616	−0.245

ZMEAN statistics

Group	1	2	3	4	5
1	—	1.6	1.5	2.3	0.9
2	—	—	0.1	1.2	0.2
3	—	—	—	1.2	0.1
4	—	—	—	—	1.0

Table 7.21. The relation of the residuals to head's education

Group	Max value (years)	N	R^2	$\bar{e}$	BMED	ZMED	$\bar{C}$ ($1,000s)	STDC ($1,000s)	RU^2	$\overline{eu}/\bar{C}$
1	8	185	0.467	0.010	0.470	0.809	4.344	3.157	0.531	−0.033
2	11	140	0.724	−0.029	0.543	1.014	5.954	3.343	0.746	−0.049
3	12	206	0.605	0.057	0.461	1.115	7.065	4.578	0.573	0.020
4	15	83	0.575	0.091	0.494	0.110	8.667	6.081	0.130	0.025
5	—	138	0.554	0.039	0.558	1.362	10.806	7.962	0.605	0.014

ZMEAN statistics

	Group				
Group	1	2	3	4	5
1	—	1.7	0.6	0.1	0.8
2		—	1.2	1.3	0.8
3			—	0.4	0.2
4				—	0.6

Table 7.22. The relation of the residuals to the number of children

Group	Max value	N	R^2	$\bar{e}$	BMED	ZMED	$\bar{C}$ ($1,000s)	STDC ($1,000s)	RU^2	$\overline{eu}/\bar{C}$
1	0	305	0.620	0.079	0.495	0.172	6.464	6.573	0.637	−0.001
2	1	118	0.421	0.037	0.517	0.368	7.910	5.357	0.758	0.015
3	2	146	0.510	−0.017	0.486	0.331	7.327	5.541	0.426	−0.002
4	3	97	0.532	0.087	0.515	0.305	7.321	3.535	0.574	−0.016
5	—	86	0.245	0.052	0.500	0.000	7.190	2.950	0.299	0.003

ZMEAN statistics

	Group				
Group	1	2	3	4	5
1	—	0.6	1.4	0.1	0.3
2		—	0.7	0.5	0.2
3			—	1.2	0.8
4				—	0.4

decline with wealth, (2) of all ten group pairs, only $\bar{e}_1 - \bar{e}_4$ and $\bar{e}_1 - \bar{e}_5$ are different than zero at the 5% level of significance, (3) *BMED* monotonically increases with net worth, and (4) the population value for *BMED* most probably increases with net worth. Apparently wealthy families tend to consume less than the model predicts but, as is indicated by the *ZMEAN* statistics, these differences tend not to be quantitatively significant.

Table 7.15 concerns home and automobile wealth and tells a story similar to that of Table 7.14. Table 7.16 indicates that renters (home owners) tend to consume more (less) than the model's predictions. The difference, however, is not quantitatively significant.

These results suggest that tastes are randomly distributed in the sample and are correlated with net worth (see Section 6.4 of Chapter 6). Our objective, in this case, is to obtain consistent estimates of the mean parameter vector. If this objective is achieved, the residuals will be correlated with net worth. Hence the findings of Tables 7.14–7.16 do not reflect unfavorably on the estimates. Indeed, it would be disturbing if the residuals were not correlated with net worth, since this would suggest that the parameters are biased in such a way as to accommodate the behavioral differences of low-wealth and high-wealth families.

Tables 7.17, 7.18, and 7.19 investigate the relationship of the residuals to disposable income, the head's labor income, and the spouse's labor income, respectively. The results are very supportive of the model's specification. Only two of the thirty *ZMEAN* test statistics, and two of the fifteen *ZMED* test statistics, are significant at the 5% level.

Tables 7.20, 7.21, and 7.22 test the model's specification for the head's age, the head's education, and the number of children in the household, respectively. None of the fifteen *ZMED* statistics, and only one of the thirty *ZMEAN* test statistics, are significant at the 5% level.

7.4 Summary and Conclusion

The empirical results are extremely encouraging. The model fits the data well in spite of its tight theoretical structure. Furthermore, there is no evidence that the model is misspecified with respect to disposable income, the head's labor income, the spouse's labor income, the head's age, the head's education, or family size. There is evidence that tastes vary across families and are correlated with net worth. This, however, is consistent with the hypothesis that our parameter estimator is a consistent estimator of the population mean parameter vector.

Liquidity constraints are apparently quite important. It is estimated that liquidity-constrained families constitute 19.4% of the population sampled. This finding is in rough agreement with the conclusions of Hall and Mishkin (1982) and Hayashi (1984) (see Section 3.3.1 of Chapter 3). These studies are unable to detect short multiperiod horizons, however. Such families constitute about half of the families that our model identifies as liquidity constrained.

I estimate that liquidity-constrained families are responsible for 16.7% of total consumption undertaken by the population sampled. I am aware of no other comparable findings. The models of Hall and Mishkin and Hayashi, it is recalled, do not identify liquidity-constrained families and, therefore, are unable to assess the importance of such families for aggregate consumption.

8 Social Security, Intergenerational Transfers, and Consumption

The estimated models of Chapter 7 assume that the social security system affects a family's consumption behavior entirely through its *direct* effect on the family's net noninterest receipts in each period. Barro (1974) shows that this assumption is not correct for families who are linked to past *or* future generations through operative intergenerational transfers.

The primary objective of this chapter is to test whether families do, in fact, view their net social security receipts the same as they do their other forms of net noninterest income when making consumption decisions. Such a test is an implicit test of the prevalence of operative intergenerational transfers. Independent evidence pertaining to the importance of planned bequests also is presented. This is done to check our conclusions regarding social security and also because bequest behavior is of independent interest.

The chapter is organized as follows. Section 8.1 generalizes our empirical model to take into account the possibility of operative intergenerational transfers. The generalized model contains one additional parameter whose value measures the impact of net social security receipts on consumption. The estimates of this generalized model are presented in Section 8.2. Section 8.3 presents evidence bearing more directly on the importance of intergenerational transfers. Finally, Section 8.4 gives a brief conclusion.

8.1 The Model with Intergenerational Transfers

This section begins with a review of the theory relating to intergenerational transfers and the effect of an unfunded social security system on consumption. The discussion is limited to the microeconomic aspects of these issues and summarizes results that are discussed extensively in Section 2.3 of Chapter 2. The general model, which incorporates intergenerational transfers, is then presented.

The effects of an unfunded social security system on the macro economy are discussed in Chapter 11.

8.1.1 A Review

Consider the effect of the social security system on a family that does not receive any planned net transfers. (Planned transfers given by a family are regarded as a negative transfer received.) Provided labor-leisure choices are unaffected, the social security system affects this family's consumption entirely through the effect of social security taxes and benefits on the family's lifetime budget constraint. If there are no constraints on net worth prior to the time of death, then this effect is completely summarized by the family's lifetime social security wealth, which is simply the discounted value of lifetime social security benefits minus the discounted value of lifetime social security taxes. If there are inequality constraints on net worth prior to the time of death, then the social security system makes binding liquidity constraints either more likely or, if already present, more severe. This is because social security taxes and benefits tilt the time profile of the family's net noninterest receipts upward. In such cases positive lifetime social security wealth may reduce the family's consumption when young but increase it substantially when old.

If intergenerational transfers are operative (that is, planned and altruistically motivated), then the relevant decision-making unit is the extended family which we define here as the succession of generations of a family that are linked by operative transfers (see Section 2.3 of Chapter 2). The effect of social security on an extended family's consumption takes place entirely through its effect on the extended family's budget constraint. Again, if there are no liquidity constraints and labor-leisure choices are unaffected, social security's effect on this budget constraint is completely summarized by the social security increment to the extended family's "lifetime" full wealth. To the extent that the social security system increases the lifetime full wealth of one constituent generation at the expense of another, the extended family's consumption is unaffected. Since liquidity constraints are unlikely to be binding for the case where intergenerational transfers are operative (see Section 2.3 of Chapter 2), this conclusion continues to be valid when there are inequality constraints on net worth.

An important consideration that has been ignored thus far is the effect of the social security system on the age of retirement. There are two reasons for such an effect: the social security increment to lifetime full wealth has an income effect on the demand for leisure, and the social security earnings test puts a high implicit tax on income earned when a worker is eligible for social security.[1] It is likely that the net effect is to reduce the age of retirement and induce the family to save more, and perhaps take less leisure, during its working life so it is able to provide for a longer period of retirement. Note that this retirement effect will be present even if intergenerational transfers are operative.

8.1.2 The Generalized Model

Net noninterest receipts in each period equals the sum of net labor income, net social security receipts, and net intergenerational transfers. Employers' social security tax contributions are a positive component of net labor income and a negative component of net social security receipts. Let $WN(i,j)$, $SSW(i,j)$, and $TR(i,j)$ be, respectively, the present values at time i of receipts during the interval (i,j) due to net labor income, net social security receipts, and net intergenerational transfers. Then full wealth in the current period t, defined for the interval (t,s), can be written

$$W(t,s) = A_t + WN(t,s) + SSW(t,s) + TR(t,s), \qquad (8.1)$$
$$s = t, t+1, \ldots, T.$$

The optimal level of current consumption when transfers are non-zero is conceptually the same as for the case where they are zero; the only difference is that full wealth for the interval (t,s), given by (8.1), contains an additional term (see Section 2.3 of Chapter 2). Implementing any reasonable theory that makes transfers endogenous, however, requires data pertaining to the extended family. Such data, if they exist at all, are rare.

The natural procedure in this situation is to treat $TR(t,s)$; $s = t, t+1, \ldots, T$; as unobservable random variables. The cogent questions concern the properties of these random variables. In particular, are they correlated with the right-hand-side variables of the consumption function?

One would expect that $TR(t,s)$ and $A_t + WN(t,s)$ are negatively correlated. That is, the size of a wealth transfer tends to increase with the wealth of the donor. This phenomenon would cause wealthy families, on average, to consume less than the model of Chapter 7 would predict.

Also, the inclusion of wealthy families in the sample may render the parameter estimates inconsistent. The results reported in Section 7.3 of Chapter 7 confirm the first expectation but indicate that the parameter estimates are not sensitive to whether the wealthiest families are included in the sample. We return to these issues in Section 8.3.

The controversy regarding the effect of social security on consumption concerns the relationship between intergenerational transfers $[TR(t,s)]$ and social security wealth $[SSW(t,s)]$. The opposing views are represented by Barro (1979) and Feldstein (1976a). Barro argues that lifetime social security wealth, $SSW(0,\tau)$, is a government-induced transfer from children to parents that tends to be offset by private lifetime intergenerational transfers so that

$$SSW(0,\tau) + TR(0,\tau) \simeq v_\tau^B, \tag{8.2}$$

where τ is the time of death, time zero represents the beginning of economic life, and v_τ^B is a random variable that is independent of $SSW(0,\tau)$.[2] Feldstein, however, maintains that operative intergenerational transfers are not prevalent so that

$$TR(t,s) \simeq \eta_s^F, \qquad s = t, t+1, \ldots, T, \tag{8.3}$$

where η_s^F is a random variable that is independent of $SSW(t,s)$.

Additional assumptions must be combined with the Barro hypothesis (8.2), which concerns *lifetime* transfers, to infer the relationship of the time profile of transfers to the social security system. To this end we make the following important assumption:

$$\begin{aligned} TR(0,s) &= v_s^B, &&\text{for } s \text{ such that } SSW(0,s) \leqslant 0, \\ &= v_s^B - SSW(0,s), &&\text{for } s \text{ such that } SSW(0,s) > 0 \end{aligned}$$

or equivalently,

$$TR(0,s) = v_s^B + \text{Min}[0, -SSW(0,s)]. \tag{8.4}$$

To interpret (8.4), note that in 1963 nearly all participants in the social security system enjoyed positive lifetime social security wealth. It follows since social security taxes precede social security benefits that there exists a date after retirement, say q, such that $SSW(0,s) \leqslant 0$, for $s \leqslant q$, and $SSW(0,s) > 0$, for $s > q$. Equation (8.4) simply states that the social security system reduces the family's consumable resources prior to period q but, after period q, positive social security wealth is entirely offset by private transfers. In other words, the family treats social security taxes as if they are deductions from labor income, and social security benefits as if they are increments to labor income up until the time that the family has received a market rate of return on all past social security taxes paid, including those paid by the employer.

An important implication of this interpretation of the Barro hypothesis is that social security will exacerbate, or perhaps cause, binding liquidity constraints if the first cutoff date, v, occurs before period q.[3] In this case, social security affects the timing of consumption but not the present value of lifetime consumption. If, conversely, $v > q$ then (8.4) implies that social security has absolutely no effect on current consumption.

Equation (8.4) is conveniently rewritten as

$$TR(t,s) = (1 + R)^t\{v_s^B - TR(0,t-1) + \text{Min}[0,-SSW(0,s)]\} \quad (8.5)$$
$$= \eta_s^B + Z(t,s) - SSW(t,s),$$

where

$$\eta_s^B = (1 + R)^t[v_s^B - TR(0,t-1)],$$
$$Z(t,s) = SSW(t,s) + \text{Min}[0,-SSW(0,s)(1 + R)^t]$$
$$= \text{Min}[SSW(t,s), -SSW(0,t-1)(1 + R)^t],$$

and R is the real net rate of return. As is discussed in the next subsection, it is necessary to restrict the sample to preretirement families when estimating β_8. According to (8.4), $TR(0,t-1)$ is v_{t-1}^B for these families so that η_s^B in (8.5) is $(1 + R)^t(v_s^B - v_{t-1}^B)$ and is independent of $SSW(0,i)$, $i = 0,1, \ldots ,T$. In other words, all past transfers are independent of $SSW(0,i)$, $i = 0,1, \ldots ,T$, for preretirement families. This is a crucial assumption. If the Barro hypothesis is correct and all intergenerational transfers already have taken place, then the family's consumption behavior will appear to be entirely consistent with the Feldstein hypothesis.

The Feldstein hypothesis (8.3) and the Barro hypothesis (8.5) may be placed in a common framework as follows:

$$TR(t,s) = \eta_s + Z(t,s) - SSW(t,s) + \beta_8[SSW(t,s) - Z(t,s)], \quad (8.6)$$

where in the Feldstein view $\eta_s = \eta_s^F$ and β_8 is one, and in the Barro view $\eta_s = \eta_s^B$ and β_8 is zero. In either case, η_s is independent of $SSW(t,s)$ and $Z(t,s)$. Note that an estimate of β_8 enables us to test the validity of these competing views.

Substituting the nonstochastic portion of (8.6) into (8.1) gives our parametric decomposition of full wealth:

$$W(t,s) = A_t + WN(t,s) + Z(t,s) + \beta_8[SSW(t,s) - Z(t,s)], \quad (8.7)$$
$$s = t,t+1, \ldots ,T.$$

Equation (8.7) gives the specification for full wealth that is utilized throughout this chapter. Note that if β_8 is one (the Feldstein hypothesis), then the specification reduces to the Chapter 7 specification. As already noted, Section 8.3 investigates the possibility that η_s of Equation (8.6) is negatively correlated with $A_t + WN(t,s)$.

To this point, our interpretation of the Barro hypothesis is overly simplified. This is because the social security system tends to redistribute full wealth across extended families so that one generation's social security wealth is positively correlated with the extended family's full wealth and, hence, will influence the consumption of all generations.[4] This would cause β_8 to be positive, but less than one, even if intergenerational transfers are operative. This phenomenon is kept in mind when interpreting the empirical results.

The specification of this chapter does not allow for the possibility that the age of retirement, and hence $WN(t,s)$, is related to social security wealth. Feldstein (1974) argues that the retirement age is negatively related to social security wealth so that $WN(t,s)$ and $SSW(t,s)$ are negatively related. Blinder, Gordon, and Wise (1980) argue, however, that the social security system discourages retirement prior to age 65 so that $WN(t,s)$ and $SSW(t,s)$ may be positively related.

The projected retirement ages are consistent, however, with the possibility that social security affects the retirement age of all individuals by an equal amount, regardless of the size of their social security wealth. This is because data on actual retirement behavior are used to project the retirement dates of the working families in the sample (see Section 5.1.3 of Chapter 5).

We note that Kotlikoff (1979b) and Kurz (1981) do allow the retirement age to depend on social security wealth but find that this allowance has little effect on the parameter estimates for their respective net worth equations.

MEASURED SOCIAL SECURITY WEALTH

Measuring full wealth, as given in (8.7), requires an estimate of the accumulated value of past social security tax contributions. For working families, this quantity is given by $-SSW(0,t-1)(1+R)^t$ in (8.5).

Past social security taxes are imputed by the same method as future social security taxes are imputed (see Section 5.1.3 of Chapter 5). Wage profiles for each of ten sex and education categories are used to backcast labor income for each individual in the sample to age 20. (Chronological age 20 corresponds to economic age 0 in the above discussion.) The statutory social security tax rates (including the employer's contribution), as well as the maximum taxable earnings, then are applied to these estimated labor income profiles to estimate social security taxes paid in each past year. These taxes are accumulated to the present using a 3% real net rate of interest.

These imputations cannot be made for retired individuals, for it is impossible to backcast their labor income. The sample shrinks, therefore, to 623 preretirement families.

The imputation of future social security benefits is explained in Section 5.1.3 of Chapter 5.

8.2 The Parameter Estimates

In Table 8.1 are presented the parameter estimates for five versions of the generalized model. Each of these models is estimated using 623 preretirement observations for which it is possible to estimate the current accumulated value of past social security tax contributions. The value of δ used to estimate the normalization factor is 0.85 for all the estimations presented in this chapter.

Model 1 is the base-case model applied to the 623 preretirement observations for which it is possible to estimate the current accumulated value of all past social security tax contributions. The value of β_7 is constrained to equal one, as the theoretical model requires, for each estimation presented in this chapter. All the parameter estimates are reasonable and have low asymptotic standard errors.

The parameter that is of most interest here is β_8. Its point estimate is 0.5945 and the hypothesis that it is as small as 0.2472 can be rejected with 95% confidence. Furthermore, the hypothesis that β_8 is one cannot be rejected with 95% confidence.

Since the asymptotic variance-covariance matrix for the estimates is dependent on the local properties of the likelihood function, the model is estimated subject to each of the restrictions $\beta_8 = 0$ (model 2) and $\beta_8 = 1$ (model 3) to obtain likelihood ratio statistics testing each hypothesis. The restricted estimates are reported in columns 2 and 3 of Table 8.1. The row the table labeled "$\chi^2 STAT$" gives statistics that are asymptotically distributed as chi-square random variables under the null hypothesis that the model of the given column is the true model (see Section 6.3 of Chapter 6 for a discussion of these statistics). These statistics indicate that the hypothesis that β_8 is zero is rejected with more than 99.9% confidence, and the hypothesis that β_8 is one cannot be rejected with 95% confidence.

The restricted parameter estimates are quite illuminating. Note that the estimated value of β_2 increases monotonically with the value of β_8 for models 1, 2, and 3. Furthermore, when β_8 is fixed, the asymptotic

Table 8.1. Parameter estimates: the effect of social security in the context of the preferred model

Parameter	Model 1	Model 2	Model 3	Model 4	Model 5
$ED1(\beta_1)$	1.0014	1.0014	1.0008	1.0001	0.9952
	(0.0024)	(0.0025)	(0.0023)	(0.0021)	(0.0022)
$ED2(\beta_1)$	1.0053	1.0063	1.0044	1.0038	1.0011
	(0.0022)	(0.0022)	(0.0021)	(0.0019)	(0.0020)
$ED3(\beta_1)$	1.0072	1.0089	1.0062	1.0057	1.0036
	(0.0019)	(0.0018)	(0.0017)	(0.0015)	(0.0016)
$ED4(\beta_1)$	1.0093	1.0113	1.0080	1.0076	1.0062
	(0.0022)	(0.0022)	(0.0021)	(0.0019)	(0.0020)
$ED5(\beta_1)$	1.0116	1.0139	1.0102	1.0098	1.0086
	(0.0022)	(0.0021)	(0.0020)	(0.0017)	(0.0018)
β_2	0.4464	0.3271	0.5316	0.5316*	0.5316*
	(0.0554)	(0.0275)	(0.0378)		
β_3	0.3981	0.3783	0.4095	0.4269	0.5359
	(0.0651)	(0.0645)	(0.0655)	(0.0635)	(0.0687)
β_4	0.2601	0.2558	0.2620	0.2575	0.2725
	(0.0413)	(0.0420)	(0.0408)	(0.0406)	(0.0448)
β_5	0.1120	0.1103	0.1126	0.1133	0.1151
	(0.0427)	(0.0424)	(0.0428)	(0.0428)	(0.0395)
β_6	0.1436	0.1428	0.1472	0.1429	0.1412
	(0.0415)	(0.0417)	(0.0415)	(0.0416)	(0.0408)
β_7	1.0000*	1.0000*	1.0000*	1.0000*	1.0000*
β_8	0.5945	0.0000*	1.0000*	0.8470	0.0000*
	(0.2111)			(0.1431)	
$SSR \times 10^{-2}$	2.5903	2.6432	2.6052	2.5999	2.7938
R^2	0.6159	0.6081	0.6137	0.6145	0.5858
$\chi^2\ STAT$		12.5950[a]	3.5754[a]		44.8122[b]
			1.2687[b]		

Note: Asymptotic standard errors are in parentheses. An asterisk indicates that the parameter is constrained to equal the value shown. The sample includes 623 preretirement families.

a. The unrestricted model is model 1.
b. The unrestricted model is model 4.

standard error for $\hat{\beta}_2$ decreases substantially from its value in model 1. These facts indicate that there is a large positive covariance between $\hat{\beta}_2$ and $\hat{\beta}_8$. The implication is that a substantial portion of the variation in normalized consumption can be explained by *either β_2 or β_8*. It follows that imposing a prior on the value of β_2, if that is possible, will lead to a much more precise estimate of β_8.

This is an important observation given that β_2 is implausibly low for models 1 and 2. For example, a value of 0.4464 for β_2 (its value in model 1) implies that an elderly couple's consumption falls by 55.36%, relative to its basic growth rate, at age 65 (see Section 4.4 of Chapter 4 for the determinants of the consumption growth rate). A reasonable assumption, therefore, is that β_2 is no smaller than 0.5316, its estimated value in model 3. The estimates that follow, therefore, fix β_2 at 0.5316. This is equivalent, of course, to requiring that β_2 be no smaller than 0.5316.

Model 4 gives the base-case parameter estimates when β_2 is fixed at 0.5316. Relative to model 1, $\hat{\beta}_8$ rises to 0.8470 and its asymptotic standard error falls by 32%. Conditional on the reasonable hypothesis that $\beta_2 \geqslant 0.5316$, therefore, it is 95% certain that β_8 is no smaller than 0.6116. Furthermore, the hypothesis that β_8 is one cannot be rejected with 75% confidence.

As before, this alternative base-case model is estimated subject to each of the additional restrictions $\beta_8 = 0$ (model 5) and $\beta_8 = 1$. (The latter model is identical to model 3 with respect to fit and the parameter estimates. The asymptotic standard errors, of course, are different.) The asymptotic chi-square statistics testing these restrictions are, respectively, 44.81 and 1.27. The hypothesis that β_8 is zero can be rejected, therefore, with far greater than 99.9% confidence (the 0.1% critical value is 10.8). The hypothesis that β_8 is one, conversely, cannot be rejected with 75% confidence.

The reader may have noticed that the estimated values of β_5 and β_6 are quite different in model 3 than they are for the preferred model of Chapter 7, which is the same specification estimated with data for the entire sample. This result is discussed in Section 8.3.3.

SUMMARY

We find that β_8 is significantly greater than 0.61 and is not significantly different than one. This suggests that in each period net social security receipts and receipts from other sources have identical effects on consumption behavior.

I believe the estimates of β_8 are too high to be entirely explained by the existence of social security induced interfamily transfers. It appears, therefore, that our results support the Feldstein hypothesis concerning the effect of social security on consumption.

8.2.1 The Modified-Constraint Model

To check the robustness of our findings with respect to the specification of liquidity constraints, the five models of Table 8.1 are estimated for the case where the family's net worth is unconstrained prior to the 65th birthday of the family head (see Section 7.2.2 for a discussion of this model). The results are given in Table 8.2. Each model in Table 8.2 corresponds to the model of the same number (column) in Table 8.1.

Note that β_5 and β_6 are constrained to be zero in model 5. This is because the unconstrained estimates of these parameters are negative

Table 8.2. Parameter estimates: the effect of social security in the context of the modified-constraint model

Parameter	Model 1	Model 2	Model 3	Model 4	Model 5
$ED1(\beta_1)$	1.0048	1.0051	1.0044	1.0038	1.0008
	(0.0021)	(0.0022)	(0.0021)	(0.0019)	(0.0018)
$ED2(\beta_1)$	1.0073	1.0081	1.0068	1.0063	1.0038
	(0.0021)	(0.0021)	(0.0020)	(0.0018)	(0.0018)
$ED3(\beta_1)$	1.0097	1.0111	1.0089	1.0086	1.0069
	(0.0018)	(0.0018)	(0.0017)	(0.0014)	(0.0014)
$ED4(\beta_1)$	1.0112	1.0128	1.0102	1.0100	1.0087
	(0.0022)	(0.0021)	(0.0020)	(0.0018)	(0.0018)
$ED5(\beta_1)$	1.0138	1.0156	1.0127	1.0125	1.0111
	(0.0021)	(0.0021)	(0.0019)	(0.0017)	(0.0017)
β_2	0.4044	0.3197	0.4641	0.4641*	0.4641*
	(0.0548)	(0.0402)	(0.0369)		
β_3	0.4195	0.4015	0.4330	0.4369	0.5439
	(0.0662)	(0.0659)	(0.0669)	(0.0653)	(0.0658)
β_4	0.2612	0.2655	0.2609	0.2597	0.2552
	(0.0380)	(0.0391)	(0.0378)	(0.0374)	(0.0388)
β_5	0.0936	0.0324	0.2427	0.0649	0.0000*
	(0.3704)	(0.3538)	(0.3914)	(0.3571)	
β_6	0.3640	−0.2435	0.5821	0.1861	0.0000*
	(0.6465)	(0.7622)	(0.2858)	(0.6559)	
β_7	1.0000*	1.0000*	1.0000*	1.0000*	1.0000*
β_8	0.5859	0.0000*	1.0000*	0.7438	0.0000*
	(0.2139)			(0.1852)	
$SSR \times 10^{-2}$	2.6701	2.7220	2.6817	2.6754	2.8382
R^2	0.6041	0.5964	0.6024	0.6033	0.5792
$\chi^2\ STAT$		11.9934[a]	2.7007[a]		36.8013[b]
			1.4653[b]		

Note: Asymptotic standard errors are in parentheses. An asterisk indicates that the parameter is constrained to equal the value shown. The sample includes 623 preretirement families.

a. The unrestricted model is model 1.

b. The unrestricted model is model 4.

and statistically significant. Since negative values for these parameters cannot be rationalized their values are constrained to be zero.

The estimates of β_8 for the models of Table 8.2 are slightly lower than the corresponding estimates in Table 8.1. The reason is that young liquidity-constrained families are assumed to consume in accordance with their lifetime social security wealth, which requires that they borrow currently, for the models of Table 8.2. This misspecification biases the estimated value of β_8 downward.

Nevertheless, the models of Table 8.2 tell a story remarkably similar to those of Table 8.1. The probability statements implied by the estimates given in Table 8.2, corresponding to each of the probability statements made with regard to the estimates given in Table 8.1, are listed below.

(1) It is 95% certain that β_8 in model 1 exceeds 0.2340.
(2) The hypothesis that β_8 in model 1 is one cannot be rejected with 95% confidence.
(3) Model 2 can be rejected in favor of model 1 with 99.9% confidence.
(4) Model 3 cannot be rejected in favor of model 1 with 90% confidence.
(5) It is 95% certain that β_8 in model 4 exceeds 0.4391.
(6) The hypothesis that β_8 in model 4 is one cannot be rejected with 85% confidence.
(7) Model 5 can be rejected in favor of model 4 with 99.9% confidence.
(8) Model 3 cannot be rejected in favor of model 4 with 80% confidence.

It is apparent that our conclusions regarding social security are not sensitive to the model's specification of liquidity constraints.

8.2.2 The Role of Wealthy Families

The estimates given in Tables 8.1 and 8.2 are for a sample that includes all preretirement families. It was discovered in Chapter 7 that the preferred model appears to be misspecified for families with net worth exceeding \$250,000. The normalization factor, however, is such that the parameter estimates are not much affected by the inclusion of these families in the sample.

It is natural to ask, however, if the conclusions of this section are sensitive to the inclusion of wealthy families in the sample. To answer this question, model 4 of Table 8.1 (the preferred model of this section) is reestimated for a restricted sample including all 603 preretirement families whose net worth is less than $250,000. The parameter estimates and their standard errors are virtually unchanged from those in Table 8.1. (The estimates of this model are not displayed.) The estimate of β_8 for this restricted sample is 0.8376 and its standard error is 0.1436.

8.3 Evidence Relating Directly to Intergenerational Transfers

The evidence presented in the last section suggests that families view net social receipts the same as they do net receipts from other sources when making their consumption decisions. This is indirect evidence that operative intergenerational transfers are not prevalent.

Here we scrutinize the consumption behavior of the families in the sample to uncover evidence relating directly to the importance of bequests. This section includes (1) a discussion of our earlier finding that families in the sample apparently do not plan to consume 79% of the value of their home(s) and automobile(s), (2) an analysis of the predictive performance of our preferred model for groups of families stratified by net worth to determine if high-wealth families behave as if they plan bequests, and (3) a closer look at the consumption behavior of older families for whom an intention to leave a bequest should be most evident.

It is important to keep in mind the fact that operative transfers must be altruistically motivated (see Section 3.1.4 of Chapter 3). This section concerns only the prevalence and size of bequests and not the motivation of the donors.

The analysis of this section concerns the preferred model of Chapter 7, which is estimated with data for the entire sample and which maintains that β_8 is one. The parameter estimates for this model, it is recalled, are given in column 1 of Table 7.3.

8.3.1 Consumption and the Value of Home(s) and Automobile(s)

Our preferred model suggests that families do not intend to consume 79% of the value of their home(s) and automobile(s). This would appear to be prima facie evidence of operative intergenerational transfers for home and automobile owners.

This finding can be explained, however, by lifetime uncertainty and the fact that annuities tend to pay low rates of return due to the self selection problem. This uncertainty will cause the family to accumulate a precautionary asset reserve that, one would expect, is larger the larger are the family's resources. The value of the family's home(s) and automobile(s) may simply be proxying for this precautionary asset reserve.

Alternatively, the family's precautionary asset reserve may be held in the form of home(s) and automobile(s). This would be prudent given the facts that (1) owner-occupied housing and user-owned automobiles are given tax preference over rental housing and rental automobiles respectively, and (2) a principal component of an elderly family's consumption is its expenditure on housing services, and owning a home provides a perfect hedge against the possibility that the price of these services will rise. The hypothesis that families who accumulate a precautionary asset reserve hold it in the form of home(s) and automobile(s) is given support by the fact that families whose heads are older than 64 and who rent their residences (62 families) consume more, on average, than our model predicts. The mean residual for this group of families is 0.2020, as compared to a mean residual of -0.0270 for the 113 older families who own their residences. If the value of home(s) and automobile(s) were simply a proxy for the desired precautionary asset reserve, the consumption of these elderly families without a home would be overestimated.

Also, the estimated value of β_6 is as high as it is primarily because of the behavior of elderly families. This is demonstrated in Section 8.3.3 where the model is estimated for young and old families separately. This is further evidence that the value of home(s) and automobile(s) constitutes a precautionary asset reserve for older families.

One should not infer, therefore, that the apparent desire of families to accumulate equity in their homes and automobiles, which on average is not consumed, is indicative of operative intergenerational transfers.

8.3.2 The Relation of Consumption to Net Worth

One would expect that the amount of gifts and bequests that a family intends to leave its relatives are positively related to its lifetime full wealth. This is because earnings capacity tends to regress to the societal mean so that wealthy parents tend to have relatively less wealthy children (see Section 2.3 of Chapter 2).

Evidence is presented in Section 7.3 of Chapter 7 that supports the contention that planned bequests tend to increase with a family's net worth. It is pointed out there that the preferred model grossly overestimates the consumption of extremely wealthy families. This is shown in Table 8.3 where the predictive performance of the preferred specification, for each of thirteen net worth categories, is shown. The table gives the mean residual, the mean denormalized residual, and the mean consumption level for the group of families falling into each of these net

Table 8.3. The predictive performance of the preferred model for thirteen net-worth categories

Group number	Net worth[a] (in $1,000s)	N[b]	Mean residual	Mean denormalized residual (in $)	Mean consumption (in $)
I. The central tendency of the residuals by net-worth classification					
1	≤0	48	0.2706	231	3,737
2	0–10	350	0.0918	147	5,313
3	10–20	140	0.0019	28	6,742
4	20–30	71	−0.0251	−134	8,016
5	30–40	44	−0.0112	26	8,662
6	40–50	25	0.1297	749	10,107
7	50–75	32	−0.1694	−1,873	10,000
8	75–100	8	−0.3429	−4,769	13,737
9	100–150	22	0.0363	291	17,374
10	150–250	12	0.0235	1,306	25,449
11	250–500	16	−0.2759	−15,911	25,166
12	500–1000	12	−0.4528	−42,539	26,470
13	>1000	18	−0.4161	−173,450	81,956

II. Group pairs whose residual means are different at the 5% level of significance

(1,3)(1,4)(1,5)(1,7)(1,8)(1,11)(1,12)(1,13)
(2,7)(2,11)(2,12)(2,13)
(3,12)(3,13)
(4,12)(4,13)
(5,12)(5,13)
(6,12)(6,13)

a. Each category for net worth excludes the lower limit but includes the upper limit.
b. Number of observations in the respective groups.

worth categories. Part II of the table lists those group pairs for which the group residual means are different at the 5% level of significance (see Section 6.3 of Chapter 6 for a discussion of these statistics).

Apparently families with wealth exceeding $250,000 in 1963 consume considerably less than the model predicts. Groups 12 and 13 have residual means that are significantly different than those for the first six groups. Also, the mean denormalized residual is negative, and large in absolute value relative to mean consumption, for the last three groups.

The evidence suggests that many of the 46 wealthiest families in the sample do indeed plan positive bequests. It is surprising that there is no evidence of planned bequests for groups with lower levels of net worth.

CONSUMPTION BEHAVIOR

In 1963, only 0.9% of families had net worth exceeding $250,000. It is important to note, however, that they held approximately 30% of the total wealth in that year.[5]

8.3.3 The Consumption Behavior of the Elderly

A family that intends to leave a bequest will consume less, relative to the case where it does not intend to leave a bequest, in all years for which it is not liquidity constrained. It follows that such a family will accumulate an ever-increasing asset reserve earmarked for bequests. The tendency of our model to overestimate the consumption of families that intend to leave bequests will be most apparent, therefore, for older families.

These considerations suggest that we take a closer look at the consumption behavior of the elderly. In particular, we wish to determine if our model tends to overstate their consumption and, if so, by how much.

In Table 8.4 are tabulated the residual means and the within-group R^2s for subsamples classified by age. Given the findings of the previous subsection, families with net worth exceeding $250,000 are not included in the tabulation of Table 8.4. The table contains no information that suggests older families have a tendency to consume less than the model predicts. In fact, the model tends to understate the consumption of all age groups except for the youngest! The statistics in Part II of the table show that only groups one and four have residual means that are different at the 5% level of significance. The table also shows that the model explains 60% and 51% of the within-group variances of the fourth and fifth age groups, respectively. The fourth column of the table gives the proportion of the families in each age group whose residual is below the overall median residual, which is -0.0087. Column 5 of the table gives a statistic for each age group that is approximately a standard normal random variable under the null hypothesis that the true probability that a family's residual is below the overall median is 50%. They indicate that each statistic given in column 4 is within a 88% confidence interval centered on 0.5. For groups 1 and 4, this statistic is within a 34% confidence interval. The difference between the residual means for groups 1 and 4, therefore, appears to be due to outliers.

Table 8.4 suggests that our model does quite well at explaining the consumption behavior of the elderly and that no misspecification is evident. The residuals may be misleading, however, since they are normalized by $ZNORM$, which is an increasing function of the family's net worth. Since families that plan to leave a bequest tend to be wealthy,

Table 8.4. Analysis of the residuals of the preferred model for five age groups[a]

I. Mean and median residual by age

Age	N^b	Mean	Within group R^2	Proportion below median	$STAT^c$
25–30	83	−0.0797	0.0414	0.5181	0.3293
31–45	281	0.0566	0.5089	0.4552	1.4914
46–60	211	0.0477	0.6075	0.5450	1.3080
61–75	127	0.1415	0.6032	0.4803	0.4437
76–92	50	0.0335	0.5126	0.5800	1.1314

II. Asymptotically standard normal variables under the null hypothesis that the respective group residual means are equal

	Group				
Group	1	2	3	4	5
1	—	1.6	1.5	2.3	0.9
2	—	—	0.1	1.2	0.2
3	—	—	—	1.2	0.1
4	—	—	—	—	1.0

a. The preferred model is model 1 of Table 7.3. The tabulation here includes the 752 families with net worth less than $250,000.

b. Number of observations in the respective groups.

c. *STAT* is approximately a standard normal random variable under the null hypothesis that the true probability of a family's residual being below the overall median is 50%.

their residuals are given relatively little weight in the residual means of Table 8.4. To investigate this possibility, Table 8.5 gives the group means of the denormalized residuals, which of course are measured in dollars. It is seen there that our suspicions are verified for the oldest age group. On average, the model overstates the consumption of the 50 families whose head is older than 75, and whose net worth is less than $250,000, by $798. Note, however, that the average denormalized residual for the 127 families whose head is between the ages of 61 and 75, and whose net worth is less than $250,000, is *positive* and near zero. The table also shows that the model explains about 60% of the within-group variance of consumption (unnormalized) for each of the last three age groups. These groups include all families whose head is older than 45. Note that the consumption behavior of younger families is more difficult to explain.

Table 8.5. Analysis of the denormalized residuals of the preferred model for five age groups[a]

Age	N[b]	Mean denormalized residual (in \$s)	Within-group R^2
25–30	83	302	0.1971
31–45	281	50	0.5157
46–60	211	−44	0.5989
61–75	127	79	0.6391
76–92	50	−798	0.6158

a. The preferred model is model 1 of Table 7.3. The tabulation here includes the 752 families with net worth less than \$250,000.
b. Number of observations in the respective groups.

Table 8.6 sheds further light on the consumption behavior of elderly families. *PFIT* is defined as the ratio of actual consumption to fitted consumption. Table 8.6 tabulates the number of families in each of two subsamples having a value of *PFIT* that falls into each of six categories. The first column of the table is for all 175 families in the sample whose head is at least 65 years of age. Column 2 of the table is for 149 families of the first subsample with net worth less than \$250,000. The table indicates that 56% of older families, and 51% of the less wealthy older families, consume less than the preferred model predicts; 68% of older families, and 78% of the less wealthy older families, consume at least

Table 8.6. The number of older families falling into each of six categories for *PFIT*

PFIT[a]	All old families[b]	Less wealthy old families[c]
<0.25	14	1
0.25–0.50	18	10
0.50–0.75	24	22
0.75–0.90	21	20
0.90–1.00	22	22
≥1.00	76	74

a. *PFIT* is the ratio of actual consumption to fitted consumption. Each category for *PFIT* includes the lower limit but excludes the upper limit.
b. Old families are those whose head is at least 65 years old.
c. Less wealthy families are those with net worth less than \$250,000.

75% as much as the preferred model predicts; and only 18.3% of older families, and 7.4% of the less wealthy older families, consume less than 50% as much as the preferred model predicts.

Table 8.6 suggests that only a small minority of older families with net worth less than $250,000 plan substantial bequests. Those cases where the model overstates the consumption of older families by small amounts may be due to the fact that the model abstracts from risk associated with lifetime uncertainty. The model assumes that families behave as if future family size is certain to be as expected. It was pointed out in Section 4.2 of Chapter 4 that this assumption probably causes the model to overestimate the consumption of older families for whom the variance of future family size is particularly high.

A final look at the consumption behavior of the elderly is provided in Table 8.7. The table gives parameter estimates of the preferred model for two subsamples. The first subsample is made up of 175 retired families, and the second subsample is made up of the remaining 623 preretirement families who constitute the sample that was used to estimate the effects of social security on consumption. The coefficient on "other adults" (β_3) is not identified in the postretirement sample since older families with more than two adults are excluded from the sample (see Section 5.2 of Chapter 5). The retirement weight (β_2) does not take effect until all children have left the home. The postretirement sample includes a few families with children so that β_2 is identified in the postretirement sample, but it is not estimated very precisely.

Models 1 and 2 of Table 8.7 give the parameter estimates for the postretirement sample and the preretirement sample, respectively. (Ignore model 3 for now.) The estimates of β_5, β_6, and the five β_1 parameters are quite different between the two samples. Relative to the young sample, the old sample has lower consumption growth rates (except for the fourth education group), has a lower demand for liquid assets, and plans to consume less of the value of its home(s) and automobile(s). These differences are significant at the 0.1% level; a Chow test of the equality of the two sets of parameters yields an asymptotic chi-square test statistic of 33.1.

The parameter estimates in Table 8.7 offer no evidence that the older families in the sample consume significantly less, relative to younger families, than the preferred model predicts. The demand for liquid assets is lower and, on the whole, the consumption growth rate is lower for the postretirement sample, which suggests that older families have *higher* propensities to consume full wealth when controlling for age. Conversely, the estimated portion of the value of home(s) and automobile(s) that the family does not plan to consume (β_6) is larger for

Table 8.7. Parameter estimates: the preferred model for subsamples stratified according to age

Parameter	Model 1[a]	Model 2[b]	Model 3[c]
$ED1(\beta_1)$	0.9558	1.0008	0.9984
	(0.0120)	(0.0023)	(0.0029)
$ED2(\beta_1)$	0.9970	1.0044	1.0034
	(0.0142)	(0.0021)	(0.0025)
$ED3(\beta_1)$	0.9922	1.0062	1.0076
	(0.0162)	(0.0017)	(0.0019)
$ED4(\beta_1)$	0.9765	1.0080	1.0104
	(0.0217)	(0.0021)	(0.0022)
$ED5(\beta_1)$	1.0485	1.0102	1.0107
	(0.0210)	(0.0020)	(0.0021)
β_2	0.9665	0.5316	0.5214
	(0.8835)	(0.0378)	(0.0412)
β_3	—	0.4095	0.4231
		(0.0655)	(0.0683)
β_4	0.3250	0.2620	0.3128
	(1.5042)	(0.0408)	(0.0516)
β_5	−0.0270	0.1126	0.0248
	(0.0619)	(0.0428)	(0.0323)
β_6	0.9669	0.1472	0.7124
	(0.0351)	(0.0415)	(0.0826)
β_7	1.0000*	1.0000*	1.0000*
β_8	1.0000*	1.0000*	1.0000*
$SSR \times 10^{-2}$	0.7190	2.6052	2.6375
R^2	0.6914	0.6137	0.6089

Note: Asymptotic standard errors are in parentheses. An asterisk indicates that the parameter is constrained to equal the value shown.

a. The preferred model for 175 postretirement observations.

b. The preferred model for 623 preretirement observations.

c. Estimates corresponding to a local peak of the likelihood function for 623 preretirement observations.

older families. This has the effect of reducing their propensity to consume full wealth relative to that of younger families.

Model 3 of Table 8.7 indicates that the values of β_5 and β_6 for the preretirement sample are much less certain than the asymptotic standard errors for model 2 would indicate. Model 3 is a preliminary estimation that turned out to be a local peak, and not a global peak, of the likelihood function. The estimates of β_5 and β_6 for model 3 are 0.0248 and 0.7124, respectively. Furthermore, the fit of model 3 is not much worse than that of model 2. It is apparent that the behavior of the postretirement and preretirement samples is not nearly so different as models 1 and 2 would suggest.[6]

Nevertheless, there does appear to be a significant difference in the estimated value of $\hat{\beta}_6$ in the two samples. This may be due to measurement error. It is probable that many of the younger families in the sample who do not currently own a home plan to own one in the future. Our estimations assume that such families never intend to own a home. This error in the measurement of future home and automobile equity for younger families biases $\hat{\beta}_6$ downward. This bias will not be as serious for the postretirement sample. Evidence verifying this hypothesis is given in Table 8.8, where the group residual means, by tenure class, for our preferred model are given. As before, the 46 families with net worth exceeding $250,000 are not included in the tabulation of Table 8.8. Part I of the table indicates that home owners consume less, relative to the model's prediction, than do renters. The asymptotic standard normal variable testing the equality of these means is 1.4, which is not significant at the 10% level. Part II of the table gives these group residual means for families whose head is age 45 or younger. It is seen there that the pattern is reversed; now home owners consume more, relative to the model's prediction, than do renters. The asymptotic standard normal random variable testing the equality of these means is

Table 8.8. Analysis of the preferred model's residuals for two tenure classes[a]

I. All families with net worth less than $250,000

Tenure class	N[b]	Mean residual	Within-group R^2
Renter	222	0.1044	0.4577
Home owner	530	0.0298	0.6155

II. All families with net worth less than $250,000 and whose head is age 45 or under

Tenure class	N[b]	Mean residual	Within-group R^2
Renter	135	−0.0325	0.3105
Home owner	229	0.0596	0.4680

a. The preferred model is model 1 of Table 7.3.
b. Number of observations in the respective groups.

1.3, which again is not significant at the 10% level. A likely explanation of these findings is that many of the young renters in the sample are saving to make a down payment on a home.

We conclude that the behavior of older families in the sample does not deviate significantly from the predictions of our model. These results stand in marked contrast to those of Mirer (1979) who concludes that the cross-section profile of net worth by age indicates that older families consume much less than the standard life-cycle consumption model predicts.[7]

8.3.4 A Synthesis

Our analysis indicates that a small minority of families, most of whom are extremely wealthy, plan bequests. This subsection attempts to estimate the amount of net worth held by each older family in the sample that is held for the purpose of leaving a bequest. The aggregate amount of bequest wealth, and its distribution, then are investigated.

Table 8.6 indicates that 99 of the 175 families whose head is older than 64 consume less than the preferred model predicts. For reasons that will become apparent, this sample of 99 families is referred to as the donor sample. For each family in the donor sample, the following variable is constructed:

$$BEQ = (1 - PFIT)(FW - DEHA) + DEHA$$

where FW is net worth at the end of the current period plus the discounted value of net noninterest income projected for each future year until the family's first cutoff date, and DEHA is the discounted value of the equity the family is required to have in its home(s) and automobile(s) at the end of its horizon. PFIT, it is recalled, is tabulated in Table 8.6 and gives the family's actual consumption as a portion of fitted consumption. BEQ, therefore, gives the amount of net worth the family could currently set aside and continue to consume PFIT times the optimal amount of consumption, as given by our preferred model, in each future year until the family's cutoff date.[8] The cutoff date occurs at a time when the family head is well into his or her nineties in all cases where net worth is large, which of course includes all cases where BEQ is potentially large. If BEQ exceeds the family's current net worth, BEQ is set equal to the family's current net worth.

The variable BEQ is clearly a noisy measure of actual bequest wealth for older families. All older families that consume less than our model predicts are attributed some bequest wealth. Families with large values of *BEQ*, however, probably do plan substantial bequests. It is demonstrated below that these families hold the overwhelming majority of bequest wealth, as measured by *BEQ*.

Column 1 of Table 8.9 gives the portion of families with heads aged 65 or over (the "old sample") who have a positive value of *BEQ* *(PDONOR)*; total bequests in the old sample as a portion of total net worth in the old sample *(BEQ/AOLD)*; and the ratio of total net worth in the old sample to total net worth in the entire sample *(AOLD/ATOT)*. It is important to note that wealthy families are *not* excluded from any of these samples. The table indicates that 60% of aggregate net worth in the entire sample is held by families in the old sample and, of this amount, 79% is attributed to planned bequests. The second column of the table gives the corresponding quantities for the population represented by the donor sample, the old sample, and the entire sample. The population of older families holds 34% of the total wealth and, of this amount, 55% is attributed to bequests. If these results could be applied to the entire U.S. population, they would imply that 18.7% of the U.S. capital stock in 1963 was held by older families for the purpose of leaving a bequest. Additional bequest wealth, of course, was held by younger families. Note that our sample is not representative of the U.S. population. In particular, self-employed persons are excluded from the sample. This may have the effect of overstating the portion of wealth held by older families. Also, many of the wealthy older families already may have distributed much of their wealth to their offspring who, one would expect, have a tendency to be self-employed.

Tables 8.10 and 8.11 show that bequest wealth is very unevenly distributed among the 99 families in the donor sample. Table 8.10 indicates that one family holds 34.89% of the bequest wealth, two families hold nearly half the bequest wealth, and sixteen families (16.1% of

Table 8.9. The values of *PDONOR, BEQ/AOLD,* and *AOLD/ATOT* for the sample and the population sampled[a]

Variable	Sample	Population sampled
PDONOR	0.57	0.49
BEQ/AOLD	0.79	0.55
AOLD/ATOT	0.60	0.34

Note: See the text for definitions of variables.

a. Wealthy families are *not* excluded from this tabulation.

Table 8.10. The distribution of bequest wealth in the donor sample

Number of highest donors	Percentage of donors	Percentage of bequest wealth
1	1.01	34.89
2	2.02	48.80
3	3.03	55.60
6	6.06	70.28
10	10.10	81.01
16	16.16	90.53
21	21.21	95.15
27	27.27	97.48
43	43.43	99.05
99	100.00	100.00

the donor sample) hold 90.53% of the bequest wealth. In interpreting these figures, it is important to keep in mind that the donor sample constitutes 57% of the old sample.

Table 8.11 gives the same information as Table 8.10 for the population of families represented by the donor sample. It shows, for example, that the 28 families with the most bequest wealth represent 3.25% of the donor *population*, a group which holds 42.49% of the bequest wealth in the donor population. The table indicates that bequest wealth is con-

Table 8.11. The distribution of bequest wealth in the population represented by the donor sample

Number of highest donors	Percentage of donor population represented	Percentage of bequest wealth in donor population
23	1.02	31.05
28	3.25	42.49
36	11.21	59.66
43	17.73	69.77
50	28.96	80.35
64	42.02	90.55
74	62.25	95.00
81	71.92	97.37
87	82.09	99.06
99	100.00	100.00

centrated among a very small portion of the donor population. Again it is important to note that the donor population represents only 49% of the old population.

8.4 Summary and Conclusion

We find that in each period net social security receipts and receipts from other sources have identical effects on consumption behavior. These results are very significant and hold up for both our preferred model and the model that does not impose liquidity constraints until the family head is age 65.

Our social security results suggest that planned intergenerational transfers are not prevalent. Independent evidence is given supporting this contention. An analysis of the consumption behavior of wealthy families, as well as that of older families, reveals that only a very small minority of families, most of whom are extremely wealthy, appear to plan substantial bequests. Despite their small numbers, however, the bequest behavior of these families is potentially responsible for a significant portion of the capital stock. Our results concerning social security may be reconciled, therefore, with those of Kotlikoff and Summers (1981), who find that the majority of the U.S. capital stock is due to intergenerational transfers.

In sum our results give strong support to the hypothesis that the standard life-cycle consumption model, modified to allow for liquidity constraints, explains the consumption behavior of the vast majority of families.

9 Liquidity Constraints and Preretirement Saving: A Simulation Approach

This chapter presents simulated consumption plans for five representative families whose preferences are consistent with our parameter estimates. We have two primary objectives: (1) to gain a deeper understanding of the model and (2) to determine the probable effects of liquidity constraints on consumption. The implications of the simulations for the optimal amount of preretirement saving also are noted.

We begin in Section 9.1 with a description of the simulation methodology. The simulations are discussed in Section 9.2 and Section 9.3 summarizes our major findings.

9.1 The Simulation Methodology

Substituting the preferred parameter estimates (model 1 of Table 7.3) into Equation (4.16) of Chapter 4 gives the optimal level of current consumption:

$$C_t^* = C_t^u(t,v), \tag{9.1}$$

$$v = \{\text{Max } s | C_t^u(t,s) \leq C_t^u(t,k), \qquad t \leq k,s \leq T\},$$

where for an arbitrary $s \geq t$:

$$C_t^u(t,s) = b(t,s)[W(t,s) - (1 + R)^{t-s-1}B_{s+1}],$$

$$W(t,s) = A_t + \sum_{i=t}^{s} (1 + R)^{t-i}YL_i^+,$$

$$B_{s+1} = \text{Min}\{[WHA_t + EHA(t,s)], 0.7947VHA_t\},$$

$$b(t,s) = \left[1 + \frac{AD_t ZD(t,s) + 0.2922CH_t ZC(t,s)}{AD_t + 0.4160AO_t + 0.2922CH_t}\right]^{-1},$$

$$ZD(t,s) = \sum_{i=t+1}^{s} 1.0069^{i-t}[_tE(AD_i)/AD_t]\{d(i,65) + [1 - d(i,65)]0.5300\},$$
$$\text{for } s = t + 1, t + 2, \ldots, T,$$
$$= 0, \quad \text{for } s = t,$$

$$ZC(t,s) = 0.5\left(\sum_{i=t+1}^{a} 1.0069^{i-t} + \sum_{i=t+1}^{b} 1.0069^{i-t}\right),$$
$$\text{for } s = t + 1, t + 2, \ldots, T,$$
$$= 0, \quad \text{for } s = t,$$

$$a = \text{Min}(s, t + 19 - AGO),$$

$$b = \text{Min}(s, t + 19 - AGY).$$

This consumption function applies to families whose head has 12 years of education. The corresponding consumption function for each of the other education groups is given by the above equations with the appropriate estimated value of β_1 substituted for 1.0069 in the expressions for $ZD(t,s)$ and $ZC(t,s)$. Note that this consumption function is much simpler than the version given in Chapter 4 because the demand for liquid assets is estimated to be zero for the preferred model.

The above equations predict the consumption of a family, whose head has received 12 years of education, conditional on: (1) current family composition (AD_t, AO_t, CH_t, and the age of each family member), (2) the value, and equity value, of the family's home(s) and automobile(s) (VHA_t and WHA_t), and (3) the family's current net worth as well as noninterest income, net of taxes and a life insurance premium, in each future period, which gives $W(t,s)$ for arbitrary s. The age of the youngest child (AGY) and of the oldest child (AGO) enter explicitly as determinants of a and b in the expression for $ZC(t,s)$. The age of each core adult (that is, the head and spouse) implicitly enters the expression for $ZD(t,s)$ through its effect on the expected number of core adults in each future period, $_tE(AD_i), i = t + 1, t = 2, \ldots, T$.

The version of the model that leaves net worth unconstrained prior to the 65th birthday of the family head is identical to that given in (9.1) except that the minimal levels of net worth are given by

$$B_{s+1} = -\infty, \quad \text{for } t \leq s \leq 65,$$
$$= \text{Min}\{[WHA_t + EHA(t,s)], 0.7947VHA_t\}, \quad \text{for } s > 65.$$

The minimum levels of net worth are set arbitrarily small prior to the time that the family head reaches age 65 so that they cannot possibly be binding. After age 65 the minimum levels of net worth are the same as they are in (9.1).

Given the model's prediction of the family's consumption in period t, C_t^*, its net worth in period $t+1$ is

$$A_{t+1} = 1.03(A_t + YL_t^+ - C_t^*),$$

where it is assumed that the real net rate of return is 3%.

The family's consumption in period $t+1$ is conditional on family composition in that period. Our simulations assume that core adults do not die until age 100. The family, of course, does not know this and uses actual mortality statistics to determine the appropriate level of current consumption in each period. This assumption is fairly innocuous. If both core adults have identical and independent mortality probabilities, and if the children have already left the home, this assumption yields the optimal consumption path that is contingent on at least one core adult being alive. This is because under these circumstances the relative expected family sizes in future periods is independent of the number of core adults currently in the family.

The consumption profiles generated in this chapter are used as a basis for simulations of the aggregate variables in the next two chapters. This task is made much simpler if no children are orphaned. It is assumed, therefore, that the probability of a core adult dying while his/her children are still dependent is zero. The probability that a core adult is alive the year his or her child leaves the home, however, is equal to its actual value computed from mortality statistics. This, of course, implies a relatively high probability that a core adult dies in the year that his or her children become independent.

9.2 The Simulations

This section simulates the lifetime consumption path given by our model for various assumptions about the time profiles of net noninterest receipts, the minimum level of net worth, and the effective family size. For comparison, the corresponding simulations for the case where the family's net worth is unconstrained prior to the 65th birthday of the family head also are presented.

These simulations are designed to approximate the consumption paths of households made up of a two 20-year-olds in 1963. The family's future net noninterest receipts therefore may be projected using the exact same method as was employed to generate the data that were used to estimate the model (see Section 5.1.3 of Chapter 5).

9.2.1 The Base-Case Simulation

The base-case simulation is given in Table 9.1 part A.

The family is composed of a husband and wife who begin their adult lives at age 20 and have three children who, for simplicity, are all assumed to arrive simultaneously when their parents are age 26. The children leave the family, after their 19th year of life, when their parents are 45 years old. As explained in the previous section, the household head and spouse die at age 100. Children are assumed to live to age 20 with certainty. The column of the table labeled FAMS gives the effective family size at the beginning of each period. It changes three times: first, when children arrive, then when they leave, and finally when the weight on old-age consumption takes effect.

Only the husband works. He has 12 years of education and receives $4,000 in wages at age 20, which is approximately the median income of a 20-year-old man in 1963. His income profile is assumed to follow the 1963 cross-section profile for men with 12 years of education, augmented by a 2% secular growth in real income. He retires at age 65. His future income taxes, social security taxes, and social security benefits are computed so as to be consistent with the expectations of a 20-year-old man in 1963. Our methods for projecting these variables into the future are explained in Section 5.1.3 of Chapter 5. Noninterest receipts, net of taxes and a life insurance premium, are displayed in the column of the table labeled YL. Note that the husband's annual social security benefits are $3,162. Total social security benefits are 1.5 times the husband's benefits when both core adults are alive and are 0.825 times the husband's benefits when only the wife is alive. The benefits that are conditional on the husband living are, therefore, $2,134. Similarly, $1,581 in annual benefits are conditional on the wife being alive. These marginal contributions of the husband and wife to total social security benefits in each period are insured against the possibility that one partner is deceased and the other is alive. This is why total retirement income, conditional only on at least one core adult being alive, declines over time.

The family is assumed not to own a home or automobile ever, so that the minimal level of net worth is zero throughout the family's life. This is shown in the column of the table labeled MIN ASSETS.

The constraint on net worth is binding at age 44 (the last year that the children are dependent) and every year after the family head reaches age 83. These years are marked with an asterisk in the table. The first constraint is binding because the family would like to move resources, earned after the family shrinks in size, backward to the time interval

Table 9.1. Simulated life-cycle consumption plans: renter with social security and three children[a]

Age	CONS	ASSETS	MIN ASSETS	FAMS	YL	MPC	AYR
A. Net worth constrained in all periods							
20	3,123.52	360.89	0.00	2.00	3,473.90	0.03	0.10
21	3,235.39	850.14	0.00	2.00	3,699.88	0.03	0.23
22	3,351.13	1,473.91	0.00	2.00	3,931.96	0.03	0.37
23	3,470.89	2,238.50	0.00	2.00	4,170.29	0.03	0.54
24	3,594.90	3,150.44	0.00	2.00	4,415.09	0.03	0.71
25	3,723.37	4,216.49	0.00	2.00	4,666.61	0.03	0.90
26	5,547.41	3,805.33	0.00	2.88	5,025.42	0.05	0.76
27	5,746.37	3,456.80	0.00	2.88	5,297.15	0.05	0.65
28	5,952.40	3,173.10	0.00	2.88	5,576.27	0.06	0.57
29	6,165.67	2,967.93	0.00	2.88	5,874.06	0.06	0.51
30	6,386.38	2,849.13	0.00	2.88	6,184.59	0.06	0.46
31	6,614.87	2,740.51	0.00	2.88	6,426.44	0.07	0.43
32	6,851.17	2,640.37	0.00	2.88	6,674.13	0.07	0.40
33	7,095.36	2,546.74	0.00	2.88	6,927.56	0.08	0.37
34	7,347.58	2,457.37	0.00	2.88	7,186.64	0.09	0.34
35	7,608.00	2,369.76	0.00	2.88	7,451.37	0.10	0.32
36	7,876.62	2,281.06	0.00	2.88	7,721.47	0.11	0.30
37	8,153.65	2,188.12	0.00	2.88	7,996.98	0.12	0.27
38	8,438.98	2,087.41	0.00	2.88	8,277.48	0.14	0.25
39	8,732.71	1,975.09	0.00	2.88	8,562.87	0.16	0.23
40	9,034.83	1,846.91	0.00	2.88	8,852.84	0.20	0.21
41	9,345.81	1,596.64	0.00	2.88	9,049.03	0.25	0.18
42	9,664.95	1,213.22	0.00	2.88	9,246.20	0.33	0.13
43	9,992.10	685.05	0.00	2.88	9,443.98	0.50	0.07
44*	10,326.78	−0.02	0.00	2.88	9,641.73	1.00	0.00

45	7,940.41	1,759.39	0.00	2.00	9,648.57	0.04	0.18
50	9,173.92	10,477.71	0.00	2.00	10,590.43	0.05	0.99
55	10,349.94	18,086.64	0.00	2.00	11,202.66	0.07	1.61
60	11,288.66	23,969.60	0.00	2.00	11,648.44	0.09	2.06
64	11,715.56	27,935.15	0.00	2.00	11,887.87	0.13	2.35
65	6,228.94	26,289.50	0.00	1.06	3,817.57	0.08	
70	5,999.10	17,000.19	0.00	1.06	3,566.07	0.10	
75	5,303.74	7,687.43	0.00	1.06	3,342.63	0.15	
80	4,106.55	1,214.62	0.00	1.06	3,156.53	0.29	
85*	3,015.44	0.00	0.00	1.06	3,015.39	1.00	
90*	2,969.92	0.00	0.00	1.06	2,969.89	1.00	
95*	2,926.50	0.00	0.00	1.06	2,926.43	1.00	
99*	2,892.99	0.00	0.00	1.06	2,893.03	1.00	

B. Net worth unconstrained prior to the 65th birthday of the family head

20	3,248.13	232.54	−1,000,000.00	2.00	3,473.90	0.02	0.07
21	3,363.81	585.67	−1,000,000.00	2.00	3,699.88	0.02	0.16
22	3,483.39	1,065.27	−1,000,000.00	2.00	3,931.96	0.02	0.27
23	3,607.03	1,677.38	−1,000,000.00	2.00	4,170.29	0.02	0.40
24	3,734.97	2,428.23	−1,000,000.00	2.00	4,415.09	0.02	0.55
25	3,867.42	3,324.25	−1,000,000.00	2.00	4,666.61	0.02	0.71
26	5,760.54	2,666.80	−1,000,000.00	2.88	5,025.42	0.03	0.53
27	5,965.56	2,058.34	−1,000,000.00	2.88	5,297.15	0.03	0.39
28	6,177.77	1,500.25	−1,000,000.00	2.88	5,576.27	0.03	0.27
29	6,397.28	1,006.66	−1,000,000.00	2.88	5,874.06	0.03	0.17
30	6,624.28	583.98	−1,000,000.00	2.88	6,184.59	0.03	0.09
31	6,859.11	155.84	−1,000,000.00	2.88	6,426.44	0.03	0.02
32	7,101.72	−279.91	−1,000,000.00	2.88	6,674.13	0.03	−0.04
33	7,352.12	−725.61	−1,000,000.00	2.88	6,927.56	0.03	−0.10

Table 9.1. *(continued)*

Age	CONS	ASSETS	MIN ASSETS	FAMS	YL	MPC	AYR
B. Net worth unconstrained prior to the 65th birthday of the family head *(continued)*							
34	7,610.35	−1,183.80	−1,000,000.00	2.88	7,186.64	0.03	−0.16
35	7,876.53	−1,657.22	−1,000,000.00	2.88	7,451.37	0.04	−0.22
36	8,150.50	−2,148.83	−1,000,000.00	2.88	7,721.47	0.04	−0.28
37	8,432.39	−2,661.77	−1,000,000.00	2.88	7,996.98	0.04	−0.33
38	8,721.86	−3,199.34	−1,000,000.00	2.88	8,277.48	0.04	−0.39
39	9,018.88	−3,765.02	−1,000,000.00	2.88	8,562.87	0.04	−0.44
40	9,323.15	−4,362.39	−1,000,000.00	2.88	8,852.84	0.04	−0.49
41	9,635.11	−5,096.92	−1,000,000.00	2.88	9,049.03	0.05	−0.56
42	9,953.46	−5,978.33	−1,000,000.00	2.88	9,246.20	0.05	−0.65
43	10,277.63	−7,016.33	−1,000,000.00	2.88	9,443.98	0.05	−0.74
44	10,606.53	−8,220.58	−1,000,000.00	2.88	9,641.73	0.06	−0.85
45	7,605.77	−6,363.10	−1,000,000.00	2.00	9,648.57	0.04	−0.66
50	8,787.29	3,058.38	−1,000,000.00	2.00	10,590.43	0.05	0.29
55	9,913.76	11,761.84	−1,000,000.00	2.00	11,202.66	0.07	1.05
60	10,812.91	19,156.18	−1,000,000.00	2.00	11,648.44	0.09	1.64
64	11,221.83	24,621.05	−1,000,000.00	2.00	11,887.87	0.14	2.07
65	5,966.44	23,146.33	0.00	1.06	3,817.57	0.08	
70	5,746.28	14,769.86	0.00	1.06	3,566.07	0.11	
75	5,080.23	6,399.39	0.00	1.06	3,342.63	0.16	
80	3,933.50	790.12	0.00	1.06	3,156.53	0.37	
85*	3,015.44	0.00	0.00	1.06	3,015.39	1.00	
90*	2,969.92	0.00	0.00	1.06	2,969.89	1.00	
95*	2,926.50	0.00	0.00	1.06	2,926.43	1.00	
99*	2,892.99	0.00	0.00	1.06	2,893.03	1.00	

a. An asterisk indicates that liquidity constraints are binding.

when the family is larger and has greater consumption needs. Note also that the family accumulates assets during the interval (20,25) to help finance consumption while the children are present. Liquidity constraints are effective in the latter years of life because the conditional probability of living becomes sufficiently small that the family wishes to borrow against future social security benefits to ensure that it is able to consume these resources.

Consumption is given in the first column of the table and generally rises with time except for two discontinuous drops that occur when children leave the home and when the old-age weight takes effect, respectively. Consumption also falls after age 65 due to the decreasing conditional probability of living.

The column of the table labeled MPC gives the marginal propensity to consume a small unexpected increment to noninterest income at each age. (Large unexpected increments to noninterest income may lengthen the horizon, thereby reducing the MPC.) It is seen there that the MPC monotonically rises in each year of the first two unconstrained intervals [(20,44) and (45,83)] up to a maximum of one in the last period of each interval. For each year after age 83, the propensity to consume unexpected increments to noninterest income is one.

Finally the last column of the table gives the ratio of net worth to net noninterest income. It peaks at 2.35 when the family head retires.

Table 9.1 part B gives the simulated consumption plan of the same family for the case where net worth is unconstrained prior to the 65th birthday of the family head. The computer program that generates this plan is identical to the one that generates the plan in Table 9.1 part A. The only difference is that the minimum net worth levels are set at very small levels prior to age 65 to ensure that the constraints are not binding prior to age 65.

Liquidity constraints, in this case, are not binding until age 82. Relative to the case simulated in Table 9.1 part A, consumption is greater between ages 20 and 44 but is less between ages 45 and 82. Net worth reaches a minimum at age 45 when it is − $6,363.

9.2.2 The Case Where the Family Purchases a Home

Table 9.2 parts A and B simulate the case where the family purchases a home when the family head is age 32. The home's value is equal to twice the family's gross income at age 40. It is assumed that a 10% down payment is required and that the family must make equal annual payments until it owns 79% of its home. The annual payments are such that at a 4% mortgage rate, the family's mortgage debt would be paid off in

Table 9.2. Simulated life-cycle consumption plans: home owner with social security and three children

Age	CONS	ASSETS	MIN ASSETS	FAMS	YL	MPC	AYR
A. Net worth constrained in all periods							
20	3,024.02	463.38	0.00	2.00	3,473.90	0.03	0.13
21	3,132.33	1,061.86	0.00	2.00	3,699.88	0.03	0.29
22	3,244.38	1,801.93	0.00	2.00	3,931.96	0.03	0.46
23	3,360.33	2,690.24	0.00	2.00	4,170.29	0.03	0.65
24	3,480.39	3,733.69	0.00	2.00	4,415.09	0.03	0.85
25	3,604.76	4,939.40	0.00	2.00	4,666.61	0.03	1.06
26	5,370.70	4,731.95	0.00	2.88	5,025.42	0.05	0.94
27	5,563.31	4,599.76	0.00	2.88	5,297.15	0.05	0.87
28	5,762.78	4,545.65	0.00	2.88	5,576.27	0.06	0.82
29	5,969.26	4,583.96	0.00	2.88	5,874.06	0.06	0.78
30	6,182.94	4,723.18	0.00	2.88	6,184.59	0.06	0.76
31	6,404.15	4,887.83	0.00	2.88	6,426.44	0.07	0.76
32	6,632.93	5,076.90	2,434.91	2.88	6,674.13	0.07	0.76
33	6,869.34	5,289.17	2,768.45	2.88	6,927.56	0.08	0.76
34	7,113.52	5,523.15	3,115.34	2.88	7,186.64	0.09	0.77
35	7,365.65	5,777.14	3,476.11	2.88	7,451.37	0.10	0.78
36	7,625.71	6,049.08	3,851.30	2.88	7,721.47	0.11	0.78
37	7,893.91	6,336.71	4,241.51	2.88	7,996.98	0.12	0.79
38	8,170.15	6,637.35	4,647.32	2.88	8,277.48	0.14	0.80
39	8,454.53	6,948.05	5,069.36	2.88	8,562.87	0.16	0.81
40	8,747.01	7,265.49	5,508.29	2.88	8,852.84	0.20	0.82
41	9,048.09	7,484.43	5,964.77	2.88	9,049.03	0.25	0.83
42	9,357.07	7,594.76	6,439.51	2.88	9,246.20	0.33	0.82
43	9,673.78	7,585.91	6,933.24	2.88	9,443.98	0.50	0.80
44*	9,997.81	7,446.71	7,446.73	2.88	9,641.73	1.00	0.77

45	8,022.71	9,344.76	7,980.75	2.00	9,648.57	0.04	0.97
50	9,269.00	18,780.12	10,988.87	2.00	10,590.43	0.05	1.77
55	10,457.21	27,151.68	14,648.71	2.00	11,202.66	0.07	2.42
60	11,405.66	33,859.03	16,801.44	2.00	11,648.44	0.10	2.91
64	11,836.99	38,548.48	16,801.44	2.00	11,887.87	0.14	3.24
65	6,293.51	37,154.71	16,801.44	1.06	3,817.57	0.08	
70	6,061.28	29,248.26	16,801.44	1.06	3,566.07	0.11	
75	5,358.69	21,567.15	16,801.44	1.06	3,342.63	0.18	
80	4,149.10	17,042.27	16,801.44	1.06	3,156.53	0.53	
85*	3,504.79	16,801.36	16,801.44	1.06	3,015.39	1.00	
90*	3,459.33	16,801.40	16,801.44	1.06	2,969.89	1.00	
95*	3,415.86	16,801.43	16,801.44	1.06	2,926.43	1.00	
99*	3,382.27	16,801.43	16,801.44	1.06	1.00	1.00	

B. Net worth unconstrained prior to the 65th birthday of the family head

20	3,205.85	276.08	−1,000,000.00	2.00	3,473.90	0.02	0.08
21	3,320.03	675.62	−1,000,000.00	2.00	3,699.88	0.02	0.18
22	3,438.05	1,204.61	−1,000,000.00	2.00	3,931.96	0.02	0.31
23	3,560.10	1,869.24	−1,000,000.00	2.00	4,170.29	0.02	0.45
24	3,686.37	2,675.90	−1,000,000.00	2.00	4,415.09	0.02	0.61
25	3,817.11	3,631.16	−1,000,000.00	2.00	4,666.61	0.02	0.78
26	5,685.61	3,060.10	−1,000,000.00	2.88	5,025.42	0.03	0.61
27	5,887.98	2,543.34	−1,000,000.00	2.88	5,297.15	0.03	0.48
28	6,097.44	2,082.84	−1,000,000.00	2.88	5,576.27	0.03	0.37
29	6,314.11	1,692.08	−1,000,000.00	2.88	5,874.06	0.03	0.29
30	6,538.17	1,378.67	−1,000,000.00	2.88	6,184.59	0.03	0.22
31	6,769.96	1,066.20	−1,000,000.00	2.88	6,426.44	0.03	0.17
32	7,009.43	752.82	−1,000,000.00	2.88	6,674.13	0.03	0.11
33	7,256.58	436.51	−1,000,000.00	2.88	6,927.56	0.03	0.06

Table 9.2. (continued)

Age	CONS	ASSETS	MIN ASSETS	FAMS	YL	MPC	AYR
B. Net worth unconstrained prior to the 65th birthday of the family head *(continued)*							
34	7,511.48	115.02	−1,000,000.00	2.88	7,186.64	0.03	0.02
35	7,774.21	−214.05	−1,000,000.00	2.88	7,451.37	0.04	−0.03
36	8,044.65	−553.34	−1,000,000.00	2.88	7,721.47	0.04	−0.07
37	8,322.89	−905.64	−1,000,000.00	2.88	7,996.98	0.04	−0.11
38	8,608.63	−1,273.91	−1,000,000.00	2.88	8,277.48	0.04	−0.15
39	8,901.81	−1,661.24	−1,000,000.00	2.88	8,562.87	0.04	−0.19
40	9,202.16	−2,070.87	−1,000,000.00	2.88	8,852.84	0.05	−0.23
41	9,510.09	−2,607.89	−1,000,000.00	2.88	9,049.03	0.05	−0.29
42	9,824.33	−3,281.61	−1,000,000.00	2.88	9,246.20	0.05	−0.35
43	10,144.30	−4,101.38	−1,000,000.00	2.88	9,443.98	0.05	−0.43
44	10,468.95	−5,076.48	−1,000,000.00	2.88	9,641.73	0.06	−0.53
45	7,507.12	−3,023.07	−1,000,000.00	2.00	9,648.57	0.04	−0.31
50	8,673.31	7,519.06	−1,000,000.00	2.00	10,590.43	0.05	0.71
55	9,785.17	17,603.99	−1,000,000.00	2.00	11,202.66	0.07	1.57
60	10,672.65	26,671.43	−1,000,000.00	2.00	11,648.44	0.10	2.29
64	11,076.26	33,699.59	−1,000,000.00	2.00	11,887.87	0.14	2.83
65	5,889.04	32,576.95	16,801.44	1.06	3,817.57	0.09	
70	5,671.74	26,119.29	16,801.44	1.06	3,566.07	0.12	
75	5,014.30	19,938.94	16,801.44	1.06	3,342.63	0.20	
80*	3,882.39	16,801.44	16,801.44	1.06	3,156.53	1.00	
85*	3,504.79	16,801.36	16,801.44	1.06	3,015.39	1.00	
90*	3,459.33	16,801.40	16,801.44	1.06	2,969.89	1.00	
95*	3,415.86	16,801.43	16,801.44	1.06	2,926.43	1.00	
99*	3,382.27	16,801.43	16,801.44	1.06	2,893.03	1.00	

Note: An asterisk indicates that liquidity constraints are binding.

30 years. As before, the first table is for the case where net worth is constrained in all years and the second table is for the case where the net worth of the family is constrained only after the family head's 65th birthday.

The tables tell a story similar to that told by Table 9.1 parts A and B. The cutoff dates, which determine the unconstrained intervals, are nearly the same. The only differences are that the last string of one-period intervals begins at age 81 and 80 in Table 9.2 parts A and B, respectively.

Note that in Table 9.2 part B net worth is negative until age 45 even though the family sets aside $16,801 at age 65 that it does not intend to consume.

9.2.3 The Case of a Smaller Family

Table 9.3 parts A and B give the simulations for the case where the family includes only one child.[1]

For the case of Table 9.3 part A, the constraints on net worth are effective only in the first two years and in every year beginning when the family head is age 83. The lone child does not increase consumption needs sufficiently to induce the family to desire to move resources backward from the later years of life. Liquidity constraints, therefore, are no longer present between the ages of 22 and 44.

The family's peak ratio of net worth to net labor income is about the same as in the base-case simulation although assets are accumulated much more gradually.

9.2.4 The Case of No Social Security

Table 9.4 gives the simulation results for the case where there is no social security system. It is seen there that liquidity constraints are only present in the last year of life. This is because the family is induced to save in all its working years to finance its retirement consumption.

Note that the peak ratio of net worth to net noninterest income is 6.92, far greater than its level in the base-case simulation.

Recall that social security benefits and taxes are computed so as to be consistent with the expectations of a 20-year-old in 1963. The fact that the social security system yields the family a high rate of return is evidenced by the fact that the consumption levels simulated for the base-case with no liquidity constraints (Table 9.1 part B) exceed the consumption levels in Table 9.4 at all ages.

Table 9.3. Simulated life-cycle consumption plans: renter with social security and one child

Age	CONS	ASSETS	MIN ASSETS	FAMS	YL	MPC	AYR
A. Net worth constrained in all periods							
20*	3,473.90	0.00	0.00	2.00	3,473.90	1.00	0.00
21*	3,699.88	0.00	0.00	2.00	3,699.88	1.00	0.00
22	3,839.43	95.31	0.00	2.00	3,931.96	0.02	0.02
23	3,975.01	299.30	0.00	2.00	4,170.29	0.02	0.07
24	4,115.24	617.13	0.00	2.00	4,415.09	0.02	0.14
25	4,260.37	1,054.06	0.00	2.00	4,666.61	0.02	0.23
26	5,055.76	985.80	0.00	2.29	4,958.79	0.02	0.20
27	5,234.81	1,007.23	0.00	2.29	5,226.91	0.02	0.19
28	5,420.11	1,122.14	0.00	2.29	5,502.33	0.02	0.20
29	5,611.76	1,345.90	0.00	2.29	5,796.32	0.03	0.23
30	5,809.92	1,688.09	0.00	2.29	6,102.95	0.03	0.28
31	6,014.91	2,075.37	0.00	2.29	6,341.75	0.03	0.33
32	6,226.65	2,508.12	0.00	2.29	6,586.34	0.03	0.38
33	6,445.12	2,986.57	0.00	2.29	6,836.58	0.03	0.44
34	6,670.39	3,510.85	0.00	2.29	7,092.41	0.03	0.50
35	6,902.52	4,081.01	0.00	2.29	7,353.82	0.03	0.55
36	7,141.39	4,696.94	0.00	2.29	7,620.54	0.03	0.62
37	7,387.12	5,358.47	0.00	2.29	7,892.58	0.03	0.68
38	7,639.41	6,065.29	0.00	2.29	8,169.57	0.03	0.74
39	7,898.25	6,816.98	0.00	2.29	8,451.38	0.04	0.81
40	8,163.42	7,613.00	0.00	2.29	8,737.72	0.04	0.87
41	8,435.37	8,352.36	0.00	2.29	8,931.45	0.04	0.94
42	8,713.00	9,028.47	0.00	2.29	9,126.15	0.04	0.99
43	8,995.90	9,634.64	0.00	2.29	9,321.46	0.04	1.03
44	9,283.26	10,164.16	0.00	2.29	9,516.73	0.04	1.07

45	8,354.06	11,802.43	0.00	2.00	9,648.57	0.04	1.22
50	9,651.82	19,652.10	0.00	2.00	10,590.43	0.05	1.86
55	10,889.10	25,908.72	0.00	2.00	11,202.66	0.07	2.31
60	11,876.72	29,924.01	0.00	2.00	11,648.44	0.09	2.57
64	12,325.85	32,036.87	0.00	2.00	11,887.87	0.13	2.69
65	6,553.43	30,180.04	0.00	1.06	3,817.57	0.08	
70	6,311.61	19,763.21	0.00	1.06	3,566.07	0.10	
75	5,580.02	9,286.76	0.00	1.06	3,342.63	0.15	
80	4,320.47	1,747.68	0.00	1.06	3,156.53	0.29	
85*	3,015.44	0.00	0.00	1.06	3,015.39	1.00	
90*	2,969.92	0.00	0.00	1.06	2,969.89	1.00	
95*	2,926.50	0.00	0.00	1.06	2,926.43	1.00	
99*	2,892.99	0.00	0.00	1.06	2,893.03	1.00	

B. Net worth unconstrained prior to the 65th birthday of the family head

20	3,579.28	−108.54	−1,000,000.00	2.00	3,473.90	0.02	−0.03
21	3,706.15	−118.26	−1,000,000.00	2.00	3,699.88	0.02	−0.03
22	3,837.26	−24.26	−1,000,000.00	2.00	3,931.96	0.02	−0.01
23	3,972.75	178.47	−1,000,000.00	2.00	4,170.29	0.02	0.04
24	4,112.91	495.07	−1,000,000.00	2.00	4,415.09	0.02	0.11
25	4,257.96	930.83	−1,000,000.00	2.00	4,666.61	0.02	0.20
26	5,052.90	861.82	−1,000,000.00	2.29	4,958.79	0.02	0.17
27	5,231.84	882.59	−1,000,000.00	2.29	5,226.91	0.02	0.17
28	5,417.03	996.92	−1,000,000.00	2.29	5,502.33	0.02	0.18
29	5,608.58	1,220.21	−1,000,000.00	2.29	5,796.32	0.03	0.21
30	5,806.63	1,562.02	−1,000,000.00	2.29	6,102.95	0.03	0.26
31	6,011.50	1,949.04	−1,000,000.00	2.29	6,341.75	0.03	0.31
32	6,223.12	2,381.62	−1,000,000.00	2.29	6,586.34	0.03	0.36
33	6,441.47	2,860.04	−1,000,000.00	2.29	6,836.58	0.03	0.42

Table 9.3. *(continued)*

Age	CONS	ASSETS	MIN ASSETS	FAMS	YL	MPC	AYR
B. Net worth unconstrained prior to the 65th birthday of the family head *(continued)*							
34	6,666.60	3,384.42	−1,000,000.00	2.29	7,092.41	0.03	0.48
35	6,898.61	3,954.82	−1,000,000.00	2.29	7,353.82	0.03	0.54
36	7,137.34	4,571.14	−1,000,000.00	2.29	7,620.54	0.03	0.60
37	7,382.93	5,233.22	−1,000,000.00	2.29	7,892.58	0.03	0.66
38	7,635.08	5,940.74	−1,000,000.00	2.29	8,169.57	0.03	0.73
39	7,893.78	6,693.29	−1,000,000.00	2.29	8,451.38	0.04	0.79
40	8,158.79	7,490.37	−1,000,000.00	2.29	8,737.72	0.04	0.86
41	8,430.59	8,230.98	−1,000,000.00	2.29	8,931.45	0.04	0.92
42	8,708.06	8,908.53	−1,000,000.00	2.29	9,126.15	0.04	0.98
43	8,990.79	9,516.36	−1,000,000.00	2.29	9,321.46	0.04	1.02
44	9,278.00	10,047.75	−1,000,000.00	2.29	9,516.73	0.04	1.06
45	8,349.32	11,687.42	−1,000,000.00	2.00	9,648.57	0.04	1.21
50	9,646.34	19,547.02	−1,000,000.00	2.00	10,590.43	0.05	1.85
55	10,882.93	25,819.20	−1,000,000.00	2.00	11,202.66	0.07	2.30
60	11,869.99	29,855.92	−1,000,000.00	2.00	11,648.44	0.09	2.56
64	12,318.87	31,989.96	−1,000,000.00	2.00	11,887.87	0.13	2.69
65	6,549.72	30,135.55	0.00	1.06	3,817.57	0.08	
70	6,308.04	19,731.67	0.00	1.06	3,566.07	0.10	
75	5,576.86	9,268.52	0.00	1.06	3,342.63	0.15	
80	4,318.05	1,741.61	0.00	1.06	3,156.53	0.29	
85*	3,015.44	0.00	0.00	1.06	3,015.39	1.00	
90*	2,969.92	0.00	0.00	1.06	2,969.89	1.00	
95*	2,926.50	0.00	0.00	1.06	2,926.43	1.00	
99*	2,892.99	0.00	0.00	1.06	2,893.03	1.00	

Note: An asterisk indicates that liquidity constraints are binding.

Table 9.4. Simulated life-cycle consumption plans: renter without social security and with three children

Age	CONS	ASSETS	MIN ASSETS	FAMS	YL	MPC	AYR
20	3,089.46	581.37	0.00	2.00	3,653.90	0.02	0.16
21	3,199.46	1,312.13	0.00	2.00	3,892.00	0.02	0.34
22	3,313.18	2,199.59	0.00	2.00	4,136.57	0.02	0.53
23	3,430.77	3,251.28	0.00	2.00	4,387.76	0.02	0.74
24	3,552.43	4,475.02	0.00	2.00	4,645.83	0.02	0.96
25	3,678.39	5,878.87	0.00	2.00	4,911.01	0.02	1.20
26	5,478.95	5,854.40	0.00	2.88	5,283.96	0.03	1.11
27	5,673.92	5,923.25	0.00	2.88	5,570.25	0.03	1.06
28	5,875.72	6,089.27	0.00	2.88	5,864.38	0.03	1.04
29	6,084.46	6,356.35	0.00	2.88	6,166.41	0.03	1.03
30	6,300.32	6,728.42	0.00	2.88	6,476.42	0.03	1.04
31	6,523.63	7,130.21	0.00	2.88	6,717.74	0.03	1.06
32	6,754.33	7,561.00	0.00	2.88	6,964.89	0.03	1.09
33	6,992.43	8,019.91	0.00	2.88	7,217.75	0.03	1.11
34	7,237.99	8,505.90	0.00	2.88	7,476.24	0.03	1.14
35	7,491.08	9,017.79	0.00	2.88	7,740.33	0.04	1.17
36	7,751.60	9,554.22	0.00	2.88	8,009.75	0.04	1.19
37	8,019.62	10,113.70	0.00	2.88	8,284.53	0.04	1.22
38	8,294.87	10,694.56	0.00	2.88	8,564.24	0.04	1.25
39	8,577.28	11,295.03	0.00	2.88	8,848.77	0.04	1.28
40	8,866.58	11,913.26	0.00	2.88	9,137.83	0.04	1.30
41	9,163.19	12,445.61	0.00	2.88	9,333.04	0.05	1.33
42	9,465.89	12,884.13	0.00	2.88	9,529.15	0.05	1.35
43	9,774.12	13,220.86	0.00	2.88	9,725.78	0.05	1.36
44	10,086.88	13,447.92	0.00	2.88	9,922.26	0.05	1.36
45	7,233.14	16,626.79	0.00	2.00	9,927.73	0.04	1.67
50	8,356.77	33,433.23	0.00	2.00	10,860.78	0.05	3.08
55	9,428.04	50,948.74	0.00	2.00	11,460.38	0.06	4.45
60	10,283.15	68,748.13	0.00	2.00	11,890.00	0.08	5.78
64	10,672.03	83,782.04	0.00	2.00	12,114.79	0.12	6.92
65	5,674.12	80,451.12	0.00	1.06	0.00	0.07	
70	5,464.75	62,713.00	0.00	1.06	0.00	0.08	
75	4,831.32	44,656.50	0.00	1.06	0.00	0.10	
80	3,740.80	28,669.31	0.00	1.06	0.00	0.12	
85	2,309.52	17,278.41	0.00	1.06	0.00	0.12	
90	1,847.33	8,782.03	0.00	1.06	0.00	0.18	
95	1,108.24	2,314.67	0.00	1.06	0.00	0.33	
99*	256.50	0.00	0.00	1.06	0.00	1.00	

Note: An asterisk indicates that liquidity constraints are binding.

Table 9.5. Simulated life-cycle consumption plans: renter with social security and three children; old age weight = 1

Age	CONS	ASSETS	MIN ASSETS	FAMS	YL	MPC	AYR
A. Net worth constrained in all periods							
20	3,344.64	133.13	48.16	2.00	3,473.90	0.05	0.04
21	3,435.03	409.92	49.46	2.00	3,699.88	0.06	0.11
22	3,527.74	838.56	50.80	2.00	3,931.96	0.06	0.21
23	3,622.88	1,427.54	52.17	2.00	4,170.29	0.06	0.34
24	3,720.61	2,185.68	53.58	2.00	4,415.09	0.07	0.50
25	3,821.08	3,122.15	55.02	2.00	4,666.61	0.07	0.67
26	5,818.18	2,399.26	83.78	2.96	5,025.42	0.11	0.48
27	5,976.16	1,771.86	86.06	2.96	5,297.15	0.13	0.33
28	6,138.36	1,246.07	88.39	2.96	5,576.27	0.14	0.22
29	6,304.82	839.77	90.79	2.96	5,874.06	0.17	0.14
30	6,475.59	565.23	93.25	2.96	6,184.59	0.20	0.09
31	6,650.87	351.02	95.77	2.96	6,426.44	0.25	0.05
32	6,830.54	200.45	98.36	2.96	6,674.13	0.33	0.03
33	7,014.53	116.88	101.01	2.96	6,927.56	0.50	0.02
34*	7,202.83	103.71	103.72	2.96	7,186.64	0.99	0.01
35*	7,450.92	107.29	107.29	2.96	7,451.37	0.99	0.01
36*	7,720.83	111.17	111.18	2.96	7,721.47	0.99	0.01
37*	7,996.35	115.14	115.15	2.96	7,996.98	0.99	0.01
38*	8,276.91	119.18	119.19	2.96	8,277.48	0.99	0.01
39*	8,562.35	123.30	123.30	2.96	8,562.87	0.99	0.01
40	8,789.73	192.00	126.57	2.96	8,852.84	0.20	0.02
41	9,016.21	231.56	129.83	2.96	9,049.03	0.25	0.03
42	9,246.18	238.51	133.15	2.96	9,246.20	0.33	0.03
43	9,479.34	209.25	136.50	2.96	9,443.98	0.50	0.02
44*	9,715.16	139.89	139.90	2.96	9,641.73	0.99	0.01

45	7,526.58	108.38	2,329.74	2.00	9,648.57	0.04	0.24
50	8,334.91	120.02	14,732.22	2.00	10,590.43	0.04	1.39
55	9,013.12	129.79	29,182.24	2.00	11,202.66	0.05	2.60
60	9,422.60	135.69	45,844.25	2.00	11,648.44	0.06	3.94
64	9,452.89	136.12	61,668.24	2.00	11,887.87	0.08	5.19
65	9,402.83	135.40	57,765.43	2.00	3,817.57	0.08	
70	8,680.04	124.99	37,635.44	2.00	3,566.07	0.10	
75	7,355.43	105.92	18,925.22	2.00	3,342.63	0.13	
80	5,458.79	78.61	5,264.85	2.00	3,156.53	0.20	
85	3,230.30	46.52	137.62	2.00	3,015.39	0.51	
90*	2,971.31	42.79	42.82	2.00	2,969.89	0.99	
95*	2,927.87	42.16	42.10	2.00	2,926.43	0.99	
99*	2,894.33	41.68	41.73	2.00	2,893.03	0.99	

B. Net worth unconstrained prior to the 65th birthday of the family head

20	3,644.98	-176.22	-1,000,000.00	2.00	3,473.90	0.02	-0.05
21	3,743.00	-225.93	-1,000,000.00	2.00	3,699.88	0.02	-0.06
22	3,843.43	-141.52	-1,000,000.00	2.00	3,931.96	0.02	-0.04
23	3,946.36	84.89	-1,000,000.00	2.00	4,170.29	0.02	0.02
24	4,051.94	461.48	-1,000,000.00	2.00	4,415.09	0.02	0.10
25	4,160.32	996.79	-1,000,000.00	2.00	4,666.61	0.02	0.21
26	6,333.08	-320.19	-1,000,000.00	2.00	5,025.42	0.03	-0.06
27	6,503.28	-1,572.11	-1,000,000.00	2.96	5,297.15	0.03	-0.30
28	6,677.92	-2,753.97	-1,000,000.00	2.96	5,576.27	0.03	-0.49
29	6,856.99	-3,849.00	-1,000,000.00	2.96	5,874.06	0.03	-0.66
30	7,040.52	-4,846.07	-1,000,000.00	2.96	6,184.59	0.03	-0.78
31	7,228.73	-5,817.81	-1,000,000.00	2.96	6,426.44	0.03	-0.91
32	7,421.38	-6,762.02	-1,000,000.00	2.96	6,674.13	0.03	-1.01
33	7,618.35	-7,676.40	-1,000,000.00	2.96	6,927.56	0.04	-1.11

Table 9.5. *(continued)*

B. Net worth unconstrained prior to the 65th birthday of the family head *(continued)*

Age	CONS	ASSETS	MIN ASSETS	FAMS	YL	MPC	AYR
34	7,819.53	−8,558.56	−1,000,000.00	2.96	7,186.64	0.04	−1.19
35	8,024.86	−9,406.02	−1,000,000.00	2.96	7,451.37	0.04	−1.26
36	8,234.05	−10,216.16	−1,000,000.00	2.96	7,721.47	0.04	−1.32
37	8,447.07	−10,986.25	−1,000,000.00	2.96	7,996.98	0.04	−1.37
38	8,663.45	−11,713.40	−1,000,000.00	2.96	8,277.48	0.04	−1.42
39	8,883.00	−12,394.54	−1,000,000.00	2.96	8,562.87	0.04	−1.45
40	9,105.31	−13,026.43	−1,000,000.00	2.96	8,852.84	0.05	−1.47
41	9,330.65	−13,707.30	−1,000,000.00	2.96	9,049.03	0.05	−1.51
42	9,557.67	−14,439.35	−1,000,000.00	2.96	9,246.20	0.05	−1.56
43	9,785.70	−15,224.51	−1,000,000.00	2.96	9,443.98	0.05	−1.61
44	10,013.65	−16,064.34	−1,000,000.00	2.96	9,641.73	0.05	−1.67
45	6,908.19	−13,723.68	−1,000,000.00	2.00	9,648.57	0.04	−1.42
50	7,650.11	−280.48	−1,000,000.00	2.00	10,590.43	0.05	−0.03
55	8,272.60	15,709.51	−1,000,000.00	2.00	11,202.66	0.05	1.40
60	8,648.44	34,395.77	−1,000,000.00	2.00	11,648.44	0.07	2.95
64	8,676.24	52,134.85	−1,000,000.00	2.00	11,887.87	0.08	4.39
65	8,630.29	48,741.79	124.28	2.00	3,817.57	0.08	
70	7,966.88	31,232.72	114.72	2.00	3,566.07	0.11	
75	6,751.11	15,074.35	97.22	2.00	3,342.63	0.15	
80	5,010.30	3,621.76	72.15	2.00	3,156.53	0.25	
85*	3,021.85	43.53	43.51	2.00	3,015.39	0.99	
90*	2,971.31	42.82	42.79	2.00	2,969.89	0.99	
95*	2,927.87	42.10	42.16	2.00	2,926.43	0.99	
99*	2,894.33	41.73	41.68	2.00	2,893.03	0.99	

Note: An asterisk indicates that liquidity constraints are binding.

9.2.5 The Case Where "Needs" Do Not Vary with Age

Finally, Table 9.5 parts A and B simulate the case where the model's parameters are as estimated for model 4 of Table 7.3. Recall that this model requires that the weight on old-age consumption, β_2, be one. The estimated demand for liquid assets as a portion of consumption is 0.0144 for this model. The demand for liquid assets in each year is given in the column of Table 9.5 part A labeled MIN ASSETS.

The case where net worth is constrained in all years is presented in Table 9.5 part A. The cutoff dates display an interesting pattern. Now the family desires to move resources forward from the interval (20,25) and backward from the interval (40,43) to finance consumption in the interval (26,39). The reason is that the consumption growth rate per effective family member is smaller for this model than it is in the base-case model, which indicates that the family values early consumption relatively more. The implication is that the unconstrained consumption plan for the interval (20,44) violates the constraints on net worth and the first cutoff date, therefore, occurs before age 44.

Note that the peak ratio of net worth to net noninterest income is 5.19 and is far greater than in the base-case simulation.

The simulation results for the case where net worth is unconstrained prior to age 65 are given in Table 9.5 part B. The most interesting feature of this simulation is that net worth is negative until age 50, even though the utility of retirement consumption is on a par with the utility derived from earlier consumption. Again, the reason is that the consumption growth rate in each year is smaller than it is in the base-case simulation. Assets are quickly accumulated, however, during the fifteen years prior to retirement so that the peak ratio of net worth to net noninterest income is 4.39.

9.3 Summary and Conclusion

The simulations suggest that liquidity constraints are likely to be important for cases where the family has more than one child. Furthermore, it appears as though liquidity constraints would not be important in the absence of social security or some other sort of pension income.

These findings are sensitive to the estimated weight on retirement consumption. If it is constrained to be one, then liquidity constraints have a much larger effect on consumption.

The preferred parameter estimates indicate that the peak ratio of net worth to net labor income is between 2 and 3. This conclusion is drawn from simulations that portray the social security system as a 20-year-old in 1963 would have expected it to evolve over his/her lifetime. Annual social security benefits in our simulations replace about 30% of the family's previous peak earnings. The social security system actually grew much more rapidly than this; currently annual benefits replace 65% of previous peak labor earnings of a family with the median level of income.

This suggests that the optimal peak ratio of net worth to net labor income may currently be substantially below 2. This conclusion contrasts with that of Diamond (1977), who suggests that this ratio should be between 2.0 and 2.5. The discrepancy is explained by the fact that Diamond assumes that the family desires to maintain a constant level of consumption over its lifetime. Our model, however, suggests that it is optimal for the family to consume substantially less when its members are old because when the family is old, (1) the effective family size is smaller due to the absence of children and the weight on retirement consumption is substantially below one and (2) the effective family size is expected to shrink rapidly due to an ever-increasing conditional probability of dying.

10 Temporary Taxes and Aggregate Consumption

The life-cycle consumption model predicts that families respond to a temporary tax by decreasing their consumption in each year of their remaining lifetimes. This implies that the first-year impact of a temporary tax on aggregate consumption is relatively small. Our liquidity-constraints model, conversely, predicts that families spread the burden of a temporary tax over the remainder of their horizons, which may be as short as one year.[1] Liquidity constraints, therefore, lead to a much larger initial response of aggregate consumption to a temporary tax.

The objective of this chapter is to estimate the responsiveness of aggregate consumption to temporary taxes when liquidity constraints are and are not imposed. Two approaches are taken, each of which assumes that preferences are in accord with our preferred parameter estimates. First we consider the immediate effect of various temporary incremental labor income taxes on the consumption of the families in our sample. Second we consider the effect of a temporary labor income tax on a hypothetical population of families. As is explained below, the latter approach enables us to consider tax changes that are consistent with the government's intertemporal budget constraint.

10.1 Sample Estimates

This section estimates the change in consumption in the population of families represented by our sample due to various one-year incremental taxes on labor income.

Recall that each family in our sample has been classified into one of three horizon groups. Groups 1 and 2 are each composed of liquidity-constrained families, the horizon extending either one year (group 1) or

Table 10.1. Distribution of labor income by horizon group

Horizon group	Percentage of labor income
1. One year	7.49
2. Child independent	9.69
3. All others	82.82

to a time when a child becomes independent (group 2). Group 3 is the residual category and is composed almost entirely of families with lengthy horizons (see Table 7.5 of Chapter 7). The effect of an incremental tax on labor income on aggregate consumption depends on the relative amounts of labor income earned by families in each of these three horizon groups. This information is provided in Table 10.1, which gives the labor income earned by the population of families represented by each horizon group as a percent of labor income earned by families represented by the entire sample. It is seen there that 17.18% of labor income is earned by liquidity-constrained families.

Table 10.2 gives the changes in current consumption, as a percentage of incremental tax paid, for various incremental tax rates. When the incremental tax rate is 10%, consumption falls by 100%, 29.2%, and 9.7% of the incremental tax paid for horizon groups 1, 2, and 3, respectively. Aggregate consumption falls by 18.4% of the total incremental tax revenue. Lower tax rates result in smaller proportionate consumption changes. This is because large positive incremental taxes exacerbate liquidity constraints, and negative incremental taxes have the effect of relaxing liquidity constraints.[2] Note that consumption rises when tax rates are negative, but the incremental revenue is negative so that the numbers in the table are all negative.

Table 10.2. Sample estimates of the effect of a one-year incremental labor income tax on aggregate consumption: the preferred model

Incremental tax rate (%)	Change in consumption (percentage of incremental tax revenue)			
	Group 1	Group 2	Group 3	Total
10.0	−100.0	−29.2	−9.7	−18.4
5.0	−100.0	−20.5	−7.3	−15.5
−5.0	−86.7	−14.8	−5.6	−12.6
−10.0	−74.4	−13.9	−5.5	−11.5

Table 10.3. Sample estimates of the effect of a one-year incremental labor income tax on aggregate consumption: the modified-constraint model

Incremental tax rate	Change in consumption (percentage of incremental tax revenue)			
	Group 1	Group 2	Group 3	Total
All	−3.6	−4.4	−4.7	−4.6

Table 10.3 gives the results for the case where liquidity constraints are not imposed until the 65th birthday of the family head. (This is the modified-constraint model explained in Section 7.2.2 of Chapter 7.) The model's parameters, however, are as estimated for our preferred model. The results are independent of the tax rate (to the degree of accuracy given in the table) and indicate that consumption falls by 4.6% of the incremental tax revenue. So, depending on the tax rate, our estimates indicate that liquidity constraints cause a one-year temporary tax to be 2.5 to 4.0 times more potent in its immediate effect on aggregate consumption.

10.2 Estimates for a Hypothetical Population

The previous section considered the first-year impact of a one-year tax change. In reality it is not possible to change taxes in only one year if the time profile of government spending remains unchanged. In this case an increase in current taxes leads to lower future taxes. If these lower future taxes are anticipated, then the initial impact of a tax increase may be significantly less than is implied by the results of the last section.

This section, therefore, considers the effect of a change in the timing of taxes that is consistent with government's intertemporal budget constraint. In particular, we consider a one-year additional 10% labor income tax which is refunded with interest to taxpayers ten years later. The tax refund is assumed to take the form of a reduction in the rate of tax on labor income.

The simulations assume a hypothetical population made up of identical families, except that labor income grows secularly at a 2% rate, at various stages of the life cycle. In particular, each family has the characteristics of the family whose consumption plan is given in the base-case simulation of Chapter 9. Namely, it has three children, the head has 12 years of education, and it does not own a home or automobile (see

Tables 9.1A and 9.1B of Chapter 9). The fact that each family has three children when the parents are age 26 implies that the population grows at an annual rate of 1.63% (that is, $1.0163 = 1.5^{1/25}$).

For simplicity it is assumed that all families survive to age 99, although they take into account the uncertainty of life in planning their consumption in each year.

10.2.1 The Simulation Methodology

Aggregate labor income grows 43.3% over ten years; (that is, $1.433 = (1.0163 \cdot 1.02)^{10}$. Hence the initial 10% increase in the tax rate on labor income calls for a 9.38% reduction in the rate of tax on labor income ten years later (that is, $1.0938 = 1.03^{10}/1.433$, where the net rate of return is assumed to be 3%).

We suppose that the government unexpectedly announces its new tax plan in year 0. That is, taxes are unexpectedly increased in year 0 and the tax reduction in year 10 is anticipated as of year 0. Henceforth the tax increase and the subsequent tax reduction is referred to as the "tax change."

Consider a family aged 20 in year k who is age i at the time of the tax increase. Let $D(i,j,k)$ be the change in this family's consumption at age j due to the tax change. Then the total change in aggregate consumption in year h is given by

$$DT(h) = \sum_{i=10}^{99} D(i, i + h, 20 - i) PP_{20-i}, \qquad 0 < h < 89, \quad (10.1)$$

where PP_{20-i} is the number of 20-year-old couples alive in period $20 - i$. (Recall that all families live to age 99.) Note that the summation in (10.1) includes "families" aged 10 to 19. These families have not yet formed at the time of the initial tax but do enjoy a tax reduction in year 10.

The population growth rate is 0.0163 and the secular growth rate of labor income is 0.02. It follows that

$$PP_{20-i} = PP_0(1.0163)^{20-i}, \qquad (10.2)$$

$$D(i, i + h, 20 - i) = D(i, i + h, 0)(1.02)^{20-i}. \qquad (10.3)$$

Equation (10.3) is implied by the fact that consumption is homogeneous of degree one with respect to the vector of net noninterest receipts. Substituting from Equations (10.2) and (10.3), Equation (10.1) can be written as

$$DT(h) = PP_0 \sum_{i=10}^{99} D(i, i+h, 0)(1.0163 \cdot 1.02)^{20-i}, \qquad (10.4)$$
$$0 < h < 89.$$

Hence, according to (10.4) the effects of the tax change on aggregate consumption in each year can be determined by considering only a representative family that is age 20 in year 0. We simply simulate the consumption path of such a family for each possible age at the time of the initial incremental tax, compute the vector of induced consumption changes, and fill in the appropriate row of matrix D. Given this matrix, Equation (10.4) gives the total change in aggregate consumption in each year.

The tax change affects families differently according to their age at the time of the initial incremental tax. Families who are older than 64 in year 0 have no labor income and hence are unaffected. Families between the ages of 55 and 64 pay additional tax in year 0 but receive no compensation in year 10. Their lifetime resources are significantly decreased. Families between the ages of 20 and 54 in year 0 are affected by both the tax increase and the subsequent tax decrease. Their lifetime resources are increased provided their labor income grows by more than 43.3% over ten years. In our simulations this is true for families aged 31 or under at time 0. The tax change decreases lifetime resources of families between the ages of 32 and 54 at time 0. Finally, ten age cohorts are not in the labor force at the time of the initial tax but benefit from the tax decrease in year 10. These families enjoy a significant increase in lifetime resources.

These results are summarized in Table 10.4. The last column of the table gives the years in which the consumption changes of each age group potentially has an effect on aggregate consumption. Those in the youngest group, for example, are not economically independent before

Table 10.4. The qualitative effects of the tax change on the lifetime consumption of various age groups

Age in year 0	Effect on lifetime consumption	Years aggregate consumption potentially affected
10–19	++	1–89
20–31	+	0–79
32–54	–	0–67
55–64	– –	0–44

year 1. The last age cohort of this group is economically independent in year 10 and dies in year 89. Hence, the youngest group potentially has an influence on aggregate consumption between years 1 and 89.

10.2.2 The Simulation Results

Table 10.5 gives the results of our simulations for two cases: where liquidity constraints are imposed and where they are not. As before, the latter simulations employ the modified-constraint model and the preference parameters estimated for our preferred model.

Our preferred model indicates that consumption falls, relative to the base case, initially and in each of the first eight years after the tax. Naturally the largest fall in consumption is in year 0 when it falls by 9.0% of the incremental tax revenue. After eight years the tax change has the effect of increasing consumption. Note that the tax reduction does not take place until year 10. Consumption is increased in year 9

Table 10.5. The effect of a one-year additional 10% labor income tax, refunded to taxpayers after ten years, on aggregate consumption

| Years after initial tax | Change in aggregate consumption (percentage of incremental tax revenue) | |
	Preferred model	Modified-constraint model
0	−9.0	−1.8
1	−6.5	−1.7
2	−5.1	−1.6
3	−4.1	−1.5
4	−3.2	−1.3
5	−2.5	−1.2
6	−1.7	−1.1
7	−1.0	−0.9
8	−0.3	−0.8
9	0.4	−0.6
10	2.3	−0.5
12	1.5	−0.3
14	1.9	−0.2
16	2.2	0.0
18	2.4	0.1
20	2.7	0.3
30	1.9	0.8
40	0.5	1.2

because families aged 11 – 19 in year 0 are economically independent in year 9 and have increased their consumption, in anticipation of the tax decrease in year 10, by enough to offset the consumption decreases of older cohorts. The tax change has no effect on aggregate consumption after year 48. In that year only the consumption of 83-year-olds is affected. These individuals are age 35 in year 0 and age 45 in year 10. According to Table 10.4, their lifetime resources are decreased by the tax change. But since liquidity constraints are binding at age 44 and age 83 (see Table 9.1A of Chapter 9), these individuals reduce their consumption between the ages of 35 and 44 and increase their consumption between the ages of 45 and 83. Note that families age 10 in year 0 enjoy an increase in their lifetime resources and are still alive in year 89. Because of liquidity constraints, however, these families increase their consumption only between the ages of 20 and 44.

The modified-constraint model gives strikingly different results. The initial decline in consumption is only 1.8% of the incremental tax revenue. In other words, the initial impact of the tax change is nearly five times greater when liquidity constraints are imposed.

This first-year difference is entirely due to the behavior of families aged 35 to 44 in year 0. Since liquidity constraints are binding at age 44, these families are unable to borrow against their future tax decrease and hence are forced to reduce their consumption significantly between year 0 and the time they reach age 45.

10.2.3 The Case of No Offsetting Tax Reduction

Our simulations make very simplified assumptions regarding the characteristics of the hypothetical population. It is important, therefore, to determine if the results of Section 10.1, concerning the population of families represented by our sample, are consistent with these assumptions.

For this purpose, we simulate the effect of a one-year incremental 10% labor income tax, with no offsetting future tax reduction, for the hypothetical population. Table 10.6 gives the results. The preferred model simulation indicates that consumption falls by 11.8% of the incremental tax revenue in the year of the tax. The modified-constraint model simulation indicates that consumption falls by 4.9% of the incremental tax revenue in the year of the tax. Hence, liquidity constraints cause a one-year incremental tax to be about 2.4 times more effective at changing aggregate consumption in the year of the tax.

The corresponding sample estimates, reported in Table 10.2 and 10.3, are 18.4% and 4.6%, respectively.

Table 10.6. The effect of a one-year additional 10% labor income tax on aggregate consumption: estimates for the hypothetical population

Years after tax	Change in aggregate consumption (percentage of incremental tax revenue)	
	Preferred model	Modified-constraint model
0	−11.8	−4.9
1	−9.6	−4.9
2	−8.5	−4.8
3	−7.8	−4.8
4	−7.3	−4.8
5	−6.8	−4.8
6	−6.4	−4.8
7	−6.1	−4.8
8	−5.7	−4.8
9	−5.4	−4.7
10	−5.1	−4.7
12	−4.6	−4.6
14	−4.0	−4.5
16	−3.4	−4.4
18	−2.9	−4.3
20	−2.2	−4.0
30	−0.5	−2.7
40	0.0	−1.6

Liquidity constraints appear to be relatively more important for the sample estimates. This suggests that the results of Table 10.5 are conservative in their implications for the importance of liquidity constraints.

10.3 Summary and Conclusion

Liquidity constraints have important implications for the effects of short-term government debt policy. We find that aggregate consumption is three to five times more responsive to temporary taxes than would be the case if capital markets were "perfect." This result is in agreement with the simulation results of Dolde (1978).[3]

The first-year impact of a temporary tax, however, is still rather small in the presence of liquidity constraints. If the initial tax increase is offset by a tax decrease ten years later, our simulations suggest that the first-year propensity to consume the initial change in disposable income is only 9%. This policy has significant lagged effects on consumption. In fact, the combined year 1 and year 2 effects exceed the year 0 effect. These findings suggest that temporary taxes are not effective instruments for short-term aggregate demand management and that they may have adverse long-term effects on capital accumulation.

The implications of our findings are usefully illustrated with reference to current government fiscal policy in the United States. The federal deficit in 1983 was 10.7% of labor income. Supposing taxpayers anticipate paying off this debt in 1993, our simulations indicate that eliminating this debt with an additional tax on labor income in 1983 would have resulted in an immediate increase in saving equal to 9% of the increased tax revenue. This translates to an increase of 0.72% in the rate of saving out of national income. Also, greater capital accumulation would be induced in each year up until 1991. Our simulations suggest that this policy would augment gross saving between 1983 and 1991 by 33.4% of the initial deficit reduction. As in the simulations, these calculations assume factor prices are unresponsive to the policy change.

The 1984 and 1985 federal deficits are also on the order of 10% of labor income. Suppose, for simplicity, that each is equal to the 1983 deficit. Consider the case where an incremental tax is unexpectedly levied on labor income in 1983, 1984, and 1985 so as to balance the government's budget in each year. Then, if it is expected that the tax on labor income will be reduced by the appropriate amounts in 1993, 1994, and 1995, our simulations suggest that gross saving between 1983 and 1991 would be augmented by 32.9% of the combined three-year deficit reduction.[4] Hence, since the 1983 deficit was $179 billion (43.7% of 1983 gross saving), this policy would lead to approximately $177 billion (1983 dollars) more gross saving between 1983 and 1991. Of course, announcing the 1984 and 1985 tax increases in 1983 would lead to a more rapid augmentation of the capital stock.

11 Life-Cycle Savings, Social Security, and Steady-State Capital Intensity: Theory and Simulations

This chapter uses a simulation methodology to study the effect of an unfunded social security system on the steady-state capital intensity of an economy consisting of agents who consume in accordance with the consumption model estimated in Chapter 7. The analysis also sheds light on the important question of whether life-cycle savings are sufficiently large to explain the size of the U.S. capital stock.

Section 11.1 gives the supply and demand for productive inputs and describes the procedure used to solve for the steady-state equilibrium. Section 11.2 discusses the effect of an unfunded social security system on the steady-state equilibrium. The simulations are presented in Section 11.3. Section 11.4 summarizes our findings and contrasts them with those of previous studies.

11.1 The Steady-State Equilibrium

The economy consists of two factor markets and one output market. Walras' law states that only two of these markets are independent. Hence we only consider the factor markets. Output is the numeraire.

Section 11.1.1 considers the factors supplied by a representative family over the life-cycle. Section 11.1.2 sums these factor supplies over the entire population assuming a steady-state: namely, that the population and the wage grow at constant rates and the rate of return on capital is constant. Section 11.1.3 gives the economy-wide demand for factors. Finally, Section 11.1.4 explains our method of solving for the equilibrium factor prices.

11.1.1 The Supply of Capital and Labor by an Individual Family

Labor input is measured in units equal to the annual labor input of a 20-year-old male with twelve years of education. Laborers of other age-sex-education categories are measured in accordance with their relative earnings (see Chapter 5). It is assumed that only males work and all families are headed by a male with twelve years of education. In this case, labor input of a family whose head is alive at age i is given by:

$$L_i = YLT(i), \qquad i = 20,21, \ldots ,T,$$

where $YLT(i), i = 20,21, \ldots ,T$, is the cross-section profile of earnings of males with twelve years of education, by age; normalized so that $YLT(20) = 1$. Laborers of different ages are assumed to be perfect substitutes in production so that $YLT(j)/YLT(i)$ i-year-old laborers are equivalent, for the purposes of production, to one j-year-old laborer. There is only one wage, therefore, and it is defined as the annual compensation of a 20-year-old laborer.

The family's supply of capital in each period is given by its net worth. The wage rate has a proportional effect on the family's consumption, and hence its net worth in all periods. A change in the rate of return, however, has an indeterminate effect on consumption since the income effect will tend to offset the substitution effect of such a change. This is because net worth is constrained to be positive in all periods so that the income effect of an increase in the rate of return induces greater consumption in all periods. Our parameter estimates suggest that γ is positive, however, so that an increase in the rate of return reduces the propensity to consume full wealth in all periods except the last. (Recall that $1/(1 - \gamma)$ is the elasticity of intertemporal substitution.) Since full wealth is also decreased by an increase in the rate of return, it follows that an increase in the rate of return increases the family's supply of capital in all periods. Simulations where γ is negative also are presented. In this case the family's supply of capital, at any given age, does not necessarily increase with the net rate of return.

11.1.2 The Aggregate Supply of Capital and Labor in a Steady State

The population is made up of identical families, except that real income grows secularly at a 2% annual rate, at various stages in the life cycle. In particular, each family is made up of a couple who begin their adult life at age 20 and have three children at age 26. The children leave the home after their 19th year of life to set up their own households. Two cases are considered: when the family does, and when it does not, own a home.

So far these assumptions parallel those made in Chapter 9 for the families whose optimal consumption plans, contingent on at least one core adult being alive, are given in Tables 9.1A – 9.2B. There are two important differences, however. First, families do dissolve due to the death of both core adults prior to age 100, although this is assumed not to occur prior to the time their children become independent.[1] Second, in each year, the social security system pays out in benefits precisely the amount that it receives in taxes. Benefits are computed so as to replace 65% of the family's labor income earned when the family is age 40. This is approximately the current replacement rate for a family with median earnings. The computation of income taxes is also simplified. It is assumed that these taxes are 20% of labor income and 50% of capital income. This ensures that the size of the government, relative to the rest of the economy, is independent of factor returns provided the production technology is Cobb-Douglas. This is because factor shares are constant under these circumstances.

Given these assumptions, total factor supplies are easily computed. First, consider the supply of labor. Let $RM(i)$ be the probability that a man lives to age i. Then the total supply of labor is given by:

$$LT = \sum_{i=20}^{64} RM(i)YLT(i)PP_{20-i}, \qquad (11.1)$$

where PP_{20-i} is the number of 20-year-old men alive in year $20 - i$. Similarly, total life-cycle assets are given by:

$$AT = \sum_{i=20}^{99} \{1 - [1 - RM(i)]^2\}AA(i,20 - i)PP_{20-i}, \qquad (11.2)$$

where $AA(i,20 - i)$ is net worth of a surviving family whose core adults were age 20 in year $20 - i$, at age i; and $1 - [1 - RM(i)]^2$ is the probability that a family survives to age i. Female survival probabilities are assumed to be identical to male survival probabilities, so $1 - [1 - RM(i)]^2$ is the probability that at least one core adult is alive at age i.

These assumptions imply that the population grows at 1.63% annually. This, in addition to the facts that in steady-state equilibrium the wage rate grows at 2% annually and the rate of return is constant, implies that (11.1) and (11.2) can be rewritten as:

$$LT = PP_0 \sum_{i=20}^{64} RM(i)YLT(i)(1.0163)^{20-i}, \qquad (11.3)$$

$$AT = PP_0 \sum_{i=20}^{99} \{1 - [1 - RM(i)]^2\} AA(i,0)(1.0163 \cdot 1.02)^{20-i}, \quad (11.4)$$

where we have made use of the fact that consumption and net worth in each period are homogeneous of degree one with respect to the wage rate.

According to (11.4), the problem of computing total life-cycle assets reduces to simulating a single family's consumption path to determine $AA(i,0)$, $i = 20,21, \ldots ,99$, as was done in Chapter 9. There is one complication, however, deriving from the fact that families dissolve over time according to mortality probabilities. It is necessary to distribute the net worth of such families to surviving families. In so doing we assume that the net worth of a dissolved family is equally distributed among surviving families who are 25 years younger (that is, members of the deceased families' children's generation).

The problem of simulating a family's consumption plan, conditional on at least one core adult being alive, is made much more difficult by the necessity of taking these bequests into account. The following iterative solution algorithm is used to solve the problem. The optimal consumption plan is first solved assuming no bequests. The implied time profile of net worth is then used to determine bequests received in each period by the representative surviving family. The optimal consumption plan is then resolved treating these bequests as though they are increments to the family's labor income. This procedure is repeated until the implied vector of bequests received converges.

11.1.3 The Demand for Factors

The economy's productive technology is assumed to be described by a Cobb-Douglas production function:

$$Q = A1 \cdot L^{A2} K^{1-A2}.$$

Equating the marginal products of capital and labor to their respective gross prices yields the inverse demand functions:

$$R = (1 - A2)A1(KD/LD)^{-A2},$$

$$W = A2 \cdot A1(KD/LD)^{1-A2},$$

where KD and LD are the amounts of capital demanded and labor demanded respectively. R and W are gross factor payments. The supply of capital depends on net factor returns.

It is assumed that $A2$ is 0.8 so that labor is paid 80% of the total output. The determination of $A1$ is explained in Section 11.2.

11.1.4 Solving for the Steady-State Equilibrium

The following procedure is used to compute the economy's steady-state general equilibrium.

(1) Total labor supply is computed using (11.3). This supply is independent of factor prices.

(2) The social security tax rate necessary to support retired families at 65% of their age-40 labor earnings is computed. This tax rate is independent of factor prices.

(3) A guess of the equilibrium wage and rate of return, say (W_0, R_0), is made.

(4) The representative family's consumption plan is simulated given the assumed factor prices. The total supply of capital is computed using (11.4).

(5) Let $(W_1, R_1) = (W_0, R_0 + 0.01)$. The representative family's consumption plan is simulated assuming factor prices (W_1, R_1). The total supply of capital is then recomputed.

(6) From the supplies of capital found in steps (4) and (5), the elasticity of life-cycle asset supply with respect to the net rate of return, say ES, is estimated. The steady-state capital supply function is estimated as $KS = KS_0(R/R_0)^{ES}(W/W_0)$ where KS_0 is the capital supply computed in step (4). (Note that the elasticity of KS with respect to W is exactly one.) Using this approximation, the wage and interest rates that clear the factor markets, say (W_2, R_2), are computed.

(7) Assuming factor prices (W_2, R_2), the supply of capital is recomputed using (11.4). The estimated elasticity of capital supply is updated, the capital supply function is reapproximated, and the equilibrium factor prices are again found. This procedure is repeated until the factor prices converge.

This iterative procedure works quite well; convergence is usually achieved in less than seven iterations.

11.2 Social Security and Steady-State Factor Supplies

To study the effect of social security on factor supplies, it is sufficient to study its effect on the factor supplies of the representative family over time.

We begin with a partial equilibrium analysis where retirement behavior and factor returns are held constant. The discussion initially assumes that the longevity of life is certain and there are no liquidity constraints. These assumptions greatly simplify the exposition but do not affect the qualitative conclusions. The implications of relaxing these assumptions are discussed in Section 11.2.3.

11.2.1 Factor Prices and the Retirement Age Held Constant

In steady-state equilibrium, the rate of return earned on social security taxes, say R_{ss}, is given by the relation

$$1 + R_{ss} = (1 + g)(1 + n),$$

where g is the wage growth rate and n is the population growth rate. To see this, note that the social security system is entirely unfunded and expenditures equal receipts. That is,

$$\sum_{i=20}^{T} NB(i) = 0, \tag{11.5}$$

where $NB(i)$ are the current total net social security payments of families aged i, and T is the certain age of death.

Consider families currently age 20. Then, when they are age i, their total net payments to the social security system are

$$NB(i)[(1 + g)(1 + n)]^{i-20},$$

and R_{ss} is defined by the equation:

$$\sum_{i=20}^{T} NB(i)[(1 + g)(1 + n)]^{i-20}(1 + R_{ss})^{20-i} = 0. \tag{11.6}$$

Equations (11.5) and (11.6) indicate that

$$1 + R_{ss} = (1 + g)(1 + n),$$

which is the desired result.

Consider the case where the rate of return on saving is equal to that on social security taxes. Then each family's lifetime full wealth is unaffected by the social security system and, if there are no liquidity constraints, the family's consumption plan is the same with, as it is without, the social security system. In this case, social security tax payments displace private saving one for one. The net worth of the representative family is reduced in each year by the accumulated value of past social security taxes paid and benefits received. The net worth profile of the representative family, with and without social security, is shown in Figure 11.1. Net worth increases less rapidly until retirement and declines less rapidly after retirement with social security than without it. Only in the initial and final periods of the representative family's life is net worth as great in the case with social security as it is in the case without it.

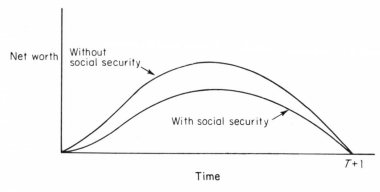

Figure 11.1

The partial equilibrium effect of the social security system is clearly to reduce the capital stock in this case.

It may seem paradoxical that consumption is unaffected by social security in this case but that the capital stock is reduced. Would this not imply that saving is also unaffected by social security and, if the capital stock is indeed smaller, capital must be growing too quickly to be a steady-state partial equilibrium? The apparent paradox is resolved once it is realized that capital income is smaller because of the smaller capital stock. It follows that saving is reduced, in the presence of social security, by the rate of return times the reduction in the capital stock. Since the rate of return is $n + g$, saving is precisely as it must be to keep the capital stock per effective laborer constant.

When the rate of return on social security taxes is greater than that on capital, the social security system yields a positive increment to the family's lifetime full wealth and increases the consumption of the representative family at all ages. The social security system, therefore, lowers the time profile of net worth for the representative family even more than in the case where the rate of return on social security taxes is equal to that on capital.

Finally, consider the case where the rate of return on social security taxes is less than that on capital so that the lifetime full wealth of the representative family, and consumption in each period, is lowered by the social security system. Let t be the age at which the social security increment to the discounted value of the family's remaining noninterest receipts is zero. It can be shown that the representative family's net worth is necessarily reduced by the social security system at all ages after age t. It is possible, but not likely, that net worth is increased at ages less than t.

For cases such as the one we consider — where social security taxes in each period are proportional to labor income, and consumption in each perod is proportional to lifetime full wealth (where the proportionality factor is independent of full wealth) — the net worth of the representative family is reduced by the social security system in all periods for which, in the absence of social security, the family's net worth is positive.

This can be shown as follows. Let β be the social security tax rate and let α be the proportionate social security induced reduction in the lifetime full wealth of the representative family. Then

$$C_i^1 = (1 - \alpha)C_i^0 \tag{11.7}$$

where C_i denotes consumption at age i, a 0 superscript denotes "with no social security," and a 1 superscript denotes "with social security." Equation (11.7) implies that

$$A_j^1 = (1 - \beta) \sum_{i=20}^{j-1} YL_i(1 + R)^{j-i} - (1 - \alpha) \sum_{i=20}^{j-1} C_i^0(1 + R)^{j-i}, \tag{11.8}$$

$$= A_j^0 - \beta \sum_{i=20}^{j-1} YL_i(1 + R)^{j-i} + \alpha \sum_{i=20}^{j-1} C_i^0(1 + R)^{j-i},$$

$$j = 21,22, \ldots ,T.$$

where, for age i, YL_i and A_i denote labor income and net worth, respectively. If social security paid no benefits, then α would equal β. It follows that α is less than β provided β is positive. Therefore, we may infer from (11.8) that

$$A_j^1 < A_j^0 - \beta \left[\sum_{i=20}^{j-1} (YL_i - C_i^0)(1 + R)^{j-i} \right] = A_j^0(1 - \beta), \tag{11.9}$$

$$j = 21,22, \ldots ,T; \beta < 1.$$

Equation (11.9) indicates that the social security system reduces the representative family's net worth in all periods for which net worth is positive in the absence of social security.

11.2.2 The Full General Equilibrium Effect

First, consider the case where social security has no effect on retirement behavior. In this case the partial equilibrium reduction in the capital stock induced by the introduction of the unfunded social security system will cause the rate of return to rise and the wage rate to fall. The increased rate of return will, in most cases, stimulate more saving and dampen the partial equilibrium reduction in the capital stock.[2] The falling wage, conversely, will have a proportionate effect on the capital stock and will tend to further reduce the capital stock. The net effect is a reduction in the capital stock.

If the social security system induces earlier retirement, then the family's saving will tend to be increased during the preretirement years to help finance consumption during the longer period of retirement. This may reverse the partial equilibrium effect discussed in the previous section so that the social security system actually has the effect of increasing the steady-state capital stock (see Feldstein, 1974). In this case, the decreased labor supply will tend to decrease the rate of return on capital thereby dampening the increase in saving. We conclude that the effect of an unfunded social security system on the steady-state equilibrium capital stock is ambiguous when earlier retirement is induced.

11.2.3 Liquidity Constraints and an Uncertain Lifetime

The existence of liquidity constraints does not affect any of our qualitative conclusions regarding the effect of an unfunded social security system on the capital stock. Liquidity constraints may dampen or magnify the social security induced changes in the capital stock depending on the relative severity of liquidity constraints with and without a social security system.

First consider the partial equilibrium effect of social security with the retirement age fixed. The social security system tilts the time profile of the family's noninterest receipts upward and, therefore, makes liquidity constraints more likely or, if already present, more severe. It follows that if liquidity constraints are effective in the presence of a social security system, then the social security–induced, partial equilibrium reduction in the capital stock is less than it would be otherwise.

If the retirement age is reduced by the existence of social security, then liquidity constraints may lead to a *larger* social security–induced, partial equilibrium reduction in the capital stock. This is because with fewer years of labor income late in life, liquidity constraints may be less severe in the presence of a social security system.

Relative to the partial equilibrium reductions in the capital stock, the general equilibrium reductions in the capital stock induced by a social security system are *greater* when liquidity constraints are imposed. This is because in general equilibrium, the net rate of return is raised by social security, and the representative family most likely will delay its consumption so that liquidity constraints are less severe.

These results are most easily understood when considering the case where liquidity constraints are binding in the absence of social security but, because of retirement and price effects, liquidity constraints are not binding in the presence of social security. Then the only consequence of imposing liquidity constraints is to make capital intensity higher in the absence of social security. In this case the social security – induced reduction in capital intensity is greater when liquidity constraints are imposed than when they are not.

To summarize, liquidity constraints have an ambiguous effect on the social security – induced change in capital intensity. If the retirement and price effects are small, then liquidity constraints dampen the reduction in capital intensity. The alternative possibility cannot be ruled out, however. In fact, our simulations suggest that liquidity constraints are likely to magnify the social security – induced reductions in capital intensity.

Finally, consider the case where lifetimes are uncertain. The crucial question here is whether total expected retirement consumption is more or less with an uncertain lifetime than it is otherwise. For illustration, suppose expected retirement consumption is greater when lifetimes are certain. Then a social security system provides a smaller portion of the family's retirement consumption when lifetimes are certain and a social security system will have a smaller proportionate effect on the capital stock.

11.3 The Simulations

This section presents the simulated values of key variables for various hypothetical economies in steady-state equilibrium. Our purpose is to ascertain the probable effect that a social security system, like the one in the United States, is likely to have on capital intensity.

As was explained in the previous section, all families are identical in the economies that we simulate. The annual population growth rate is 1.63% and the wage rate grows at 2%.

Eight basic cases are considered. The representative family may, or may not, own a home (see Section 9.2 of Chapter 9 for details). In addition, the following four pairs of values for ρ and γ are considered. (Recall that ρ is the pure rate of time preference and $1/[1 - \gamma]$ is the elasticity of intertemporal substitution.)

$$\rho = 0.00, \quad \gamma = 0.19,$$
$$\rho = 0.02, \quad \gamma = 0.73,$$
$$\rho = 0.02, \quad \gamma = -0.50,$$
$$\rho = 0.02, \quad \gamma = -2.50.$$

The first two possibilities are consistent with a net rate of return of 3% and our preferred estimate of β_1 for families whose head has 12 years of education. The high estimate of β_1 precludes the possibility that γ is negative provided ρ is nonnegative, as we require. Since the implied value of γ is probably a bit high, the second two possibilities, which are not consistent with our preferred estimate for β_1, are also considered. In all there are eight basic cases: two possible tenure situations and four possible pairs of values for the parameters (ρ,γ).

For each of these eight basic cases, we consider five possibilities regarding the social security system. The base case corresponds to the situation where workers retire at age 65 and there is a social security system that, in retirement, makes annual payments equal to 65% of the family's gross earnings when age 40. The four alternatives to the base case are listed below.

(1) No social security, retirement at age 65, factor returns as in the base case.

(2) No social security, retirement at age 65, factor returns adjust to clear the factor markets.

(3) No social security, retirement at age 67, factor returns as in the base case.

(4) No social security, retirement at age 67, factor returns clear the factor markets.

Our primary objective is to compare the capital stock associated with each of these four alternative cases to the capital stock in the base case. To help understand the results, the corresponding equilibrium factor returns are also reported. In addition, the ratio of the capital stock to labor income is given so we may ascertain whether life-cycle savings are sufficiently large to explain the size of the capital stock in the United States and other developed countries.

These forty simulations (eight basic cases and five situations regarding the social security system) are performed for each of three possibilities concerning liquidity constraints and the uncertainty of life. To ascertain the sensitivity of the results to the existence of liquidity constraints, we simulate our preferred model with liquidity constraints as well as the modified-constraint model that constrains the net worth of families only after the 65th birthday of the family head. In addition, to facilitate comparison with the findings of Kotlikoff (1979a), we simulate the case where lifetimes are certain to be 75 years long and there are no liquidity constraints. In all three cases, the preference parameters are as estimated for our preferred model (see model 1 of Table 7.3).

The results reported in the next subsection suggest that life-cycle savings are not sufficiently large to explain the size of the U.S. capital stock for reasonable rates of return. Therefore Section 11.3.2 addresses the case where some exogenous assets exist. Finally, Section 11.3.3 analyzes the contribution of unplanned bequests (partially planned for the cases where the family owns a home) to the total capital stock.

11.3.1 The Case Where All Assets Are Due to Life-Cycle Savings

Table 11.1 parts A and B give, for 24 cases, the base-case level of life-cycle assets and the percentage changes for each of the four alternatives. Each of the eight horizontal partitions of the tables (four partitions per table) correspond to different assumptions as to the values of ρ and γ and whether the representative family owns a home. The three columns of the tables correspond to the assumptions regarding liquidity constraints and the uncertainty of life. The first column is for our preferred model, the second column is for the modified-constraint model, and the third column is for the case where lifetimes last 75 years with certainty and there are no liquidity constraints.

In computing the base-case general equilibrium, the gross wage is fixed at $4,000 which, it is recalled, is the labor income of a 20-year-old. The scale parameter on the production function, $A1$, is set so as to ensure that this is the equilibrium wage. In other words, we find the scale parameter and the rate of return that clear the factor markets given that the gross wage is $4,000. The scale parameter is fixed at the base-case level for each of the four alternative cases. The base-case wage rate is chosen, somewhat arbitrarily, to reflect the situation in the United States in 1963. The results are insensitive to the base-case wage rate, since all quantities are homogeneous of degree one with respect to the wage rate. Note, however, that the cross-section profile of labor earnings is important to the results.

Table 11.1 part A gives those cases where ρ and γ are consistent with our estimate of β_1 and a 3% real net rate of return. The results are insensitive to whether or not the representative family owns a home.

Consider the case where $\rho = 0.00$ and $\gamma = 0.19$, the representative family does not own a home, and liquidity constraints are imposed. The partial equilibrium effect of eliminating the social security system in this case is to increase the capital stock by 96.0% if the retirement age is unaffected, and to increase it by 81.2% if the retirement age is delayed by two years. When factor prices adjust to clear the factor markets, the increments to the capital stock are substantially smaller, only 31.3% if the retirement age remains 65 and 26.7% if it is delayed to age 67.

The results for the modified-constraint model (column 2) are identical. This is because the base-case equilibrium real net rate of return is

CONSUMPTION BEHAVIOR

Table 11.1. The simulated effects of a social security system on the steady-state equilibrium of various simplified economies: life-cycle assets—base-case level and percentage changes (no exogenous assets exist)

Condition	Constrained	Unconstrained	Certain lifetime
A. Cases for which γ and ρ are consistent with the parameter estimates			
$\rho = 0.00$; $\gamma = 0.19$; no home			
SS/ GEN	$529,871.438	$529,871.438	$624,736.188
RET = 65: NO SS/PART	96.0%	96.0%	43.4%
NO SS/ GEN	31.3%	31.3%	16.2%
RET = 67: NO SS/PART	81.2%	81.2%	26.7%
NO SS/ GEN	26.7%	26.7%	11.6%
$\rho = 0.00$; $\gamma = 0.19$; owns home			
SS/ GEN	$535,640.875	$535,640.875	$635,733.125
RET = 65: NO SS/PART	92.0%	92.0%	42.8%
NO SS/ GEN	30.9%	30.9%	16.7%
RET = 67: NO SS/PART	77.3%	77.3%	26.1%
NO SS/ GEN	26.1%	26.1%	11.7%
$\rho = 0.02$; $\gamma = 0.73$; no home			
SS/ GEN	$669,536.625	$669,536.688	$747,253.813
RET = 65: NO SS/PART	87.5%	87.5%	37.6%
NO SS/ GEN	13.7%	13.7%	7.1%
RET = 67: NO SS/PART	76.3%	76.3%	23.9%
NO SS/ GEN	13.6%	13.6%	7.2%
$\rho = 0.02$; $\gamma = 0.73$; owns home			
SS/ GEN	$673,288.813	$673,288.938	$753,806.250
RET = 65: NO SS/PART	84.5%	84.5%	37.4%
NO SS/ GEN	13.5%	13.5%	7.2%
RET = 67: NO SS/PART	73.2%	73.2%	23.5%
NO SS/ GEN	13.4%	13.4%	7.2%

4.6% (see Table 11.2 part A), which is high enough that families are induced to delay their consumption so that liquidity constraints are not effective prior to age 65.

The results for the case of an uncertain lifetime are illuminating. In this case the social security system affects the capital stock about half as much as it does for our preferred model. The reason is that families consume much more in their retirement years when the longevity of life is certain. This is indicated by the facts that, for the base case, net worth at the time of retirement (not reported in the tables) is $2,034 for our preferred model and is $33,162 for the certain lifetime model. (This is true in spite of the fact that the equilibrium rate of return is smaller for the certain lifetime model.) Social security, therefore, provides a much

Table 11.1. *(continued)*

Condition	Constrained	Unconstrained	Certain lifetime
B. Cases for which γ is smaller than is implied by the parameter estimates			
$\rho = 0.02$; $\gamma = -0.50$; no home			
SS/ GEN	$253,212.219	$253,212.219	$293,888.563
RET = 65: NO SS/PART	97.9%	97.9%	63.3%
NO SS/ GEN	18.8%	18.6%	12.9%
RET = 67: NO SS/PART	74.3%	74.3%	34.2%
NO SS/ GEN	15.4%	15.3%	9.3%
$\rho = 0.02$; $\gamma = -0.50$; owns home			
SS/ GEN	$254,961.531	$254,962.984	$296,201.406
RET = 65: NO SS/PART	92.4%	92.4%	62.9%
NO SS/ GEN	23.1%	17.8%	13.3%
RET = 67: NO SS/PART	68.7%	68.7%	33.9%
NO SS/ GEN	18.5%	14.5%	9.4%
$\rho = 0.02$; $\gamma = -2.50$; no home			
SS/ GEN	$129,739.094	$129,732.141	$148,510.766
RET = 65: NO SS/PART	80.4%	80.4%	65.7%
NO SS/ GEN	33.0%	13.7%	11.6%
RET = 67: NO SS/PART	61.0%	56.4%	33.3%
NO SS/ GEN	24.8%	11.2%	8.4%
$\rho = 0.02$; $\gamma = -2.50$; owns home			
SS/ GEN	$139,670.938	$132,299.453	$148,729.906
RET = 65: NO SS/PART	62.7%	63.3%	65.7%
NO SS/ GEN	35.2%	11.0%	11.7%
RET = 67: NO SS/PART	44.8%	39.3%	33.3%
NO SS/ GEN	21.1%	8.5%	8.4%

Note: RET, Retirement age; SS, social security; GEN, factor prices clear the factory markets; PART, factor prices are held at the levels found in the base case.

smaller portion of retirement consumption for the case of a certain lifetime. It follows that the elimination of social security has a much smaller proportionate effect on the capital stock in this case.

Now consider the case where $\rho = 0.02$ and $\gamma = 0.73$. Here the partial equilibrium results are nearly the same as in the previous case but the general equilibrium results suggest that the capital stock is much less influenced by the social security system. This is because the interest elasticity of the savings is much greater now that γ is larger. This is shown in Appendix E, where the elasticity of life-cycle asset supply is tabulated, for various interest rates, for each of the cases simulated.

The results given in Table 11.1 part B are somewhat surprising. Here γ is negative, so the interest elasticity of capital supply should be smaller for any given interest rate. But the results suggest otherwise; the general equilibrium increase in the capital stock is smaller in the case where $\gamma = -0.50$ than for the case where $\gamma = 0.19$, although the partial equilibrium effects are quite similar. The reason is that the base-case equilibrium net rate of return is much higher, and the capital stock much smaller, for the cases given in Table 11.1B. Evidently the interest elasticity of capital supply rises with the interest rate because of a disproportionate effect on the value of human wealth. Inspection of the tables in Appendix E verify this conclusion.

Note that the general equilibrium increase in the capital stock is greater when $\gamma = -2.50$ than when $\gamma = -0.50$. This is in accord with our intuition; evidently the base-case net rates of return are sufficiently close for these two cases so that the interest elasticity of capital supply is indeed smaller when γ is -2.50 than when γ is -0.50.

A comparison of columns 1 and 2 of Table 11.1 part B reveals that liquidity constraints are effective, in some cases, for our preferred model. Eliminating the social security system has as much as three times as large an effect on the capital stock, in general equilibrium, when liquidity contraints are imposed than when they are not. This is because the reduction in the rate of return induces the representative family to desire early consumption. This desire is partially frustrated when liquidity constraints are imposed (see Section 11.2.3). Also note that the partial equilibrium increments to the capital stock, when the retirement age is 67, tend to be greater in column 1 than in column 2 of Table 11.1 part B. This is because in column 1 the two additional years of labor income cause liquidity constraints to become effective. (Again, see Section 11.2.3.)

It is important to note that in all cases here liquidity constraints make a difference, they *magnify* the increase in capital intensity caused by eliminating social security.

Table 11.1 part B suggests — as does part A — that the retirement effect of eliminating social security has a much smaller impact on the capital stock than does the asset substitution effect. Also note that Table 11.1 part B verifies our earlier conclusion that ignoring the uncertainty of life leads to conservative estimates of the effect of the social security system on capital intensity.

Table 11.2 parts A and B give the real net factor returns associated with each of the simulation results presented in Table 11.1 parts A and B. It is apparent that the base-case real net rates of return are higher than those earned in recent U.S. experience. (Recall that the tax rates on capital and labor income are 50% and 20%, respectively.)

Table 11.3 parts A and B give the ratio of the capital stock to total labor income. For our preferred model this ratio is as low as 0.901 when $\gamma = -2.5$ and is as high as 4.345 when $\gamma = 0.73$. The actual value for this ratio in the United States is about five. We believe that γ is probably closer to 0 than it is to 0.73. It appears, therefore, that life-cycle savings are not sufficiently large to explain the size of the U.S. capital stock. This conclusion is consistent with Kotlikoff and Summers (1981), who find that life-cycle savings account for less than 20% of the U.S capital stock.

The next subsection allows for the possibility that a portion of the total capital stock derives from planned bequests and not life-cycle savings.

11.3.2 The Case with Exogenous Assets

This subsection considers the case where the base-case equilibrium is computed so as to ensure that the gross wage is $4,000 and the gross real rate of return is 6%. These two assumptions entirely determine factor supplies. The production function scale parameter (A1) and the amount of exogenous assets are computed so as to ensure that factor demands are satisfied. The scale parameter and the amount of exogenous assets are held constant when computing the solutions for the four alternative cases. The implicit assumption is that the amount of outstanding exogenous assets is independent of factor prices. We view this as a tolerable approximation.

Total assets, including exogenous assets, are given in Tables 11.4A and 11.4B. Again the base-case levels and the percentage changes are given. The partial equilibrium increments to the capital stock, owing to the abolishment of social security system, are smaller than in the last subsection. The general equilibrium effects, however, are of roughly the same magnitude. The reason is straightforward; most of the total assets are exogenous, so the induced changes in life-cycle assets are smaller relative to the total capital stock and, therefore, such changes have little effect on factor returns.

The makeup of total assets is given in Table 11.5 parts A and B. For our preferred model the portion of the total capital stock made up of life-cycle assets in the base case ranges from 0.3% to 19.3% depending on the parameter values and whether the representative family owns a home.

Given the insignificance of life-cycle assets in each of the base cases, it is surprising that eliminating the social security system has such a large

Table 11.2. The simulated effects of a social security system on the steady-state equilibrium of various simplified economies: gross return net of tax and net wage (no exogenous assets exist)

Condition	Constrained	Unconstrained	Certain lifetime
A. Cases for which γ and ρ are consistent with the parameter estimates			
$\rho = 0.00; \gamma = 0.19$; no home			
SS/ GEN	1.046 /3,200.000	1.046 /3,200.000	1.041 /3,200.000
RET = 65: NO SS/PART	1.046 /3,200.000	1.046 /3,200.000	1.041 /3,200.000
NO SS/ GEN	1.037 /3,378.917	1.037 /3,378.921	1.037 /3,297.281
RET = 67: NO SS/PART	1.046 /3,200.000	1.046 /3,200.000	1.041 /3,200.000
NO SS/ GEN	1.039 /3,338.913	1.039 /3,338.916	1.039 /3,248.470
$\rho = 0.00; \gamma = 0.19$; owns home			
SS/ GEN	1.045 /3,200.000	1.045 /3,200.000	1.041 /3,200.000
RET = 65: NO SS/PART	1.045 /3,200.000	1.045 /3,200.000	1.041 /3,200.000
NO SS/ GEN	1.036 /3,376.859	1.036 /3,376.858	1.036 /3,300.125
RET = 67: NO SS/PART	1.045 /3,200.000	1.045 /3,200.000	1.041 /3,200.000
NO SS/ GEN	1.038 /3,335.918	1.038 /3,335.918	1.038 /3,249.398
$\rho = 0.02; \gamma = 0.73$; no home			
SS/ GEN	1.036 /3,200.000	1.036 /3,200.000	1.035 /3,200.000
RET = 65: NO SS/PART	1.036 /3,200.000	1.036 /3,200.000	1.035 /3,200.000
NO SS/ GEN	1.033 /3,283.355	1.033 /3,283.355	1.033 /3,244.300
RET = 67: NO SS/PART	1.036 /3,200.000	1.036 /3,200.000	1.035 /3,200.000
NO SS/ GEN	1.033 /3,267.040	1.033 /3,267.041	1.034 /3,222.734
$\rho = 0.02\ \gamma = 0.73$; owns home			
SS/ GEN	1.036 /3,200.000	1.036 /3,200.000	1.034 /3,200.000
RET = 65: NO SS/PART	1.036 /3,200.000	1.036 /3,200.000	1.034 /3,200.000
NO SS/ GEN	1.032 /3,282.111	1.032 /3,282.111	1.032 /3,245.058
RET = 67: NO SS/PART	1.036 /3,200.000	1.036 /3,200.000	1.034 /3,200.000
NO SS/ GEN	1.033 /3,265.504	1.033 /3,265.500	1.033 /3,222.867

B. Cases for which γ is smaller than is implied by the parameter estimates

$\rho = 0.02$; $\gamma = -0.50$; no home

SS/ GEN	1.096 /3,200.000	1.096 /3,200.000	1.088 /3,200.000
RET = 65: NO SS/PART	1.096 /3,200.000	1.096 /3,200.000	1.088 /3,200.000
NO SS/ GEN	1.083 /3,312.253	1.083 /3,311.310	1.080 /3,278.723
RET = 67: NO SS/PART	1.096 /3,200.000	1.096 /3,200.000	1.088 /3,200.000
NO SS/ GEN	1.087 /3,277.105	1.087 /3,276.659	1.084 /3,235.372

$\rho = 0.02$; $\gamma = -0.50$; owns home

SS/ GEN	1.095 /3,200.000	1.095 /3,200.000	1.087 /3,200.000
RET = 65: NO SS/PART	1.095 /3,200.000	1.095 /3,200.000	1.087 /3,200.000
NO SS/ GEN	1.080 /3,335.937	1.083 /3,306.662	1.079 /3,280.793
RET = 67: NO SS/PART	1.095 /3,200.000	1.095 /3,200.000	1.087 /3,200.000
NO SS/ GEN	1.085 /3,294.386	1.087 /3,271.819	1.084 /3,236.024

$\rho = 0.02$; $\gamma = -2.50$; no home

SS/ GEN	1.187 /3,200.000	1.187 /3,200.000	1.174 /3,200.000
RET = 65: NO SS/PART	1.187 /3,200.000	1.187 /3,200.000	1.174 /3,200.000
NO SS/ GEN	1.149 /3,387.575	1.168 /3,283.333	1.160 /3,270.871
RET = 67: NO SS/PART	1.187 /3,200.000	1.187 /3,200.000	1.174 /3,200.000
NO SS/ GEN	1.159 /3,328.842	1.175 /3,252.859	1.168 /3,229.842

$\rho = 0.02$; $\gamma = -2.50$; owns home

SS/ GEN	1.173 /3,200.000	1.183 /3,200.000	1.174 /3,200.000
RET = 65: NO SS/PART	1.173 /3,200.000	1.183 /3,200.000	1.174 /3,200.000
NO SS/ GEN	1.136 /3,399.186	1.168 /3,267.436	1.159 /3,271.538
RET = 67: NO SS/PART	1.173 /3,200.000	1.183 /3,200.000	1.174 /3,200.000
NO SS/ GEN	1.152 /3,308.718	1.175 /3,237.088	1.168 /3,230.053

Table 11.3. The simulated effects of a social security system on the steady-state equilibrium of various simplified economies: life-cycle assets/labor Y (no exogenous assets exist)

Condition		Constrained	Unconstrained	Certain lifetime
A. Cases for which γ and ρ are consistent with the parameter estimates				
$\rho = 0.00$; $\gamma = 0.19$; no home				
	SS/ GEN	3.420	3.420	3.773
RET = 65: NO SS/PART		6.701	6.701	5.412
	NO SS/ GEN	4.251	4.251	4.253
RET = 67: NO SS/PART		6.050	6.050	4.618
	NO SS/ GEN	4.053	4.053	4.007
$\rho = 0.00$; $\gamma = 0.19$; owns home				
	SS/ GEN	3.457	3.457	3.840
RET = 65: NO SS/PART		6.636	6.636	5.484
	NO SS/ GEN	4.287	4.287	4.343
RET = 67: NO SS/PART		5.982	5.982	4.680
	NO SS/ GEN	4.083	4.083	4.082
$\rho = 0.02$; $\gamma = 0.73$; no home				
	SS/ GEN	4.321	4.321	4.513
RET = 65: NO SS/PART		8.103	8.103	6.212
	NO SS/ GEN	4.789	4.789	4.768
RET = 67: NO SS/PART		7.434	7.434	5.403
	NO SS/ GEN	4.695	4.695	4.643
$\rho = 0.02$; $\gamma = 0.73$; owns home				
	SS/ GEN	4.345	4.345	4.553
RET = 65: NO SS/PART		8.018	8.018	6.255
	NO SS/ GEN	4.809	4.809	4.815
RET = 67: NO SS/PART		7.346	7.346	5.436
	NO SS/ GEN	4.712	4.712	4.684

proportionate effect on the total capital stock. For our preferred model the general equilibrium increment to the capital stock ranges from 6.5% to 27.7% depending on the parameter values and whether the retirement age is affected.

Liquidity constraints make a difference for all cases in Table 11.4 parts A and B. For the two cases where γ is 0.19, liquidity constraints dampen the general equilibrium increase in capital intensity due to

Table 11.3. *(continued)*

Condition	Constrained	Unconstrained	Certain lifetime
B. Cases for which γ is smaller than is implied by the parameter estimates			
$\rho = 0.02$; $\gamma = -0.50$; no home			
SS/ GEN	1.634	1.634	1.775
RET = 65: NO SS/PART	3.234	3.234	2.898
NO SS/ GEN	1.876	1.874	1.956
RET = 67: NO SS/PART	2.780	2.780	2.302
NO SS/ GEN	1.797	1.796	1.855
$\rho = 0.02$; $\gamma = -0.50$; owns home			
SS/ GEN	1.645	1.645	1.789
RET = 65: NO SS/PART	3.165	3.165	2.914
NO SS/ GEN	1.943	1.876	1.977
RET = 67: NO SS/PART	2.710	2.710	2.315
NO SS/ GEN	1.848	1.798	1.871
$\rho = 0.02$; $\gamma = -2.50$; no home			
SS/ GEN	0.838	0.837	0.897
RET = 65: NO SS/PART	1.527	1.510	1.486
NO SS/ GEN	1.052	0.928	0.979
RET = 67: NO SS/PART	1.316	1.279	1.155
NO SS/ GEN	0.981	0.894	0.931
$\rho = 0.02$; $\gamma = -2.50$; owns home			
SS/ GEN	0.901	0.854	0.898
RET = 65: NO SS/PART	1.467	1.395	1.488
NO SS/ GEN	1.148	0.928	0.981
RET = 67: NO SS/PART	1.274	1.161	1.157
NO SS/ GEN	1.030	0.894	0.933

abolishing social security. In all other cases, however, liquidity constraints *magnify* the increase in capital intensity due to eliminating social security. For the cases reported in Table 11.4 part B, this magnification is substantial.

It is interesting that for each of the last three cases in Table 11.4 part B for our preferred model, the general equilibrium increase in the capital stock is larger than the partial equilibrium increase. This is

Table 11.4. The simulated effects of a social security system on the steady-state equilibrium of various simplified economies: total assets—base-case level and percentage changes (exogenous assets exist)

Condition	Constrained	Unconstrained	Certain lifetime
A. Cases for which γ and ρ are consistent with the parameter estimates			
$\rho = 0.00; \gamma = 0.19$; no home			
SS/ GEN	807,042.188	807,042.188	862,344.250
RET = 65: NO SS/PART	42.7%	58.1%	34.1%
NO SS/ GEN	27.7%	32.5%	18.6%
RET = 67: NO SS/PART	30.2%	45.6%	19.3%
NO SS/ GEN	23.2%	25.3%	11.5%
$\rho = 0.00; \gamma = 0.19$; owns home			
SS/ GEN	807,042.188	807,042.188	862,344.250
RET = 65: NO SS/PART	33.3%	51.2%	34.1%
NO SS/ GEN	25.3%	28.9%	19.0%
RET = 67: NO SS/PART	24.0%	38.7%	19.3%
NO SS/ GEN	21.8%	21.7%	11.7%
$\rho = 0.02; \gamma = 0.73$; no home			
SS/ GEN	807,042.188	807,042.250	862,344.250
RET = 65: NO SS/PART	42.7%	58.1%	34.1%
NO SS/ GEN	19.5%	14.0%	8.3%
RET = 67: NO SS/PART	30.2%	45.6%	19.3%
NO SS/ GEN	17.3%	12.4%	7.1%
$\rho = 0.02; \gamma = 0.73$; owns home			
SS/ GEN	807,042.250	807,042.188	862,344.250
RET = 65: NO SS/PART	33.3%	51.2%	34.1%
NO SS/ GEN	18.1%	12.3%	8.3%
RET = 67: NO SS/PART	24.0%	38.7%	19.3%
NO SS/ GEN	16.0%	10.8%	7.2%

because the interest elasticity of life-cycle asset supply is negative between interest rates of 2% and 3% for these cases.

Note that the partial equilibrium increases in the capital stock are much smaller in Table 11.4 part B than in part A. This may be puzzling, given that it is not true when there are no exogenous assets. The reason is that the base-case net rate of return is the same (0.03) in Table 11.4 parts A and B. It follows that the families whose preferences are repre-

Table 11.4. *(continued)*

Condition	Constrained	Unconstrained	Certain lifetime
B. Cases for which γ is smaller than is implied by the parameter estimates			
$\rho = 0.02$; $\gamma = -0.50$; no home			
SS/ GEN	807,042.188	807,042.188	862,344.250
RET = 65: NO SS/PART	14.8%	19.7%	35.4%
NO SS/ GEN	14.6%	12.6%	22.7%
RET = 67: NO SS/PART	10.4%	3.8%	15.9%
NO SS/ GEN	10.3%	3.3%	10.9%
$\rho = 0.02$; $\gamma = -0.50$; owns home			
SS/ GEN	807,042.250	807,042.250	862,344.313
RET = 65: NO SS/PART	10.3%	12.6%	35.4%
NO SS/ GEN	10.6%	8.2%	23.4%
RET = 67: NO SS/PART	7.0%	−3.4%	15.9%
NO SS/ GEN	7.2%	−1.1%	11.1%
$\rho = 0.02$; $\gamma = -2.50$; no home			
SS/ GEN	807,042.188	807,042.250	862,344.313
RET = 65: NO SS/PART	12.9%	16.6%	35.6%
NO SS/ GEN	13.2%	12.4%	27.0%
RET = 67: NO SS/PART	9.0%	0.3%	15.6%
NO SS/ GEN	9.2%	0.9%	11.9%
$\rho = 0.02$; $\gamma = -2.50$; owns home			
SS/ GEN	807,042.188	807,042.188	862,344.250
RET = 65: NO SS/PART	8.9%	9.5%	35.6%
NO SS/ GEN	9.6%	7.3%	27.9%
RET = 67: NO SS/PART	6.2%	−6.8%	15.6%
NO SS/ GEN	6.5%	−4.1%	12.2%

sented in part B plan less retirement consumption than do families whose preferences are represented in part A. Eliminating social security therefore does little to increase saving for retirement of the families represented in part B. In other words, the social security system induces greater consumption in retirement than families represented in part B would choose if they could borrow against their social security benefits. (Note that families are not allowed to borrow against social security

CONSUMPTION BEHAVIOR

Table 11.5. The simulated effects of a social security system on the steady-state equilibrium of various simplified economies: ratio of total assets to labor Y and ratio of life-cycle assets to total assets (exogenous assets exist)

Condition	Constrained	Unconstrained	Certain lifetime	
A. Cases for which γ and ρ are consistent with the parameter estimates				
$\rho = 0.00$; $\gamma = 0.19$; no home				
SS/ GEN	5.208 /0.070	5.208 /−0.085	5.208 /	0.171
RET = 65: NO SS/PART	7.432 /0.348	8.237 / 0.314	6.984 /	0.382
NO SS/ GEN	6.333 /0.271	6.523 / 0.181	5.968 /	0.301
RET = 67: NO SS/PART	6.619 /0.285	7.404 / 0.255	6.004 /	0.305
NO SS/ GEN	6.036 /0.245	6.117 / 0.134	5.530 /	0.257
$\rho = 0.00$; $\gamma = 0.19$; owns home				
SS/ GEN	5.208 /0.193	5.208 / 0.014	5.208 /	0.229
RET = 65: NO SS/PART	6.941 /0.395	7.874 / 0.348	6.984 /	0.425
NO SS/ GEN	6.237 /0.356	6.381 / 0.235	5.984 /	0.352
RET = 67: NO SS/PART	6.303 /0.349	7.050 / 0.289	6.004 /	0.354
NO SS/ GEN	5.981 /0.337	5.980 / 0.190	5.537 /	0.310
$\rho = 0.02$; $\gamma = 0.73$; no home				
SS/ GEN	5.208 /0.070	5.208 /−0.085	5.208 /	0.171
RET = 65: NO SS/PART	7.432 /0.348	8.237 / 0.314	6.984 /	0.382
NO SS/ GEN	6.005 /0.221	5.785 / 0.049	5.550 /	0.234
RET = 67: NO SS/PART	6.619 /0.285	7.404 / 0.255	6.004 /	0.305
NO SS/ GEN	5.804 /0.207	5.610 / 0.035	5.355 /	0.226
$\rho = 0.02$; $\gamma = 0.73$; owns home				
SS/ GEN	5.208 /0.193	5.208 / 0.014	5.208 /	0.229
RET = 65: NO SS/PART	6.941 /0.395	7.874 / 0.348	6.984 /	0.425
NO SS/ GEN	5.950 /0.317	5.716 / 0.122	5.553 /	0.289
RET = 67: NO SS/PART	6.303 /0.349	7.050 / 0.289	6.004 /	0.354
NO SS/ GEN	5.751 /0.304	5.545 / 0.110	5.356 /	0.281

benefits for either of the models in columns 1 and 2.)

An interesting result reported in Table 11.4 part B is that eliminating social security decreases the capital stock in two cases. This is shown in column 2 for the cases where the representative family owns a home and the retirement age is 67 without social security. These are cases where the retirement effect outweighs the asset substitution effect. The strength of the retirement effect depends on the proportionate effect

Table 11.5. *(continued)*

Condition	Constrained	Unconstrained	Certain lifetime
B. Cases for which γ is smaller than is implied by the parameter estimates			
$\rho = 0.02$; $\gamma = -0.50$; no home			
SS/ GEN	5.208 /0.003	5.208 /−0.859	5.208 /−0.991
RET = 65: NO SS/PART	5.981 /0.132	6.236 /−0.553	7.054 /−0.470
NO SS/ GEN	5.807 /0.130	5.725 /−0.652	6.135 /−0.622
RET = 67: NO SS/PART	5.610 /0.097	5.278 /−0.791	5.835 /−0.717
NO SS/ GEN	5.524 /0.096	5.241 /−0.801	5.504 /−0.795
$\rho = 0.02$; $\gamma = -0.50$; owns home			
SS/ GEN	5.208 /0.140	5.208 /−0.753	5.208 /−0.930
RET = 65: NO SS/PART	5.745 /0.220	5.863 /−0.557	7.054 /−0.425
NO SS/ GEN	5.647 /0.223	5.545 /−0.621	6.163 /−0.564
RET = 67: NO SS/PART	5.440 /0.196	4.913 /−0.814	5.835 /−0.665
NO SS/ GEN	5.401 /0.197	5.065 /−0.772	5.512 /−0.737
$\rho = 0.02$; $\gamma = -2.50$; no home			
SS/ GEN	5.208 /0.003	5.208 /−0.948	5.208 /−1.120
RET = 65: NO SS/PART	5.881 /0.117	6.071 /−0.671	7.062 /−0.563
NO SS/ GEN	5.753 /0.119	5.718 /−0.733	6.305 /−0.669
RET = 67: NO SS/PART	5.544 /0.086	5.099 /−0.942	5.816 /−0.834
NO SS/ GEN	5.480 /0.087	5.147 /−0.929	5.547 /−0.893
$\rho = 0.02$; $\gamma = -2.50$; owns home			
SS/ GEN	5.208 /0.138	5.208 /−0.840	5.208 /−1.060
RET = 65: NO SS/PART	5.671 /0.209	5.703 /−0.681	7.062 /−0.518
NO SS/ GEN	5.603 /0.213	5.509 /−0.716	6.343 /−0.609
RET = 67: NO SS/PART	5.399 /0.189	4.738 /−0.975	5.816 /−0.781
NO SS/ GEN	5.371 /0.191	4.939 /−0.919	5.558 /−0.834

that two additional years of labor income have on the representative family's consumable full wealth. Since 79% of the value of homes purchased is deducted from consumable lifetime full wealth, these two additional years of labor income are relatively more important for the case where the representative family owns a home.

For completeness Table 11.6 parts A and B give the net factor returns associated with each of the simulations discussed in this subsection.

Table 11.6. The simulated effects of a social security system on the steady-state equilibrium of various simplified economies: gross return net of tax and net wage (exogenous assets exist)

Condition	Constrained	Unconstrained	Certain lifetime
A. Cases for which γ and ρ are consistent with the parameter estimates			
$\rho = 0.00$; $\gamma = 0.19$; no home			
SS/ GEN	1.030 /3,200.000	1.030 /3,200.000	1.030 /3,200.000
RET = 65: NO SS/PART	1.030 /3,200.000	1.030 /3,200.000	1.030 /3,200.000
NO SS/ GEN	1.025 /3,360.344	1.024 /3,385.172	1.026 /3,310.807
RET = 67: NO SS/PART	1.030 /3,200.000	1.030 /3,200.000	1.030 /3,200.000
NO SS/ GEN	1.026 /3,320.149	1.026 /3,331.333	1.028 /3,248.368
$\rho = 0.00$; $\gamma = 0.19$; owns home			
SS/ GEN	1.030 /3,200.000	1.030 /3,200.000	1.030 /3,200.000
RET = 65: NO SS/PART	1.030 /3,200.000	1.030 /3,200.000	1.030 /3,200.000
NO SS/ GEN	1.025 /3,347.424	1.024 /3,366.614	1.026 /3,313.045
RET = 67: NO SS/PART	1.030 /3,200.000	1.030 /3,200.000	1.030 /3,200.000
NO SS/ GEN	1.026 /3,312.605	1.026 /3,312.395	1.028 /3,249.285
$\rho = 0.02$; $\gamma = 0.73$; no home			
SS/ GEN	1.030 /3,200.000	1.030 /3,200.000	1.030 /3,200.000
RET = 65: NO SS/PART	1.030 /3,200.000	1.030 /3,200.000	1.030 /3,200.000
NO SS/ GEN	1.026 /3,315.850	1.027 /3,285.151	1.028 /3,251.165
RET = 67: NO SS/PART	1.030 /3,200.000	1.030 /3,200.000	1.030 /3,200.000
NO SS/ GEN	1.027 /3,287.774	1.028 /3,259.950	1.029 /3,222.301
$\rho = 0.02$; $\gamma = 0.73$; owns home			
SS/ GEN	1.030 /3,200.000	1.030 /3,200.000	1.030 /3,200.000
RET = 65: NO SS/PART	1.030 /3,200.000	1.030 /3,200.000	1.030 /3,200.000
NO SS/ GEN	1.026 /3,308.231	1.027 /3,275.346	1.028 /3,251.725
RET = 67: NO SS/PART	1.030 /3,200.000	1.030 /3,200.000	1.030 /3,200.000
NO SS/ GEN	1.027 /3,280.305	1.028 /3,250.506	1.029 /3,222.521

B. Cases for which γ is smaller than is implied by the parameter estimates

$\rho = 0.02;\ \gamma = -0.50;$ no home

SS/ GEN	1.030 /3,200.000	1.030 /3,200.000	1.030 /3,200.000
RET = 65: NO SS/PART	1.030 /3,200.000	1.030 /3,200.000	1.030 /3,200.000
NO SS/ GEN	1.027 /3,288.229	1.027 /3,276.590	1.025 /3,333.766
RET = 67: NO SS/PART	1.030 /3,200.000	1.030 /3,200.000	1.030 /3,200.000
NO SS/ GEN	1.028 /3,247.361	1.030 /3,205.052	1.028 /3,244.471

$\rho = 0.02;\ \gamma = -0.50;$ owns home

SS/ GEN	1.030 /3,200.000	1.030 /3,200.000	1.030 /3,200.000
RET = 65: NO SS/PART	1.030 /3,200.000	1.030 /3,200.000	1.030 /3,200.000
NO SS/ GEN	1.028 /3,265.389	1.028 /3,250.566	1.025 /3,337.482
RET = 67: NO SS/PART	1.030 /3,200.000	1.030 /3,200.000	1.030 /3,200.000
NO SS/ GEN	1.029 /3,229.135	1.031 /3,177.714	1.028 /3,245.670

$\rho = 0.02;\ \gamma = -2.50;$ no home

SS/ GEN	1.030 /3,200.000	1.030 /3,200.000	1.030 /3,200.000
RET = 65: NO SS/PART	1.030 /3,200.000	1.030 /3,200.000	1.030 /3,200.000
NO SS/ GEN	1.027 /3,280.502	1.027 /3,275.534	1.025 /3,356.623
RET = 67: NO SS/PART	1.030 /3,200.000	1.030 /3,200.000	1.030 /3,200.000
NO SS/ GEN	1.029 /3,240.951	1.030 /3,190.604	1.028 /3,250.724

$\rho = 0.02;\ \gamma = -2.50;$ owns home

SS/ GEN	1.030 /3,200.000	1.030 /3,200.000	1.030 /3,200.000
RET = 65: NO SS/PART	1.030 /3,200.000	1.030 /3,200.000	1.030 /3,200.000
NO SS/ GEN	1.028 /3,258.951	1.028 /3,245.149	1.025 /3,361.594
RET = 67: NO SS/PART	1.030 /3,200.000	1.030 /3,200.000	1.030 /3,200.000
NO SS/ GEN	1.029 /3,224.699	1.032 /3,157.859	1.028 /3,252.339

CONSUMPTION BEHAVIOR

11.3.3 The Effect of Unplanned Bequests on Capital Intensity

Kotlikoff and Summers (1981) give an operational method of dividing the capital stock into the portion that is due to life-cycle savings and the portion that is due to intergenerational transfers. For each family transfer wealth is defined as the accumulated value of all net transfers received in the past. The total stock of transfer wealth is simply the sum of transfer wealth held by each family. Kotlikoff and Summers (hence-forth KS) find that the stock of transfer wealth is approximately 80% as large as the entire U.S. capital stock. They estimate that each dollar of transfer wealth increases the capital stock by approximately $0.70 when factor prices are held constant. These findings imply that intergenerational transfers account for roughly 60% of the capital stock.

How much transfer wealth would we expect in an economy where all intergenerational transfers are unplanned? Table 11.7 parts A and B answer this question for the hypothetical economies that have been simulated. The tables apply to the case where all assets are generated by life-cycle savings. Bequests may be thought of as partially planned for cases where the representative family owns a home.

These tables give two quantities. The first is total accumulated bequests (transfer wealth) divided by total life-cycle assets. The second quantity is the ratio of life-cycle assets when all would-be bequests are consumed by the deceased family in its last year of life divided by total life-cycle assets in the normal case.

The results are nearly identical for the models of columns 1 and 2 and are insensitive to whether the representative family owns a home. Of course, when the length of life is known with certainty, bequests are zero except for those cases where the representative family owns a home. The results of Table 11.7 part A indicate that transfer wealth is about 20% of total life-cycle wealth in the presence of social security. Without social security, net worth is larger late in life so that total transfer wealth is larger. In Table 11.7 part B the portion of wealth that is transfer wealth rises dramatically due to the high net rates of return. When $\gamma = -2.5$ the base-case level of transfer wealth is about five times larger than total life-cycle wealth.

The second variable reported in the tables is very nearly one in all cases and shows that transfer wealth induces greater consumption so that the capital stock is little affected by whether or not unplanned bequests take place. These later results may appear to contradict Kotli-koff and Summers, who claim that any consumption induced by transfer wealth is likely to be small enough so that the capital stock is increased by 70% of total transfer wealth. Our findings have little relation, however, to the analysis of Kotlikoff and Summers. The second variable reported in our tables considers the effect of transfers on the capital stock relative to the case where all would-be transfers are consumed in the last period of life. Kotlikoff and Summers, conversely, compare the situation where transfers are increased by $1 with the situation where this $1 is consumed optimally over the donor family's lifetime. Clearly a transfer of the Kotlikoff and Summers variety will have a much larger impact on the capital stock.

It is apparent that unplanned bequests cannot explain the findings of Kotlikoff and Summers. For the cases in Table 11.7 part A, for which the equilibrium factor prices and the ratio of the capital stock to total labor income are reasonable, transfer wealth is only 20% of the capital stock. The cases in Table 11.7 part B, while able to explain the Kotlikoff and Summers finding that transfer wealth is 80% as large as the capital stock, are unable to account for observed factor returns (Table 11.2 part B) or the size of the capital stock relative to total labor income (Table 11.3 part B).

11.4 Summary and Conclusion

Our results indicate that eliminating the social security system would, in steady-state equilibrium, increase the capital stock by at least 6.5% and possibly by as much as 31.3%. For cases where the entire capital stock is generated by life-cycle savings, the increase in the capital stock is between 13.4% and 31.3%. Alternatively, for cases where exogenous assets exist, the increase in the total capital stock is between 6.5% and 27.7%.

Liquidity constraints have a significant effect on the results in many of the simulations. Of the sixteen cases considered (four cases in each of Tables 11.1 parts A and B and Table 11.4 parts A and B), liquidity constraints play a role in twelve. In ten of these twelve cases liquidity constraints *magnify* the general equilibrium increase in capital intensity due to eliminating social security.

We find that ignoring the uncertainty of life leads to conservative estimates of the proportionate effect of social security on the capital stock. (This is not always true when exogenous assets exist.) This is an interesting finding in light of the fact that Kotlikoff (1979a) uses a certain lifetime model to determine that the social security system depresses the capital stock by about 20%, which is in the upper part of our estimated range. Apparently Kotlikoff's estimate is as high as it is because the interest elasticity of steady-state life-cycle assets is smaller in his model. This is indicated by the fact that his partial equilibrium

Table 11.7. The actual and apparent contribution of unplanned bequests to the stock of life-cycle assets: ratio of accumulated bequests to life-cycle assets and ratio of life-cycle assets (no bequests) to life-cycle assets (no exogenous assets exist)

Condition	Constrained	Unconstrained	Certain lifetime
A. Cases for which γ and ρ are consistent with the parameter estimates			
$\rho = 0.00$; $\gamma = 0.19$; no home			
SS/ GEN	0.185 /0.972	0.185 /0.972	0.000 /1.000
RET = 65: NO SS/PART	0.326 /0.989	0.326 /0.989	0.000 /1.000
NO SS/ GEN	0.306 /1.006	0.306 /1.006	0.000 /1.000
RET = 67: NO SS/PART	0.338 /0.993	0.338 /0.993	0.000 /1.000
NO SS/ GEN	0.328 /1.010	0.328 /1.010	0.000 /1.000
$\rho = 0.00$; $\gamma = 0.19$; owns home			
SS/ GEN	0.217 /0.994	0.217 /0.994	0.003 /1.013
RET = 65: NO SS/PART	0.331 /0.996	0.331 /0.996	0.002 /1.009
NO SS/ GEN	0.318 /1.019	0.318 /1.019	0.002 /1.014
RET = 67: NO SS/PART	0.344 /1.001	0.344 /1.001	0.002 /1.011
NO SS/ GEN	0.339 /1.022	0.339 /1.022	0.003 /1.013
$\rho = 0.02$; $\gamma = 0.73$; no home			
SS/ GEN	0.160 /0.965	0.160 /0.965	0.000 /1.000
RET = 65: NO SS/PART	0.269 /0.971	0.269 /0.971	0.000 /1.000
NO SS/ GEN	0.275 /0.997	0.275 /0.997	0.000 /1.000
RET = 67: NO SS/PART	0.278 /0.974	0.278 /0.974	0.000 /1.000
NO SS/ GEN	0.287 /0.998	0.287 /0.998	0.000 /1.000
$\rho = 0.02$; $\gamma = 0.73$; owns home			
SS/ GEN	0.183 /0.981	0.183 /0.981	0.002 /1.008
RET = 65: NO SS/PART	0.275 /0.978	0.275 /0.978	0.002 /1.006
NO SS/ GEN	0.287 /1.010	0.287 /1.010	0.002 /1.011
RET = 67: NO SS/PART	0.285 /0.981	0.285 /0.981	0.002 /1.007
NO SS/ GEN	0.299 /1.009	0.299 /1.009	0.002 /1.009

results suggest a smaller social security–induced reduction in the capital stock than do ours. The interest elasticity of steady-state life-cycle asset supply is smaller in the Kotlikoff model because he assumes a flat cross-section earnings profile with respect to age. A change in the net rate of return therefore has a smaller influence on the value of human wealth in his model than it does in ours.

Our simulations suggest that life-cycle savings are not sufficiently large to account for the size of the U.S capital stock. This finding is consistent with that of Kotlikoff and Summers (1981). Our results conflict, however, with those of Tobin (1967), who concludes that life-cycle

Table 11.7. *(continued)*

Condition	Constrained	Unconstrained	Certain lifetime
B. Cases for which γ is smaller than is implied by the parameter estimates			
$\rho = 0.02$; $\gamma = -0.50$; no home			
SS/ GEN	0.523 /0.993	0.523 /0.993	0.000 /1.000
RET = 65: NO SS/PART	0.977 /1.053	0.977 /1.053	0.000 /1.000
NO SS/ GEN	0.943 /1.077	0.947 /1.084	0.000 /1.000
RET = 67: NO SS/PART	0.998 /1.064	0.998 /1.064	0.000 /1.000
NO SS/ GEN	0.995 /1.090	0.997 /1.094	0.000 /1.000
$\rho = 0.02$; $\gamma = -0.50$; owns home			
SS/ GEN	0.632 /1.040	0.632 /1.040	0.006 /1.051
RET = 65: NO SS/PART	0.979 /1.062	0.979 /1.062	0.004 /1.032
NO SS/ GEN	0.886 /0.992	0.966 /1.101	0.006 /1.049
RET = 67: NO SS/PART	1.003 /1.075	1.003 /1.075	0.005 /1.038
NO SS/ GEN	0.947 /0.989	1.015 /1.110	0.006 /1.049
$\rho = 0.02$; $\gamma = -2.50$; no home			
SS/ GEN	5.344 /1.008	5.365 /1.009	0.000 /1.000
RET = 65: NO SS/PART	8.213 /1.073	8.252 /1.087	0.000 /1.000
NO SS/ GEN	4.058 /0.995	5.888 /1.133	0.000 /1.000
RET = 67: NO SS/PART	7.588 /1.064	7.617 /1.097	0.000 /1.000
NO SS/ GEN	4.613 /0.982	5.914 /1.133	0.000 /1.000
$\rho = 0.02$; $\gamma = -2.50$; owns home			
SS/ GEN	4.631 /1.012	5.382 /1.069	0.014 /1.089
RET = 65: NO SS/PART	6.224 /0.996	7.558 /1.099	0.008 /1.054
NO SS/ GEN	2.967 /0.969	5.853 /1.145	0.012 /1.087
RET = 67: NO SS/PART	5.872 /0.989	6.939 /1.113	0.010 /1.067
NO SS/ GEN	3.979 /0.993	5.871 /1.144	0.013 /1.085

savings can explain the size of the capital stock. There are two reasons for the different conclusions: (1) Tobin assumes that the within-period utility function is independent of age, whereas our model gives only 53% as much weight to retirement consumption as to preretirement consumption, and (2) our results are for an economy where the social security system replaces 65% of age-40 earnings, whereas Tobin's estimates are for an economy with a social security system like that in 1964. Our results probably underestimate the current amount of life-cycle assets relative to labor income in the United States, because the economy has not had time to adjust to the current social security replacement rates. Therefore we also have performed simulations for the case where the social security replacement rate is 40%. The equilibrium ratios of the capital stock to labor income, for these simulations, are not substantially larger. We conclude that our results differ from those of Tobin primarily because we give relatively less importance to retirement consumption.

12 Summary and Conclusion

This study has taken a unique approach to analyzing consumption behavior. The estimated consumption model, which serves as the basis for all our empirical inferences, is derived from a realistic model of individual maximizing behavior. The most notable real-world features of the model are its allowance for liquidity constraints and "needs" that vary over time with changing family composition.

We find that liquidity constraints are quite prevalent. Our preferred model estimates indicate that 19.4% of the population of families represented by the sample are liquidity constrained. Less than half of these families have one-year horizons. The remaining liquidity-constrained families have horizons that extend to a time that a child becomes independent. Hall and Mishkin (1982) and Hayashi (1984) come to similar conclusions regarding the prevalence of liquidity constraints. Their estimates, however, concern the prevalence of one-period horizons. If allowance is taken for short multiperiod horizons, these two studies suggest that liquidity constraints are more prevalent than does this study.

A major advantage of our methodology is that it enables us to identify liquidity-constrained families. It is possible, therefore, to infer the importance of liquidity-constrained families for aggregate consumption. We find that 16.7% of consumption undertaken by the population of families represented by our sample is undertaken by liquidity-constrained families. It is also possible to simulate the effect of tax changes on the consumption of each family in our sample. We find, for example, that a one-time incremental tax equal to 10% of labor income would reduce the aggregate consumption of the population represented by our sample by 18.4% of the incremental tax revenue. If no families were liquidity constrained, this change would only be 4.6%. Previous studies do not identify liquidity-constrained families and hence are unable to make inferences of this type.

We find that, at any given age, net social security receipts are indistinguishable from other net receipts in their effect on consumption behavior. It is concluded that each dollar of net social security receipts is 95% certain to have at least 60% as great an effect on consumption as does other net income received on the same date. The significance of these results, relative to those of previous studies, is attributable to the fact that our consumption model incorporates the lifetime budget constraint. It is not possible, therefore, for the model to attribute social security's effect on consumption to ordinary human wealth.

Evidence is presented suggesting that a small minority of families, most of whom are extremely wealthy, plan substantial bequests. Roughly 55% of the wealth held by the population represented by our retired sample is estimated to be held for the purpose of leaving a bequest. We estimate, however, that 1.6% of retired families hold over 40% of this "bequest" wealth.

We have applied our estimated consumption model to a hypothetical population of families to trace the effects of government fiscal policies over time. It is found that a current increase in the rate of tax on labor income, offset by an anticipated reduction in the rate of tax on labor income ten years later, reduces current consumption by 9.0% of the incremental tax revenue. The lagged effects of this policy are significant in spite of liquidity constraints. Over nine years, consumption falls by 33.4% of the initial incremental tax revenue.

We also have simulated the effect of eliminating the social security system in the United States. This policy is found to increase the steady-state capital intensity by at least 6.5% and possibly by as much as 31.3%. Perhaps surprisingly, this change tends to be smaller for the case where no families are liquidity constrained. Our steady-state simulations also suggest that the bulk of the capital stock in the United States and other developed countries is due to bequests.

Our findings indicate that government debt policy, whether the debt be in the form of government bonds or promises to pay current workers retirement benefits, have important effects on the real economy. Holding the time profile of the government's real spending constant, deficits increase aggregate demand and decrease capital accumulation. It appears, however, that the short-term effects of government debt policy are small relative to the long-term effects.

Appendixes

Notes

References

Index

The Intertemporal Utility Function

The models discussed in the text assume that labor income may be treated as exogenous and that lifetime utility is an additive function of real consumption expenditure in each period. This appendix explores the implications of these assumptions.

A.1 A General Model

The agent is assumed to be certain of his life span and all future prices and interest rates. His lifetime utility is a monotonically increasing and concave function of the amounts of each of $n + 1$ goods consumed in each of the $T + 1$ periods of his life:

$$V = V(S_0, \mathbf{X}_0, S_1, \mathbf{X}_1, \ldots, S_T, \mathbf{X}_T), \tag{A.1}$$

where S_t is leisure consumption in period t and $\mathbf{X}_t = (X_{t1}, X_{t2}, \ldots, X_{tn})$ gives the consumption of each of goods, other than leisure, in period t. Henceforth the term "goods" refers to the X's and excludes leisure. Denote the prices of S_t and X_{ti} by ω_t and q_{ti}, respectively. Then the agent's problem is

$$\underset{\mathbf{Z}}{\text{Max }} V(\mathbf{Z}), \tag{A.2}$$

subject to

$$\sum_{i,t} PN(t,0) q_{ti} X_{ti} + \sum_{t} S_t PN(t,0) \omega_t \leqslant WF_0 \equiv L \sum_{t} PN(t,0) \omega_t, \qquad \mathbf{Z} \geqslant 0,$$

where

$$Z = (S_0, \mathbf{X}_0, S_1, \mathbf{X}_1, \ldots, S_T, \mathbf{X}_T),$$

$$PN(t,0) = \prod_{j=0}^{t-1} (1 + RN_j)^{-1}, \quad \text{for } t = 1, 2, \ldots, T,$$

$$= 1, \quad \text{for } t = 0,$$

RN_t is the nominal rate of interest at time t, and L is the agent's time endowment in each period. Note that labor income is endogenous. The present value of the agent's lifelong time endowment is given by WF_0, and he allocates this endowment to the purchase of the n goods and leisure in each period. In other words, the agent must buy back his leisure and his explicit labor income is therefore endogenous.

A.2 Separability Assumptions and the Indirect Utility Function

The models presented in the text assume that the timing of goods and leisure consumption are determined independently. Also, preferences for goods are additively separable through time. These assumptions imply that the direct intertemporal utility function (A.1) takes the form

$$V = V_1(\mathbf{S}) + \sum_{i=0}^{T} V_2(i, \mathbf{X}_i), \tag{A.3}$$

where $\mathbf{S} = (S_0, S_1, \ldots, S_T)$ gives leisure consumption in each period. This intertemporal utility function is said to display leisure-goods separability and temporal separability with respect to goods. The function V_1 also may be separable through time but this is not necessary.

Maximizing (A.3) with respect to the constraints in (A.2) gives $\mathbf{S}^*(\mathbf{p})$ and $X_i^*(\mathbf{p})$, $i = 0, 1, \ldots, T$, where $\mathbf{p}$ is a vector of all prices and interest rates. Conditional on $\mathbf{S}^*$, $\mathbf{X}^* = (\mathbf{X}_1^*, \mathbf{X}_2^*, \ldots, \mathbf{X}_T^*)$ maximizes

$$\sum_{i=0}^{T} V_2(i, \mathbf{X}_i),$$

subject to

$$\sum_{i,t} PN(t,0) q_{ti} X_{ti} \leq W_0 \equiv \sum_{t} PN(t,0) \omega_t (L - S_t^*) \qquad \mathbf{X} \geq \mathbf{0}.$$

An immediate implication is that $\mathbf{X}^*$ depends on $\mathbf{S}^*$ and wages entirely through the index W_0, which is referred to in the text as lifetime full wealth.

Denote total nominal expenditure on goods at time t as C_t'. Then, conditional on C_t', the agent's chooses $\mathbf{X}_t$ to maximize

$$V_2(t,\mathbf{X}_t) \tag{A.4}$$

subject to

$$\sum_{i=1}^{n} q_{ti}X_{ti} \leq C_t', \qquad \mathbf{X}_t \geq \mathbf{0}.$$

The solution is of the form $\mathbf{X}_i^*(C_t',\mathbf{q}_t)$ where $\mathbf{q}_t = (q_{t1},q_{t2}, \ldots ,q_{tm})$ is the goods price vector in period t. Substitution of this result into (A.4) gives the indirect utility function at time t:

$$U(t,C_t',\mathbf{q}_t) \equiv V_2[t,\mathbf{X}_i^*(C_t',\mathbf{q}_t)],$$

where U is monotonically increasing and strictly concave in C_t' and homogeneous of degree zero in C_t' and $\mathbf{q}_t$.

The within-period indirect utility function depends on prices as well as nominal expenditure. There are two possible justifications for purging it of the influence of prices. First, if within-period preferences are homothetic, then the indirect within-period utility function takes the form:

$$U[t,C_t'/\phi(\mathbf{q}_t)] = U(t,C_t), \tag{A.5}$$

where $\phi(\mathbf{q}_t)$, say ϕ_t, is the true cost of living index and C_t is real consumption expenditure. Note that the functional form of ϕ is time-invariant. A second possibility is that relative prices are expected to remain constant so that:

$$\mathbf{q}_i/\phi_i = \mathbf{q}_j/\phi_j \equiv \mathbf{k}, \quad \text{all } i,j,$$

where $\mathbf{k}$ is the vector of constants and ϕ_i and ϕ_j give the general price levels in periods i and j, respectively. In this case the indirect utility function takes the form

$$U(t,C_t',\mathbf{q}_t) = U(t,C_t'/\phi_t,\mathbf{q}_t/\phi_t) = U(t,C_t,\mathbf{k}), \tag{A.6}$$

where the first equality follows from the fact that U is homogeneous of degree zero in C_t' and $\mathbf{q}_t$. The vector of constants, $\mathbf{k}$, is time-invariant and may be dropped from the list of arguments for U.

The first justification for purging prices from the within-period indirect utility function is highly implausible in that it requires that all goods have an income elasticity of one, thus ruling out the existence of necessities and luxuries. Even if this assumption were realistic and relative prices were to change over time, the functional form of the true cost of living index is needed in order to convert nominal expenditure into real expenditure in each period. The second justification, conversely, would seem to be a reasonable approximation, especially given the assumption that the intertemporal utility function is separable in leisure and goods so that the wage is not included in $\mathbf{q}_t$.

Given an indirect utility function of the form (A.5) or (A.6), the agent's problem is to choose the real consumption vector, say $\mathbf{C}^*$, to maximize

$$\sum_{i=0}^{T} U(i,C_i)$$

subject to

$$\sum_{i=0}^{T} PN(i,0)C_i' \equiv \sum_{i=0}^{T} P(i,0)C_i \leq W_0,$$

where

$$P(i,0) = (\phi_i/\phi_0)PN(i,0) \equiv \prod_{j=0}^{i-1} (1 + R_j)^{-1}$$

and R_j is the real rate of interest in period j. This is the problem considered in the text.

Note that leisure is endogenous in this formulation of the agent's problem. The special feature of this model is that consumption decisions are made conditional on only one index of lifetime labor supply, lifetime full wealth. This implies that the optimal timing of goods and leisure consumption are independent of each other.

A.3 Separability of Goods and Leisure

Ghez and Becker (1975) and Heckman (1974) relax the assumption of goods-leisure separability while assuming temporal separability for both goods and leisure. In particular, they assume that the intertemporal utility function is given by

$$V = \sum_{i=0}^{T} V_3(S_i, \mathbf{X}_i), \tag{A.7}$$

where V_3 is homogeneous in leisure and goods so that a two-stage optimization process is possible: (1) given an index of prices for goods and leisure in each period, determine the optimal amount of full consumption, which includes leisure consumption, to devote to each period, and

(2) given full consumption in each period, divide it optimally between the consumption of goods and leisure as their relative prices dictate.

Many interesting conclusions emerge from this model. One which has important implications for the proportionality hypothesis is the following: An increase in the real wage in period t will decrease leisure and may increase or decrease the consumption of goods depending on the degree of complementarity and substitutability between leisure and goods.

To see the ramifications of this observation for the proportionality hypothesis, suppose that the marginal utility of goods consumption increases with leisure consumption. Individuals with a particularly high wage, in this case, will consume less than would be predicted by a model which assumes the marginal utility of goods and leisure are independent. This is because the agent will choose to enjoy the fruits of her labor at a time when she can afford to take more leisure time (for example, in retirement). In a cross section of individuals, therefore, those with higher lifetime full wealth will consume proportionately less during their working years than those with lower lifetime full wealth. This model, therefore, is consistent with the many empirical studies that appear to refute the proportionality hypothesis. (See, for example, Ando and Modigliani, 1960, and Mayer, 1972.)

If, conversely, the marginal utility of goods consumption is decreasing in leisure consumption, then high-wage individuals will tend to consume more than would be predicted by a model that assumes the marginal utility of leisure and goods to be independent. This would be the case, for example, if work-related expenses are significant.

The complementarity or substitutability of goods and leisure is only important to the extent that leisure consumption varies over the life cycle. Suppose, for example, that the optimal amount of leisure consumption is constant prior to retirement. In this case the inclusion of leisure in (A.7) has the effect of shifting the within-period indirect utility function for goods at retirement.

It follows that a within-period utility function that excludes leisure as an argument, but which is allowed to shift at retirement, would closely approximate preferences for goods over the life cycle if leisure is relatively constant prior to retirement.

A.4 Temporal Separability

An intertemporal utility function that is additive through time requires the utility experienced in different periods be independent. This has three distinct implications: (1) goods consumed at different times cannot be complementary; (2) diminishing marginal utility would seem to be violated where one time period merges into the next; and (3) tastes cannot be affected by previous consumption experience. The first two restrictions on intertemporal preferences seem reasonable provided the time period is sufficiently lengthy. Restriction (3), however, would not be consistent with the common sense notion that a given standard of living is less enjoyable to an agent the higher the standard of living to which she is accustomed, a phenomenon which would cause an agent to gradually increase her consumption over time so as not to reduce her appreciation for consumption too quickly. This seems to be what Keynes had in mind when he wrote, "it gratifies a common instinct to look forward to a gradually improving standard of life rather than the contrary, even though the capacity for enjoyment may be diminishing" (Keynes, 1936, p. 108).

I do not believe this problem to be too serious. The major behavioral implication of endogenously changing preferences is that there is a strong tendency to delay consumption. It is established in Section 2.1.3 of Chapter 2 that the standard intertemporal utility function, which is additive with an isoelastic within-period utility function, leads to an increasing consumption profile provided the pure rate of time preference is less than the real interest rate. I conjecture, therefore, that an additive intertemporal utility function is capable of predicting behavior closely approximating that which is implied by a preference function that changes as a function of previous experience.

The General Proofs of Propositions 2.1 and 2.2

The proofs of Propositions 2.1 and 2.2 given in Section 2.2.2. of Chapter 2 make assumptions which, while apparently innocuous, reduce the notational complexity of the proofs considerably. Here it is shown that these assumptions are indeed innocuous. Most of the notation used in this appendix is introduced in Section 2.2.2 of Chapter 2.

B.1 The General Proof of Proposition 2.1 — A Sketch

The proof of Proposition 2.1 given in the text assumes that $v + 1$, the first date that the constraints on net worth are binding, is the first date that net worth equals its minimal level. A sketch of the general proof is given here.

Let $q + 1$ and $r + 1$, $t < q < r \leqslant v$, be the first two dates that net worth equals its minimum allowable level. Partition $\mathbf{C}^*(t,T)$ as $[\mathbf{C}^*(t,q)$, $\mathbf{C}^*(q + 1,r),\mathbf{C}^*(r + 1,T)]$. Then the proof given in the text proves that $\mathbf{C}^*(t,q) = \mathbf{C}^u(t,q)$. Likewise, it is easily shown that $\mathbf{C}^*(q + 1,r) = \mathbf{C}^u(q + 1,r)$, where $\mathbf{C}^u(q + 1,r) = (C_{q+1}^u(q + 1,r), C_{q+2}^u[q + 1,r], \ldots, C_r^u(q + 1,r)]$ maximizes

$$V[\mathbf{C}(q + 1,r)] = \sum_{i=q+1}^{r} \alpha(i,t)U(i,C_i),$$

subject to the constraint $A_{r+1} \geqslant B_{r+1}$, given that $A_{q+1} = B_{q+1}$. Since the constraint $A_{q+1} \geqslant B_{q+1}$ is not binding (that is, $q < v$), it follows that $\mathbf{C}^*(t,r) = (\mathbf{C}^u(t,q),\mathbf{C}^u(q + 1,r)) = \mathbf{C}^u(t,r)$. Repeating the argument leads to the conclusion that $\mathbf{C}^*(t,v) = \mathbf{C}^u(t,v)$.

B.2 The General Proof of Proposition 2.2

The proof of Proposition 2.2 given in the text assumes that there exists a date, x, such that the two net worth paths depicted in Figure 2.1 intersect. (Such a date necessarily exists in the continuous time case.) The general proof given below pursues a different strategy than the proof given in the text.

Suppose, contrary to the proposition, that there exists a date p such that $\mathbf{A}^u(t,p) \geqq \mathbf{B}(t,p)$, $v < p \leqq T$. Define the integer $w + 1$ as

$$w + 1 = \{\text{Min } s | v + 1 < s \leqq p + 1; A_s[\mathbf{C}^*(t,T)] \geqq A_s[\mathbf{C}^u(t,p)]\}.$$

The date w exists, since $A_{p+1}[\mathbf{C}^u(t,p)] = B_{p+1} \leqq A_{p+1}[\mathbf{C}^*(t,T)]$. Also, define the consumption vector, $\mathbf{C}^+(t,w)$, as

$$\mathbf{C}^+(t,w) = \{\mathbf{C}'(t,w) | \mathbf{C}'(t,w) \in S^+(t,w), V[\mathbf{C}'(t,w)] \geqq V[\mathbf{C}(t,w)],$$
$$\text{for all } \mathbf{C}(t,w) \in S^+(t,w)\},$$

where

$$S^+(t,w) = \{\mathbf{C}'(t,w) | A_{w+1}[\mathbf{C}'(t,w)] = A_{w+1}[\mathbf{C}^*(t,T)]\}.$$

The concavity of the preference function ensures that $\mathbf{C}^+(t,w)$ is unique. Our strategy is to show that $[\mathbf{C}^+(t,w),\mathbf{C}^*(w + 1,T)]$ is feasible and dominates $\mathbf{C}^*(t,T)$, thereby contradicting the supposed optimality of $\mathbf{C}^*(t,T)$.

By definition of w, $\mathbf{C}^u(t,p,t,w)$ uses up at least as many resources as does $\mathbf{C}^+(t,w)$ so that, by (2.27) in the text, $\mathbf{C}^u(t,p,t,w) \geqq \mathbf{C}^+(t,w)$ and $\mathbf{A}[\mathbf{C}^+(t,w)] \geqq \mathbf{A}^u(t,p,t,w) \geqq \mathbf{B}(t,w)$. It follows then that $\mathbf{C}^{**}(t,T) = [\mathbf{C}^+(t,w),\mathbf{C}^*(w + 1,T)]$ is feasible and dominates $\mathbf{C}^*(t,T)$, provided the two plans are distinct. But the constraint $A_{v+1} \geqq B_{v+1}$ is not binding for $\mathbf{C}^+(t,w)$, as it is for $\mathbf{C}^*(t,T)$, so that $\mathbf{C}^{**}(t,T)$ and $\mathbf{C}^*(t,T)$ are distinct.

APPENDIX C

The Hall and Mishkin Study

The empirical findings of Hall and Mishkin (1982) are discussed in Section 3.3.1 of Chapter 3. It is asserted that their estimates regarding the prevalence of liquidity constraints are biased if nondeterministic income change is measured with error. It is also pointed out that the Hall and Mishkin (henceforth HM) hybrid model is appropriate only under special assumptions concerning the probability of being liquidity constrained. We support these assertions here.

The logic of the HM methodology is most easily understood with reference to a simplified version of their model. Suppose that

$$\Delta y_t = \epsilon_t + \eta_t - \eta_{t-1} \qquad (C.1)$$

where Δy_t is nondeterministic income change and ϵ_t and η_t are each distributed over time as white noise. That is, nondeterministic income change consists of a permanent component, ϵ_t, and a transitory component, η_t, that lasts only one year. (HM allow "transitory" income to follow a two-year moving average process.) As explained in the text, HM construct a measure of Δy_t that is assumed to be error-free.

HM propose an optimizing model where the change in consumption, net of a deterministic component depending on family characteristics, is

$$\Delta c_t = \epsilon_t + \beta\eta_t, \qquad (C.2)$$

where β is the annual amount paid by a fair annuity costing one dollar. HM also allow for a transitory consumption term that follows a two-year moving average process. For simplicity we assume transitory consumption is identically zero. Note that β depends on age. HM acknowledge this, but choose to treat it as constant across families.

Equations (C.1) and (C.2) constitute the essence of the HM model.

Note that

$$COV(\Delta c_t, \Delta y_t) = \beta \sigma_\eta^2 + \sigma_\epsilon^2, \qquad (C.3)$$

$$-COV(\Delta y_t, \Delta y_{t-1}) = \sigma_\eta^2, \qquad (C.4)$$

$$VAR(\Delta y_t) + 2COV(\Delta y_t, \Delta y_{t-1}) = \sigma_\epsilon^2, \qquad (C.5)$$

where COV denotes covariance, VAR denotes variance, σ_η^2 is the variance of η, and σ_ϵ^2 is the variance of ϵ. Using sample variances and covariances to estimate the left-hand sides of (C.3), (C.4), and (C.5) yields a consistent estimate of β. Note, however, that

$$COV(\Delta c_t, \Delta y_{t+1}) = -\beta \sigma_\eta^2,$$

which makes an alternative estimate of β possible. That is, β is overidentified. Assuming the ϵ's and η's are normal, the maximum-likelihood estimator yields a unique estimate of β and the other parameters, which trades off the fit between the various sample and population moments.

As explained in the text, HM uncover evidence suggesting that some portion μ of families in their sample consume their entire disposable income. They therefore propose the following hybrid consumption model:

$$\Delta c_t = (1 - \mu)(\epsilon_t + \beta \eta_t) + \mu(\epsilon_t + \eta_t - \eta_{t-1}). \qquad (C.6)$$

Note that

$$COV(\Delta c_t, \Delta y_{t-1}) = -\mu \sigma_\eta^2, \qquad (C.7)$$

which, in addition to (C.4), identifies μ. HM estimate μ to be 0.20 with a standard error of 0.065. That is, they estimate that 20% of their sample is liquidity constrained.

Measurement error in Δy_t is likely to seriously bias HM's estimate of μ. Suppose, for example, that

$$\Delta y_t = \epsilon_t + \eta_t - \eta_{t-1} + \omega,$$

where ω is a family-specific error in the measurement of Δy_t, which is time invariant. Then

$$-COV(\Delta y_t, \Delta y_{t-1}) = \sigma_\eta^2 - VAR(\omega)$$

so that the estimate of σ_η^2 from (C.4) is downward biased. This, in turn, causes the estimate of μ from (C.7) to be upward biased.

This is potentially a serious problem. HM's regression for deterministic income change explains only 14% of actual income change. Also, their regression for deterministic income change does not include a scale term. That is, two families that are identical, except that one has twice as much labor income as the other, are assumed to experience the same absolute deterministic income change! This suggests that a family-specific error in the measurement of Δy_t is indeed present.

Our analysis of measurement error is only illustrative. The HM model is quite complex and we cannot be certain that measurement error in Δy_t, that is positively correlated over time, leads to an upward-biased estimate of μ. The point is that HM's estimate of μ is much less certain than its asymptotic standard error would suggest.

Another important point is that the hybrid consumption equation (C.6) contains an error term, say τ, with a binomial distribution. In particular, τ has the value

$$(1 - \mu)[(1 - \beta)\eta_t - \eta_{t-1}]$$

with probability μ and the value

$$-\mu[(1 - \beta)\eta_t - \eta_{t-1}]$$

with probability $1 - \mu$. Since HM leave this error term out of their model, their estimates are not maximum likelihood. More important, the covariance of τ with the right-hand side of (C.6) is nonzero if $E(\eta^2)$ is different for constrained and unconstrained families. (Note that $E(\eta)$ is probably negative for liquidity-constrained families.) If these moments do differ, then σ_η^2 in (C.7) is $E(\eta^2)$ for liquidity-constrained families. To obtain a consistent estimate of μ in this case, it is necessary to divide a consistent estimate of $COV(\Delta c_t, \Delta y_{t-1})$ with a consistent estimate of $E(\eta^2)$ for liquidity-constrained families. The HM procedure instead amounts to estimating σ_η^2 in (C.7) with a weighted average of the two subsample moments.

I make this point primarily to illustrate a more general concept which is important for interpreting other studies as well. A hybrid model such as (C.6) can be given a structural interpretation only if assumptions are made concerning any systematic differences in the two populations of agents whose behavior is being modeled. HM implicitly assume the only relevant difference between the two populations is the consumption equation. This comment also applies to the Hayashi (1984) study discussed in Section 3.3.1 of Chapter 3.

It remains true, however, that equation (C.6) can be used as the basis for a valid test of the restriction $\mu = 0$. In this case, $COV(\Delta c_t, \Delta y_{t-1})$ in (C.7) is zero regardless of the value of σ_η^2. But if the hypothesis $\mu = 0$ is rejected, a structural interpretation of μ requires additional assumptions, as is demonstrated above.

The essence of this result may be understood as follows. If $E(\eta^2)$ for liquidity-constrained families differs from $E(\eta^2)$ for unconstrained families, then the probability of being liquidity constrained is not independent of η_t and η_{t-1}. Therefore, since (C.6) does not allow μ to depend on η_t and η_{t-1}, the hybrid model does not give the expectation of Δc_t conditional on η_t, η_{t-1}, and ϵ_t.

Consumption under Uncertainty

This appendix analyzes the effect of labor-income uncertainty and rate-of-return uncertainty on consumption. Many of the results presented here are referenced in Chapter 4.

D.1 Labor-Income Uncertainty

Nearly all results concerning the effect of labor-income uncertainty on consumption have been derived in the context of two-period models. The principal contributions are by Dreze and Modigliani (1972), Leland (1968), and Sandmo (1970). The results of Dreze and Modigliani (henceforth DM) are most general and are presented in Section D.1.1. Section D.1.2 extends these results to a multiperiod model for the case where the intertemporal utility function is additive and the within-period utility function is of the form $(1/\gamma)C^\gamma$.

D.1.1 A General Two-Period Model

Dreze and Modigliani consider an agent with a two-period horizon who receives a certain first-period income, YL_1, and an uncertain income, YL_2, in period two. Here it is assumed that the rate of return on savings, R, is certain although DM allow it to be random.

The agent's problem is to choose first-period consumption, C_1, to maximize his expected intertemporal utility:

$$V(C_1) = {}_1E\langle U\{C_1, [(1 + R)(YL_1 - C_1) + YL_2]\}\rangle, \qquad \text{(D.1)}$$

where ${}_1E(YL_2) = \overline{YL_2}$, ${}_1E[(YL_2 - \overline{YL_2})^2] > 0$, and U is monotonically increasing and strictly concave in its arguments. It is assumed that any constraints that are imposed on C_1, other than those that are implicit in the objective function, are not binding. Note that the utility function is not necessarily additive.

Let C_1^* maximize (D.1) and let $V^*(C_1^*)$ be the associated value of V. Define $C_1^+(X)$ as the optimal first-period consumption when YL_2 is certain to equal X and let $V^+(X)$ be the associated value of V. Also, let YL_2^+ be the certain level of period-two income which makes the agent as well off as with the uncertain income YL_2, that is $V_1^+[C_1^+(YL_2^+)] = V_1^*(C_1^*)$. Finally, let $RR(C_1,C_2)$ represent the change in absolute risk aversion as C_1 increases and C_2 decreases along budget lines with slope $\partial C_2 / \partial C_1 = -(1 + R)$:

$$RR(C_1,C_2) = \frac{\partial - (U_{22}/U_2)}{\partial C_1} - (1 + R) \frac{\partial - (U_{22}/U_2)}{\partial C_2}.$$

Then Dreze and Modigliani show that

$$RR(C_1^*,C_2) \gtreqless 0 \quad \text{for all } C_2 \to C_1^* \lesseqgtr C_1^+(YL_2^+).$$

Decreasing absolute risk aversion as C_2 increases and C_1 decreases along the budget line (that is, $RR(C_1^*,C_2) > 0$ for all C_2) is a sufficient condition for saving in the uncertainty case to exceed its level in the certainty case, where expected utility is held constant.

Furthermore, for a risk-averse agent, YL_2^+ is less than $\overline{YL_2}$ so that

$$RR(C_1^*,C_2) \geqslant 0 \quad \text{for all } C_2 \to C_1^* < C_1^+(\overline{YL_2}),$$

provided consumption is a normal good in both periods. In other words, decreasing absolute risk aversion is sufficient, but not necessary, for income uncertainty to increase saving above the level that would occur if second-period income were certain to equal its mean. Leland (1968) and Sandmo (1970) make persuasive arguments implying that $RR(C_1,C_2)$ is greater than zero for all C_1 and C_2, in which case income uncertainty necessarily increases saving.

The intuition behind this result is clear. A positive variance of YL_2 around its mean makes a risk-averse agent poorer. If consumption is a normal good in each period, the agent will respond by saving more and shifting the probability distribution of second-period consumption, provided that such a move does not increase his distaste for risk by too much.

D.1.2 Application to the Yaari Model of Chapter 2

For the case where the intertemporal utility function is additively separable and the contribution of second-period consumption to total utility is given by $U(C_2)$, the condition that absolute risk aversion decreases implies that $U'U''' - (U'')^2 > 0$. We note that the isoelastic form of U, $(1/\gamma)C_2^\gamma$, satisfies this condition so that increased income risk increases saving for all values of γ.

This result continues to be valid in the case of a multiperiod horizon. Indeed, it would be disturbing if the length of the period, and hence the number of periods, changed any qualitative implications of the model.

The proof given below assumes a three-period horizon. Extending the proof to an arbitrary number of periods is straightforward.

The agent receives labor income YL_i in period i; $i = 1,2,3$; and YL_2 and YL_3 are stochastic with means $\overline{YL}_2$ and $\overline{YL}_3$, respectively.

First, consider the agent's problem in period 2. Her objective is to choose C_2, say C_2^*, to maximize the expected value of

$$(1/\gamma)C_2^\gamma + (1/\gamma)(1 + \rho)^{-1}[(1 + R)^2(YL_1 - C_1)$$
$$+ (1 + R)(YL_2 - C_2) + YL_3]^\gamma.$$

When choosing C_2, the agent knows the values of C_1, YL_1, and YL_2. Her problem, therefore, is identical in form to the Dreze and Modigliani problem. Invoking their result, we have

$$C_2^*(C_1,YL_1,YL_2) < \overline{C}_2(C_1,YL_1,YL_2) \qquad \text{(D.2)}$$

where as before, $\overline{C}_2$ is the optimal level of consumption in period 2 when labor income in each *future* period is certain to equal its mean. As the notation indicates, C_2^* is contingent on C_1, YL_1, and YL_2.

In period 1 the agent equates the marginal utility of first-period consumption to $(1 + R)$ times the expected marginal utility of second-period consumption. More formally, C_1^* satisfies the following relation:

$$(C_1^*)^{\gamma-1} = [(1 + R)/(1 + \rho)]_1 E\{[C_2^*(C_1^*,YL_1,YL_2)]^{\gamma-1}\}, \qquad \text{(D.3)}$$

where YL_1 is nonstochastic. It follows from (D.2) and (D.3) that

$$(C_1^*)^{\gamma-1} > [(1 + R)/(1 + \rho)]_1 E\{[\overline{C}_2(C_1^*,YL_1,YL_2)]^{\gamma-1}\}, \qquad \text{(D.4)}$$

since $\gamma - 1 < 0$.

Suppose, contrary to what we wish to show, that $\overline{C}_1 < C_1^*$, where $\overline{C}_1$ is the optimal level of first-period consumption when YL_2 and YL_3 are certain to equal their respective means. In this case

$$(\overline{C}_1)^{\gamma-1} > (C_1^*)^{\gamma-1} > [(1 + R)/(1 + \rho)]_1 E\{[\overline{C}_2(\overline{C}_1,YL_1,YL_2)]^{\gamma-1}\}, \qquad \text{(D.5)}$$

where the last inequality follows from (D.4) and the fact that $\overline{C}_2(\overline{C}_1,YL_1,YL_2) > \overline{C}_2(C_1^*,YL_1,YL_2)$ for all YL_2 when $\overline{C}_1 < C_1^*$. The convexity of the marginal utility function, in addition to (D.5), implies that

$$(\overline{C}_1)^{\gamma-1} > [(1 + R)/(1 + \rho)][\overline{C}_2(\overline{C}_1,YL_1,\overline{YL}_2)]^{\gamma-1}. \qquad \text{(D.6)}$$

But $\overline{C}_2(\overline{C}_1, YL_1, \overline{YL}_2)$ is the optimal level of period-2 consumption when YL_2 and YL_3 are certain to equal their respective means. It follows that (D.6) must be an equality. The assumption that $\overline{C}_1 < C_1^*$, therefore, is contradicted.

D.2 Rate-of-Return Uncertainty

This section considers the effect of capital-income uncertainty on consumption. As in the cases of lifetime and labor-income uncertainty, the standard approach to formalizing the agent's problem is to assume that he maximizes the expected value of his lifetime utility, where the expectation is taken over the portfolio rate of return.

It turns out that the Yaari model presented in Section 2.1.3 of Chapter 2, which satisfies the proportionality hypothesis, can be generalized to the case where an arbitrary number of capital assets exist provided (1) a riskless asset is also available and (2) the rates of return on risky assets are distributed independently over time. This generalization is due to Hakansson (1970) and Merton (1971). The Hakansson model is presented below.[1]

THE HAKANSSON MODEL

Hakansson (1970) solves for the optimal multiperiod consumption-investment plan assuming the following circumstances.

(1) There are h risky assets available whose rates of return are independently and identically distributed over time.
(2) There is one riskless asset.
(3) The intertemporal utility function is additive where the within-period utility function is of the isoelastic form, $(1/\gamma)C^\gamma$, and the discount factor on utility-experienced i periods in the future is $(1 + \rho)^{-i}$.

Merton (1971) solves essentially the same problem for the continuous-time case and where asset returns follow a Weiner process.

The only difference between the Hakansson problem and the Yaari problem posed in Section 2.1.3 of Chapter 2 is that there are $h + 1$ assets, h of which are risky. The vector $\mathbf{K}_i' = (K_{1i}, K_{2i}, \ldots, K_{hi})$ is a decision vector and denotes the amounts of each capital asset held in period i. (Vector multiplication is employed in this section so that all vectors are column vectors unless they are transposed, as indicated by a superscript prime.) The associated vector of random real rates of return is $\mathbf{RK}_i' = (RK_{1i}, RK_{2i}, \ldots, RK_{hi})$. For the case where the agent's horizon is certain to be $T + 1$ periods long, the agent's problem is

$$\underset{\mathbf{C},\mathbf{K}}{\text{Max}}\, V_0 = {_0E}\left[\sum_{i=0}^{T} (1 + \rho)^{-i}(1/\gamma)C_i^{\gamma}\right], \tag{D.7}$$

subject to:

$$\mathbf{C} \geqslant \mathbf{0}$$

$$\mathbf{K} \geqslant \mathbf{0}$$

$$\text{Prob}(W_i < 0) = 0, \qquad i = 0,1, \ldots, T,$$

where

$$\mathbf{C}' = (C_0, C_1, \ldots, C_T),$$

$$\mathbf{K}' = (\mathbf{K}_0', \mathbf{K}_1', \ldots, \mathbf{K}_T'),$$

$$W_i = A_i + \sum_{k=i}^{T} P(k,i)YL_k$$

$$= (1 + R_{i-1})(W_{i-1} - C_{i-1}) + \mathbf{K}_{i-1}'(\mathbf{RK}_{i-1} - R_{i-1}),$$

$$P(k,i) = \sum_{j=i}^{k-1} (1 + R_j)^{-1}, \quad \text{for } k = i + 1, i + 2, \ldots, T,$$

$$= 1, \quad \text{for } k = i,$$

and R_i is the risk-free rate of return in period i.

It is assumed that $\mathbf{RK}_i$ is independent of $\mathbf{RK}_j$, $i \neq j$, and that the joint distributions of asset returns in each period are known in the initial period. This ensures that all the relevant information revealed in past periods is reflected in the current level of net worth, and hence full wealth. In other words, future full wealth is the only variable that is uncertain and is relevant to future consumption. The solution to problem (D.7), therefore, is a consumption-investment plan contingent on full wealth in each period. We note that if capital returns were not independently distributed over time, then consumption in each period would be contingent on full wealth and, in addition, all past realized rates of return.

Problem (D.7) is solved in the next subsection. The solution is

$$C_{T-n}^* = b_{T-n}^* W_{T-n}, \tag{D.8}$$

$$\mathbf{K}_{T-n}^* = (1 - b_{T-n}^*)\mathbf{u}_{T-n}^* W_{T-n}, \qquad n = 0,1, \ldots, T,$$

where

$$b^*_{T-n} = 1 \bigg/ \left(1 + \sum_{i=1}^{n} \delta_{i,T-n}\right),$$

$$\delta_{i,T-n} = \prod_{j=0}^{i-1} [k^*_{T-n+j}/(1 + \rho)]^{1/(1-\gamma)},$$

$$k^*_i = \gamma \max_{u_i \in R^{h+}} \langle (1/\gamma)_i E\{[1 + R_i + \mathbf{u}'_i(\mathbf{RK}_i - R_i)]^\gamma\}\rangle$$

$$= {}_i E\{[1 + R_i + \mathbf{u}^*_i{}'(\mathbf{RK}_i - R_i)]^\gamma\}.$$

Note the remarkable similarity of the optimal consumption plan to (2.20) of Chapter 2, the optimal plan for the case of complete certainty. The only difference is that $(1 + R_i)^\gamma$ in the certainty case is replaced by k^*_i. The relation of k^*_i to $(1 + R_i)^\gamma$ should be clear, for k^*_i is simply γ times the maximum expected value of the gross portfolio rate of return in period i raised to the power γ and multiplied by $1/\gamma$, where the maximization is over the h capital asset shares in the portfolio. Note that full wealth is defined here just as it is in the certainty case; that is, future labor income is discounted by the risk-free rates of return.

It was established in Section 2.1.3 of Chapter 2 that the quantity $1/(1 - \gamma)$ is the intertemporal elasticity of substitution. This model suggests another interpretation of γ. It is shown in the next subsection that the maximum expected value of intertemporal utility in an arbitrary period $T - n$ is

$$V^*_{T-n} = (1/\gamma)(C^*_{T-n})^\gamma + (1 + \rho)^{-1}V^*_{T-n+1}$$

$$= (1/\gamma)(C^*_{T-n})^\gamma + \max\{{}_{T-n}E[g(W_{T-n+1})]\},$$

where

$$g(W_{T-n+1}) = (1 + \rho)^{-1} \left[1 + \sum_{i=1}^{n-1} \delta_{i,T-n+1}\right]^{1-\gamma} (1/\gamma)W^\gamma_{T-n+1}.$$

Given C^*_{T-n}, the agent chooses her portfolio to maximize ${}_{T-n}E[g(W_{T-n+1})]$. This is the portfolio problem considered by Arrow (1971). An important concept in his theory of portfolio choice is the coefficient of relative risk aversion that is defined as $RRA = -W_{T-n+1}g''(W_{T-n+1})/g'(W_{T-n+1})$. Arrow shows that if RRA is increasing (decreasing) in wealth, then the share of the agent's portfolio devoted to risky assets decreases (increases) with her wealth. It is easily verified that the coefficient of relative risk aversion is $1 - \gamma$ in the Hakansson model and the share of the agent's portfolio devoted to risky assets is therefore independent of wealth. The asset demands given in (D.8) verify this conclusion.

It is interesting to consider how an increase in the riskiness of asset returns affects consumption in this model. To answer this question, suppose there is only one risky capital asset so that the optimal value of k in some arbitrary period j is

$$k_j^* = \gamma \, \underset{u_j}{\text{Max}} \, \langle (1/\gamma)_j E\{[1 + R_j + u_j(RK_j - R_j)]^\gamma\}\rangle \qquad \text{(D.9)}$$

$$= {}_j E\{[1 + R_j + u_j^*(RK_j - R_j)]^\gamma\}.$$

We wish to vary the riskiness of the capital asset in period j while keeping the risk-free rate of return constant. To do this it is not appropriate to compare (D.9) with the case where RK_j is certain to equal its mean, because this effectively changes the risk-free rate of return. Instead we consider the effect of adding white noise to the return to capital in period j, so that it is given by $RK_j^+ = RK_j + e_j$ where $E(e_j) = \bar{e}_j = 0$, $E(e_j^2) > 0$, and e_j is independent of RK_i for all i and j.[2] In this case the optimal value of k_j is

$$k_j^+ = \gamma \, \underset{u_j}{\text{Max}} \, \langle (1/\gamma)_j E\{[1 + R_j + u_j(RK_j + e_j - R_j)]^\gamma\}\rangle \qquad \text{(D.10)}$$

$$= {}_j E\{[1 + R_j + u_j^+(RK_j + e_j - R_j)]^\gamma\}.$$

It is apparent from (D.8) that the effect of increased capital risk in period j, holding the risk-free rate of return constant, affects consumption entirely through its effect on the optimal value of k_j. In periods up to and including period j the propensity to consume out of full wealth is decreased (increased) with an increase (decrease) in the optimal value of k_j. These early changes in consumption, as well as the increased capital risk experienced in period j, affect the value of full wealth in period $j + 1$, which in turn affects consumption in later periods.

Our problem, therefore, reduces to determining the relative magnitudes of k_j^* given in (D.9) and k_j^+ given in (D.10). Letting

$$g(RK_j, e_j, u_j) = (1/\gamma)[1 + R_j + u_j(RK_j + e_j - R_j)]^\gamma,$$

note that

$$k_j^* = \gamma \, \underset{u_j}{\text{Max}} \, \{ \underset{RK_j}{E} \, [g(RK_j, 0, u_j)]\},$$

$$= \gamma \, \underset{u_j}{\text{Max}} \, \{ \underset{RK_j}{E} \, [g(RK_j, \bar{e}_j, u_j)]\},$$

and

$$k_j^+ = \gamma \, \underset{u_j}{\text{Max}} \, \langle \underset{RK_j}{E} \, \{ \underset{e_j}{E} \, [g(RK_j, e_j, u_j)]\}\rangle.$$

It is straightforward to show that

$$\underset{RK_j}{E} \, \{ \underset{e_j}{E} \, [g(RK_j, e_j, u_j)]\} < \underset{RK_j}{E} \, [g(RK_j, \bar{e}_j, u_j)],$$

for all u_j since g is concave in e_j. In other words, the expected value of g is less with increased risk for all u_j. It follows that

$$k_j^+ \gtreqqless k_j^* \leftrightarrow \gamma \gtreqqless 0.$$

If γ is less than zero, then increased capital risk induces more early saving. Otherwise capital risk induces less early saving.

SOLVING THE HAKANSSON MODEL

Hakansson (1970) presents the solution to problem (D.7) for the case of an infinite time horizon. Here the model is solved for the case of a finite time horizon.

At age T the agent knows she will only survive to the end of the period and, since bequests have no value to her, she will consume her entire wealth in that period so that

$$V_T = a_T(1/\gamma)W_T^\gamma,$$

where

$$a_T = 1.$$

The factor a_T is included so that the current formulation of the agent's problem will generalize to earlier periods.

At age $T-1$ the value function is

$$V_{T-1} = \underset{\substack{C_{T-1} \\ \mathbf{K}_{T-1}}}{\text{Max}} \ [(1/\gamma)C_{T-1}^\gamma + (1/\gamma)(1+\rho)^{-1}a_{T\ T-1}E(W_T^\gamma)], \quad \text{(D.11)}$$

subject to

$$0 \leqslant C_{T-1} \leqslant W_{T-1},$$

$$\text{Prob}(W_T < 0) = 0,$$

$$\mathbf{K}_{T-1} \gtreqqless \mathbf{0},$$

where

$$W_j = A_j + YL_j + \sum_{i=j+1}^{T} YL_i \left[\prod_{k=j}^{i-1} (1+R_k)^{-1} \right], \quad \text{(D.12)}$$

$$= (1 + R_{j-1})(W_{j-1} - C_{j-1}) + \mathbf{K}'_{j-1}(\mathbf{RK}_{j-1} - R_{j-1}),$$

$$j = 0, 1, \ldots, T.$$

The optimal consumption level, C_{T-1}^*, and the optimal capital asset holdings, $\mathbf{K}_{T-1}^*$, may be expressed as:

$$C_{T-1}^* = b_{T-1}^* W_{T-1}, \quad \text{(D.13)}$$

$$\mathbf{K}_{T-1}^* = \mathbf{d}_{T-1}^* W_{T-1}.$$

Note that these relations constrain the solution values for C_{T-1} and $\mathbf{K}_{T-1}$ only when W_{T-1} is zero, in which case the constrained values are in accord with the constraints in (D.11). Consider the case where $C_{T-1} < W_{T-1}$. Then substituting (D.13) into the maximand (D.11) simplifies the problem, for it quickly becomes apparent that b^*_{T-1} and $\mathbf{d}^*_{T-1}$ are independent of W_{T-1}. The value function now is

$$V_{T-1} = \underset{\substack{b_{T-1} \\ \mathbf{d}_{T-1}}}{\text{Max}}\ (1/\gamma)W^\gamma_{T-1}\{b^\gamma_{T-1} + (1+\rho)^{-1}(1 - b_{T-1})^\gamma \quad \text{(D.14)}$$
$$\cdot\ a_{T\ T-1}E[(1 + RR_{T-1})^\gamma]\},$$

subject to

$$0 \leqslant b_{T-1} < 1,$$
$$\text{Prob}[(1 + RR_{T-1}) < 0] = 0,$$
$$\mathbf{d}_{T-1} \geqslant \mathbf{0},$$

where

$$(1 + RR_{T-1}) = 1 + R_{T-1} + [\mathbf{d}'_{T-1}/(1 - b_{T-1})](\mathbf{RK}_{T-1} - R_{T-1}).$$

Note that the constraints in (D.14) are equivalent to the constraints in (D.11), except for the requirement that $b_{T-1} < 1$. (It is shown below that this is a nonbinding constraint.) Since W_{T-1} factors out of the maximand, it is clear that the solution $(b^*_{T-1}, \mathbf{d}^*_{T-1})$ is independent of full wealth.

The vector $(b_{T-1}, \mathbf{d}'_{T-1})$ is isomorphic to the vector $\{b_{T-1}, [\mathbf{d}'_{T-1}/(1 - b_{T-1})]\}$, say $(b_{T-1}, \mathbf{u}'_{T-1})$, and we may carry out the maximization with respect to this latter set of variables and compute $\mathbf{d}^*_{T-1} = (1 - b^*_{T-1})\mathbf{u}^*_{T-1}$. The advantage of this transformation is that it allows a sequential solution. It is immediately apparent that

$$\mathbf{u}^*_{T-1} \text{ maximizes } (1/\gamma)_{T-1}E[(1 + RR_{T-1})^\gamma],$$

subject to

$$\text{Prob}(1 + RR_{T-1} < 0) = 0,$$
$$\mathbf{u}_{T-1} \geqslant \mathbf{0}.$$

Hakansson shows that $\mathbf{u}^*_{T-1}$ exists, is unique, and is finite, provided that the following reasonable conditions hold:

$$\text{Prob}(RK_{it} < R_t) > 0, \quad \text{all } i,t, \quad\quad \text{(D.15)}$$
$$\text{Prob}(RK_{it} < -1) = 0, \quad \text{all } i,t,$$
$$\text{Prob}(RK_{it} < Z) = 1, \quad \text{some finite } Z, \text{ all } i,t.$$

Let k^*_{T-1} be the optimal value of the expectation term. Then the conditions in (D.15), in addition to the fact that $\mathbf{u}^*_{T-1}$ is finite, ensure that

$$(1 + R_{T-1})^\gamma \leqslant k^*_{T-1} < \infty.$$

Given k^*_{T-1}, we may concentrate the maximand in (D.14) and rewrite the problem:

$$V_{T-1} = \max_{b_{T-1}} \{(1/\gamma)W^\gamma_{T-1}[b^\gamma_{T-1} + (1 + \rho)^{-1}a_T(1 - b_{T-1})^\gamma k^*_{T-1}]\}, \quad (D.16)$$

subject to

$$0 \leqslant b_{T-1} < 1.$$

Solving the first-order condition yields

$$b^*_{T-1} = 1/\{1 + [(1 + \rho)^{-1}a_T k^*_{T-1}]^{1/(1-\gamma)}\}. \quad (D.17)$$

Substituting (D.17) into (D.16) gives

$$V^*_{T-1} = a_{T-1}(1/\gamma)W^\gamma_{T-1},$$

where

$$a_{T-1} = \{[(1 + \rho)^{-1}a_T k^*_{T-1}]^{1/(1-\gamma)} + 1\}^{1-\gamma}. \quad (D.18)$$

The solution for age $T - n$ is entirely analogous. The only complication is that b^*_{T-n} depends on a_{T-n+1}. It is necessary to solve the difference equation (D.18) subject to the terminal condition $a_T = 1$. If we work backward by continual substitution, it quickly becomes apparent that

$$a_{T-n+1} = \left\{ \sum_{i=1}^{n-1} \left[(1 + \rho)^{-i} \left(\prod_{j=0}^{i-1} k^*_{T-n+j+1} \right) \right]^{1/(1-\gamma)} + 1 \right\}^{1-\gamma}. \quad (D.19)$$

The solution given in the previous subsection follows directly.

In deriving the solution we assumed that the agent does not consume his entire full wealth prior to age T (that is, $b^*_{T-n} < 1$, $t \geqslant 1$). The alternative possibility can quickly be ruled out, since if the agent did consume his entire full wealth prior to age T, say age $T - t$, then:

$$V^+_{T-t} = (1/\gamma)W^\gamma_{T-t}.$$

But the value function at time $T - t$ derived above is

$$V^*_{T-t} = a_{T-t}(1/\gamma)W^\gamma_{T-t}.$$

It is apparent from (D.19) that $V^*_{T-t} > V^+_{T-t}$ and the agent will not consume his entire full wealth prior to age T.

Steady-State Life-Cycle Asset Supply and the Real Net Rate of Return

This appendix reports the steady-state life-cycle asset supply and its arc interest elasticity, for five real net rates of return, for each of the economies simulated in Chapter 11. Appendix Table E.1 parts A and B apply to the case where the representative family does not own a home. Appendix Table E.2 parts A and B are for the case where the representative family does own a home.

In some cases steady-state life-cycle asset supply is infinite. This is shown in the tables as "N.A." and results from unplanned bequests becoming infinite owing to extremely high net rates of return. High net rates of return induce the representative family to delay its consumption, which leads to large unplanned bequests. A large portion of these bequests, in turn, are saved to finance late consumption, thus leading to even greater bequests. The result is an infinite supply of life-cycle assets. Laitner (1979) develops a model where asset supply becomes infinite, at some critical interest rate, because of infinite planned bequests. It is interesting that this result also applies to the case where all bequests are unplanned. Note that asset supply is infinite even for cases where the representative family does not own a home.

The arc elasticities given in the tables can be misleading for cases where life-cycle assets are small or negative. For this reason the asset levels for each real net rate of return are also reported.

Appendix Table E.1. Steady-state life-cycle asset supply and the net rate of return: conditions: renter

			Life-cycle assets/arc-interest elasticity				
	RGN	Constrained		Unconstrained		Certain lifetime	
A. Cases for which γ and ρ are consistent with the parameter estimates							
$\gamma = 0.19; \rho = 0.00$							
SS	1.01	0.33E+04		−0.62E+06		−0.60E+06	
	1.03	0.56E+05 /	1.8	−0.69E+05 /	1.6	0.98E+06 /	8.3
	1.08	0.30E+07 /	2.1	0.30E+07 /	2.3	0.97E+07 /	1.8
	1.13	0.45E+08 /	3.7	0.45E+08 /	3.7	0.90E+08 /	3.4
	1.18	N.A.		N.A.		0.12E+10 /	5.3
No SS	1.01	0.18E+06		−0.30E+06		0.57E+06	
	1.03	0.40E+06 /	0.8	0.40E+06 /	14.2	0.18E+07 /	1.0
	1.08	0.36E+07 /	1.8	0.36E+07 /	1.8	0.11E+08 /	1.6
	1.13	0.49E+08 /	3.6	0.49E+08 /	3.6	0.10E+09 /	3.4
	1.18	N.A.		N.A.		0.14E+10 /	5.3
$\gamma = 0.73; \rho = 0.02$							
SS	1.01	0.85E+03		−0.16E+07		−0.33E+07	
	1.03	0.56E+05 /	1.9	−0.69E+05 /	1.8	0.98E+06 /	3.7
	1.08	N.A.		N.A.		0.31E+08 /	2.1
	1.13	N.A.		N.A.		0.33E+09 /	3.5
	1.18	N.A.		N.A.		0.47E+10 /	5.4
No SS	1.01	0.48E+05		−0.16E+07		−0.17E+07	
	1.03	0.40E+06 /	1.6	0.40E+06 /	3.3	0.18E+07 /	56.0
	1.08	N.A.		N.A.		0.35E+08 /	2.0
	1.13	N.A.		N.A.		0.38E+09 /	3.5
	1.18	N.A.		N.A.		0.54E+10 /	5.4

Appendix Table E.1. *(continued)*

	RGN	Constrained		Unconstrained		Certain lifetime	
		Life-cycle assets/arc-interest elasticity					

B. Cases for which γ is smaller than is implied by the parameter estimates

$\gamma = -0.50;\ \rho = 0.02$

	RGN	Constrained		Unconstrained		Certain lifetime	
SS	1.01	0.17E+04		−0.10E+07		−0.18E+07	
	1.03	0.25E+04 /	0.4	−0.69E+06 /	0.4	−0.96E+06 /	0.6
	1.08	0.74E+05 /	2.1	−0.97E+04 /	2.1	0.64E+06 /	10.9
	1.13	0.10E+07 /	3.6	0.10E+07 /	4.3	0.35E+07 /	2.9
	1.18	0.30E+07 /	3.1	0.30E+07 /	3.1	0.13E+08 /	3.7
No SS	1.01	0.95E+05		−0.88E+06		−0.46E+06	
	1.03	0.12E+06 /	0.3	−0.53E+06 /	0.5	−0.65E+05 /	1.5
	1.08	0.26E+06 /	0.8	0.23E+06 /	5.7	0.12E+07 /	2.5
	1.13	0.13E+07 /	2.8	0.13E+07 /	2.9	0.42E+07 /	2.4
	1.18	0.34E+07 /	2.8	0.34E+07 /	2.8	0.16E+08 /	3.6

$\gamma = -2.50;\ \rho = 0.02$

	RGN	Constrained		Unconstrained		Certain lifetime	
SS	1.01	0.19E+04		−0.96E+06		−0.16E+07	
	1.03	0.23E+04 /	0.2	−0.76E+06 /	0.2	−0.11E+07 /	0.3
	1.08	0.40E+04 /	0.6	−0.40E+06 /	0.7	−0.44E+06 /	1.0
	1.13	0.18E+05 /	2.6	−0.13E+06 /	2.1	0.15E+05 /	4.5
	1.18	0.11E+06 /	4.4	0.97E+05 /	37.8	0.46E+06 /	5.8
No SS	1.01	0.11E+06		−0.77E+06		−0.27E+06	
	1.03	0.11E+06 /	0.0	−0.63E+06 /	0.2	−0.24E+06 /	0.1
	1.08	0.12E+06 /	0.1	−0.31E+06 /	0.7	−0.20E+05 /	1.9
	1.13	0.14E+06 /	0.4	−0.46E+05 /	3.1	0.31E+06 /	4.8
	1.18	0.22E+06 /	1.3	0.20E+06 /	9.9	0.73E+06 /	2.5

Note: N.A. indicates that steady-state life-cycle asset supply is infinite. SS, Social security.

Appendix Table E.2. Steady-state life-cycle asset supply and the net rate of return: Conditions: Home owner

		Life-cycle assets/Arc-interest elasticity					
	RGN	Constrained		Unconstrained		Certain lifetime	

A. Cases for which γ and ρ are consistent with the parameter estimates

$\gamma = 0.19;\ \rho = 0.00$

	RGN	Constrained		Unconstrained		Certain lifetime	
SS	1.01	0.13E+06		−0.52E+06		−0.54E+06	
	1.03	0.16E+06 /	0.2	0.11E+05 /	2.1	0.10E+07 /	6.7
	1.08	0.30E+07 /	2.0	0.30E+07 /	2.2	0.98E+07 /	1.8
	1.13	0.45E+08 /	3.7	0.45E+08 /	3.7	0.90E+08 /	3.4
	1.18	N.A.		N.A.		0.12E+10 /	5.3
No SS	1.01	0.28E+06		−0.24E+06		0.63E+06	
	1.03	0.42E+06 /	0.4	0.42E+06 /	7.2	0.18E+07 /	1.0
	1.08	0.36E+07 /	1.7	0.36E+07 /	1.7	0.11E+08 /	1.6
	1.13	0.49E+08 /	3.6	0.49E+08 /	3.6	0.10E+09 /	3.4
	1.18	N.A.		N.A.		0.14E+10 /	5.3

$\gamma = 0.73;\ \rho = 0.02$

	RGN	Constrained		Unconstrained		Certain lifetime	
SS	1.01	0.12E+06		−0.15E+07		−0.32E+07	
	1.03	0.16E+06 /	0.3	0.11E+05 /	2.0	0.10E+07 /	3.8
	1.08	N.A.		N.A.		0.31E+08 /	2.1
	1.13	N.A.		N.A.		0.33E+09 /	3.5
	1.18	N.A.		N.A.		0.47E+10 /	5.4
No SS	1.01	0.16E+06		−0.16E+07		−0.16E+07	
	1.03	0.42E+06 /	0.9	0.42E+06 /	3.5	0.18E+07 /	30.7
	1.08	N.A.		N.A.		0.35E+08 /	2.0
	1.13	N.A.		N.A.		0.38E+09 /	3.5
	1.18	N.A.		N.A.		0.54E+10 /	5.4

Appendix Table E.2. *(continued)*

	RGN	Life-cycle assets/arc-interest elasticity					
		Constrained		Unconstrained		Certain lifetime	

B. Cases for which γ is smaller than is implied by the parameter estimates

$\gamma = -0.50;\ \rho = 0.02$

	RGN	Constrained		Unconstrained		Certain lifetime	
SS	1.01	0.12E+06		−0.93E+06		−0.18E+07	
	1.03	0.11E+06 /	−0.1	−0.61E+06 /	0.4	−0.94E+06 /	0.6
	1.08	0.14E+06 /	0.3	0.43E+05 /	2.5	0.64E+06 /	11.8
	1.13	0.10E+07 /	3.2	0.10E+07 /	3.9	0.35E+07 /	2.9
	1.18	0.30E+07 /	3.1	0.30E+07 /	3.1	0.13E+08 /	3.7
No SS	1.01	0.20E+06		−0.81E+06		−0.40E+06	
	1.03	0.20E+06 /	0.0	−0.51E+06 /	0.5	−0.39E+05 /	1.6
	1.08	0.30E+06 /	0.5	0.24E+06 /	6.1	0.12E+07 /	2.4
	1.13	0.13E+07 /	2.6	0.13E+07 /	2.9	0.42E+07 /	2.4
	1.18	0.34E+07 /	2.8	0.34E+07 /	2.8	0.16E+08 /	3.6

$\gamma = -2.50;\ \rho = 0.02$

	RGN	Constrained		Unconstrained		Certain lifetime	
SS	1.01	0.12E+06		−0.85E+06		−0.15E+07	
	1.03	0.11E+06 /	−0.1	−0.68E+06 /	0.2	−0.11E+07 /	0.3
	1.08	0.95E+05 /	−0.2	−0.35E+06 /	0.7	−0.44E+06 /	1.0
	1.13	0.96E+05 /	0.0	−0.94E+05 /	2.4	0.16E+05 /	4.5
	1.18	0.15E+06 /	1.3	0.12E+06 /	51.2	0.46E+06 /	5.8
No SS	1.01	0.21E+06		−0.70E+06		−0.21E+06	
	1.03	0.18E+06 /	−0.1	−0.60E+06 /	0.2	−0.22E+06 /	0.0
	1.08	0.16E+06 /	−0.1	−0.31E+06 /	0.7	−0.17E+05 /	1.9
	1.13	0.17E+06 /	0.2	−0.45E+05 /	3.1	0.31E+06 /	4.7
	1.18	0.24E+06 /	1.0	0.20E+06 /	9.8	0.73E+06 /	2.5

Note: N.A. indicates that steady-state life-cycle asset supply is infinite. SS, Social security.

Notes

1. Introduction

1 This probability statement applies to the case where an inequality is imposed on one of the model's parameters. I argue in Chapter 8 that this prior is appropriate. The unconstrained estimates indicate it is 95% certain that, in any period, each dollar of net social security receipts has at least 25% as great an effect on consumption as does one dollar of ordinary net noninterest income.

2 Blinder, Gordon, and Wise (1981) estimate a structural equation for net worth using cross-section data. Modigliani and Ando (1963) invoke extreme assumptions to obtain a linear structural model applicable to aggregate time-series data.

2. The Theoretical Framework

1 The Friedman concept of the "horizon" is defined as the inverse of the interest rate used to discount future earnings, and is a measure of the importance of future income to current consumption (Friedman, 1963). The length of the horizon, as we define it, is not explicitly specified.

Friedman is well aware that liquidity constraints may affect consumption behavior and he represents this formally by including the ratio of human to nonhuman wealth as a determinant of the ratio of permanent consumption to permanent income. Friedman is more explicit in a footnote where he suggests that differing borrowing and lending rates will cause permanent income to track measured income in the early years of life (Friedman, 1957, p. 93).

Friedman's reluctance to make simplifying assumptions leads him to a vaguely specified consumption function. He asserts that the propensity to consume permanent income is a general function of such factors as age, family size, education, and the ratio of nonhuman to human wealth (Friedman, 1957, pp. 16–19).

2 It is shown in Appendix A that there may be good reason for the proportionality hypothesis to be invalid when labor is elastically supplied.

3 The elasticity of intertemporal substitution is defined as $\partial\log(C^*_{j+1}/C^*_j)/\partial\log(1 + R_j)$.

4 Modigliani and Brumberg (1954) make several assumptions to simplify their exposition. For example, they assume the interest rate to be zero. Arguably, their assertion that the agent desires a flat consumption profile is also made to simplify the exposition and not because they feel it is realistic.

5 Friedman (1957, p. 19) acknowledges that age may affect the propensity to consume permanent income but, in his empirical work, he assumes that this propensity does not vary with age.

6 Friedman defines permanent income to be that amount which can be consumed while keeping wealth intact. We measure consumption and wealth at the beginning of the period so that permanent income in period j is $R^*W_j/(1 + R)$.

7 Yaari (1965), Tobin (1972), Heller and Starr (1979), and Davies (1981) recognize that liquidity constraints have the effect of shortening the agent's horizon. Yaari gives necessary and sufficient conditions for the optimal consumption plan when liquidity constraints are imposed but does not suggest a solution method. Davies gives a condition for finding the cutoff date that is necessary and *not* sufficient. He identifies the cutoff date by utilizing the fact that if income is a continuous function of time and the minimal level of net worth is always zero, labor earnings will equal consumption at the cutoff date. Clearly there may be many dates that satisfy this condition. Davies' method may prove useful for quickly finding the cutoff date when the income stream is "normally" shaped but it is not generally applicable.

8 Note that $PR(i|t) = \Pi^i_{k=t+1}PR(k|k - 1)$. It follows that the intertemporal utility function, (2.28), leads to a dynamically consistent consumption plan provided the subjective discount factors satisfy (2.13).

9 The case of one individual with an uncertain lifetime is tractable for two reasons: (1) the fact that future earned income is contingent on survival does not concern the agent, and (2) the underlying random variable, survival, is dichotomous and utility is nonzero only in the event of survival. If the underlying random variable were continuous — for example, health — and the ability to enjoy consumption depended on health, then the case of one individual also would be problematic.

10 The inclusion of i as an argument of the within-period utility function for period i is meant to summarize everything that is predictable and influences preferences in period i. In particular, one would expect family size to be an argument of the within-period utility function.

11 Yaari (1965) presents a model that assumes the existence of perfect insurance and annuities markets. This model is such that the agent's assets are held entirely in the form of annuities and, since the rate of return on annuities increases as the agent ages, the tendency to borrow against future income does not increase with age. This model is discussed in Chapter 4.

12 Fama proves a more general result. He considers an agent who chooses current consumption so as to maximize expected lifetime utility, say $_tE[V(C_t,C_{t+1}, \ldots ,C_T)]$. Fama shows that the expected value of V at time t, given the agent behaves optimally in each future period, can be expressed as $Z_t(A_t,C_t|I_t)$ where A_t is current net worth and I_t denotes currently available information. The important result is that Z_t is monotonically increasing and strictly concave in its arguments provided V is monotonically increasing and strictly concave in its arguments.

3. The Importance of Consumption Behavior for the Effects of Government Fiscal Policies

1 Blinder, Gordon, and Wise (1980) argue that social security may delay retirement for many families. The reason is that in any given year an additional year's labor income may exceed the minimum income that was received previously and would be used to compute social security benefits if the individual retires. In such cases benefits increase if retirement is delayed.

2 Hayashi does not invoke the Hall hypothesis to derive his specification. Instead he invokes a deterministic life-cycle specification which he adapts to the case of uncertainty by discounting human wealth at a higher rate than nonhuman wealth. Nevertheless, the specification includes lagged consumption and current disposable income and is estimated using instruments that are uncorrelated with all forecast errors.

3 Hall and Mishkin interpret μ as the portion of total sample consumption undertaken by liquidity-constrained families. This interpretation is not correct. HM's model is formulated in first-differences and yields no information concerning consumption levels.

4 This interpretation of Hayashi's empirical results is consistent with the fact that the high-wealth sample estimates tend to overestimate the consumption of families in the low-wealth sample. This is because the propensity to consume net worth is estimated to be negative or barely positive in the high-wealth sample. (A 65-year-old couple is estimated to have propensity to consume net worth of approximately 0.01.) This is because the variance of net worth in the high-wealth sample is dominated by the taste effect. Income, however, contains a relatively small taste effect and the propensity to consume income is therefore biased upward. It is not surprising, in light of these facts, that this consumption function tends to overestimate the consumption of low-wealth families.

5 If intergenerational transfers have taken place in the past and are unobservable, then it is impossible to measure social security's effect on net worth. Suppose, for example, that intergenerational transfers are operative and have all taken place in the past. Then families in a cross section will appear to consume in accordance with the standard life-cycle model.

6 Kotlikoff reports results for two samples: one that includes families not covered by social security and one that excludes these families. The full sample

estimates lead to a rejection of the life-cycle model. The restricted sample estimates, however, are too imprecise to distinguish between the null hypothesis and the alternative. As is pointed out by Kotlikoff, using the full sample has the effect of artificially increasing the variance of social security wealth and over-states the precision of the estimates.

4. An Estimable Consumption Model with Liquidity Constraints

1 MaCurdy (1981), for example, estimates the elasticity of hours worked with respect to the wage to be between 0.10 and 0.23 for primary workers. Our sample, taken in 1963, is such that secondary workers account for relatively little income. Only 40% of the spouses in the sample work. Of the spouses that do work, 41% earn less than $1,455 and 70% earn less than $3,300. Only 17% of primary workers, in contrast, earn less than $4,500.

2 Note that no insurance is purchased if the family is made up of only one individual.

3 In actuality, (1) life insurance covering future earnings requires that premiums be paid *currently,* (2) not all earners with dependents choose to purchase insurance, (3) insurance premiums include administrative costs and, hence, are not "fair," and (4) a family presumedly has less "need" for consumption after an earner has died, so that it is suboptimal to fully insure.

4 It is established in Section 4.4 that β_2 only affects fitted consumption for families in the sample whose heads are younger than 65. The estimated retirement ages for these family heads are conditional on their current ages but, in any case, fall between the ages of 65 and 68. (The estimated retirement ages are discussed in Chapter 5.) The fitted consumption of these families, therefore, is relatively insensitive to whether β_2 takes effect at age 65 or at retirement. Hence, we occasionally will refer to β_2 as the weight on retirement consumption.

5 This is exact for the case where the within-period utility function for goods is homothetic.

6 This specification may be criticized for not allowing required home and automobile equity to fall late in life. It turns out that the parameter estimates are such that this possibility is ruled out. We elaborate on this point in Chapter 7.

7 It should not be inferred that a higher rate of interest necessarily leads to a reduction in current consumption. A higher real rate of interest can simultaneously increase current consumption and the growth rate of consumption.

8 No approximations are necessary when solving our model for the case of one individual with an uncertain lifetime (see Section 2.2.3 of Chapter 2). The exact consumption growth rate, for this case, is given by (4.21) with $PR(t + 1|t)$ raised to the power $1/(1 - \gamma)$.

9 Davies (1981) also argues that imposing inequality constraints on net worth is the appropriate procedure for modeling the effect of lifetime uncertainty on consumption.

10 Hall and Mishkin (1982) present a model where the within-period

utility function is quadratic. It is optimal, in this case, for the agent to behave as if expected future labor income is certain.

11 Nagatani (1972) argues that, on average, this phenomenon would cause consumption to track labor income.

12 A capital asset is said to become riskier if its random rate of return, R, is augmented to $R + e$, where e is distributed as white noise. Rothschild and Stiglitz (1971) persuasively argue that this is the appropriate concept of an "increase in risk."

5. The Data and Variable Definitions

1 The Advisory Commission on Intergovernmental Relations, 1962, p. 131.

2 Ibid., p. 138.

3 This method of imputing future social security benefits is very similar to the methods used by Feldstein and Pellechio (1979) and Kotlikoff (1979). There are two important differences. First, we control for age when determining the agent's relative position in the income distribution. Second, we assume that real social security benefits are expected to stay constant after retirement. (The aforementioned studies assume that real benefits are expected to grow at a 2% annual rate after retirement.)

In defense of our second deviation from standard practice, we note that holding the real average monthly wage constant, real social security benefits increased at a 0.15% annual rate between 1954 and 1958 and at a 0.8% annual rate between 1958 and 1965. Furthermore, since it makes little sense for the government to plan real benefit increases for the retired as they age, we believe it is unlikely that individuals came to expect such increases.

4 U.S. Department of Health, Education, and Welfare, Social Security Administration, 1964, p. 24.

6. The Econometric Methodology

1 The least-squares estimator is consistent when the disturbances are heteroscedastic. Heteroscedastic disturbances cause the parameter estimates to be inefficient, and the estimator for the variance-covariance matrix to be inconsistent.

2 Our estimator for $\log(\sigma)$ in (6.5) is not consistent because the disturbance term in the regression, not displayed in (6.5), has a nonzero mean. Nevertheless, our estimator for δ is consistent.

3 The parameter δ is fixed when computing the least-squares estimate of β. The role of the normalization factor, therefore, is solely to normalize the linear regression at each iteration.

4 The maximum likelihood estimator of the disturbance term variance is $SSR(\hat{\beta})/N$ which, of course, is asymptotically equivalent to the estimator given in (6.6).

5 The consumption function, of course, is everywhere continuous.

6 Generally, only $N - k$ of the estimated residuals are independent of the right-hand-side variables. (N is the sample size and k is the number of estimated parameters.) In our case, 791 of the 798 estimated residuals may be regarded as independent of the right-hand-side variables. It is reasonable, therefore, to invoke asymptotic results.

7. The Estimated Consumption Function and Its Interpretation

1 Ando and Modigliani view their findings as evidence against the proportionality hypothesis. (See Section 2.1.3 of Chapter 2.) As is seen here, however, their findings may simply reflect a correlation between tastes and education.

2 Convergence was not attained for model 3 of Table 7.1. The reason is that the cutoff dates are very sensitive to each of the five β_2 parameters. Several different starting values for the parameters have been tried and we are confident that the estimates given for model 3 are near the peak of the likelihood function.

3 Friend and Blume (1975) use cross-section data on portfolio shares devoted to risky assets to infer the coefficient of relative risk aversion $(1 - \gamma)$. In so doing they assume that human wealth is riskless, so the observed portfolios appear quite conservative. I believe human wealth is far from riskless; their procedure biases the estimated coefficient of relative risk aversion upward. Hall (1981) uses aggregate data to estimate the elasticity of intertemporal substitution. Aside from the considerable aggregation problems, the Hall procedure assumes that consumption responds to expected short-run variations in real interest rates. I do not believe this to be realistic. It is much more plausible that families consider more permanent changes in interest rates when planning their consumption. It is not surprising, therefore, that Hall finds that the growth rate of aggregate consumption is not very responsive to expected short-run deviations in real interest rates.

4 I have attempted to allow the net rate of return to vary with the family's marginal tax rate, thereby obtaining poor results. It appears that it is necessary to allow for the possibility that affluent families, who have high marginal tax rates, earn unusually high real gross rates of return on their investments. A reasonable approximation, therefore, is that the real net rate of return is the same for all families.

5 The model is blind to unusual future expenses that the family may anticipate. The model treats assets earmarked for such expenditures, therefore, as if they are a windfall. As is argued in Section 2.2.4 of Chapter 2, windfalls can lead to short multiperiod horizons.

6 The sum of the sample weights for each of the horizon groups gives the size of the population represented by each group. Dividing the population represented by each horizon group by the population represented by all three groups gives the figures in the last column of Table 7.6.

7 Hall and Mishkin (1982) estimate that 20% of food consumption is undertaken by liquidity-constrained families. A correct interpretation of their parameter estimates, however, indicates that 20% of the families in their sample are liquidity constrained. Their model utilizes first differences and is not capable of identifying the portion of consumption undertaken by liquidity-constrained families.

8 Davies (1981) also argues that the appropriate method of modeling lifetime uncertainty is to impose constraints on the net worth of older families.

9 Obtaining convergence for model 4 of Table 7.13 is difficult because the cutoff dates are very sensitive to the value of β_5. It was necessary, therefore, to fix the value of β_5 to obtain convergence. This was done as follows. After the estimation algorithm began taking minuscule steps, the value of β_5 was fixed at its current value (the value shown in the table), after which convergence was achieved on the first iteration. The standard error shown for β_5 in the table is its standard error just prior to its being fixed. The other standard errors are computed with β_5 fixed.

10 Let X be a random variable that is zero with probability $1 - \pi$ and is one with probability π. Then, given a large sample of N observations on X, the sample mean, say P, is approximately normal with mean π and variance $\pi(1 - \pi)/N$. If π is 0.5, then $2*N^{1/2}(P - 0.5)$ is approximately a standard normal variable. Wonnacott and Wonnacott (1977) assert that this is a good approximation provided $\text{Min}[\pi N,(1 - \pi)N]$ exceeds five, which requires a minimum group size of 10 in our case.

8. Social Security, Intergenerational Transfers, and Consumption

1 Blinder, Gordon, and Wise (1980) argue that social security may delay retirement for many families. This may happen when a potential retirer's current annual labor income exceeds the minimum amount earned previously, and which would be used to compute social security benefits if the individual retires currently. Benefits increase, in this case, if retirement is delayed.

2 Barro (1974) stresses that (8.2) holds with equality only if intergenerational transfers are operative, a position that he takes in subsequent publications (see, for example, Barro, 1979).

3 This statement may require clarification. Let w be the age of retirement. Then $0 < w < q < T$ and, by assumption, $v < q$. Social security constitutes forced saving (taxes) during the interval $(0,w)$; annuity payments, yielding the market return on forced savings, during interval $(w + 1,q)$; and transfer annuity payments during interval $(q + 1,T)$ which, according to (8.4), are exactly offset by private transfers and can be ignored. By the definition of v, the family would like to borrow against net receipts incoming after period v to consume more during interval (t,v) but cannot. It follows that liquidity constraints would be less severe, or perhaps nonexistent, if no social security taxes are paid during interval $(0,w)$ and no benefits are received during interval $(w + 1,q)$.

Note that our version of the Barro hypothesis is identical to the Feldstein hypothesis for the interval $(0,q)$. The two hypotheses differ with regard to the effect on consumption of the transfer annuity payments received during the interval $(q + 1,T)$.

4 In the context of this discussion, the extended family consists of currently living family members and their descendants. Earnings capacity tends to be passed on to offspring so that a family that is currently poor and has positive lifetime social security wealth expects that its descendants, on average, also will be poor and have positive lifetime social security wealth. Such an extended family is receiving a transfer from more affluent extended families which is not, even under the Barro hypothesis, offset by private transfers.

5 Projector and Weiss (1966, Table A16), using our data, estimate that 35% of total wealth in 1963 was held by families with net worth exceeding $200,000. Feldstein (1976b), using the same data, estimates that 28.4% of the wealth held by families headed by individuals aged 35 to 64 was held by families with net worth exceeding $250,000.

6 It turns out that there exists an alternative set of parameter estimates, each constituting a local peak of the likelihood function, corresponding to each of the five estimated models given in Table 8.1. (For each local-peak model, the estimates of β_5 and β_6 are in the neighborhoods of 0.02 and 0.70, respectively.) These local-peak estimates have the exact same implications for the effect of social security on consumption as do the estimates given in Table 8.1. The local-peak estimates of β_8 for models 2 and 4, for example, are 0.6311 and 0.8239, respectively. The corresponding standard errors are 0.2331 and 0.1524. Furthermore, all the probability statements made with regard to the chi-square statistics in Table 8.1 also can be made with respect to the local-peak estimates.

7 Mirer (1979) relates net worth to age for four groups stratified by educational attainment. He finds that, when taking secular income growth into account, wealth rises with age for retired families.

Part of the discrepancy between our results and those of Mirer may be explained by the fact that 79% of the value of home(s) and automobile(s) is not consumable in our model.

8 As is emphasized in Section 4.3.1 of Chapter 4, it is impossible to project the family's consumption without knowing the time path of effective family size. A technically correct interpretation of *BEQ*, therefore, is that it is the amount of net worth the family could currently set aside and consume *PFIT* times the level of consumption that would be optimal in each future period if effective family size and expectations in each future period are in exact agreement with current expectations.

9. Liquidity Constraints and Preretirement Saving

1 Net noninterest receipts are slightly different in Tables 9.3, parts A and B, because of the tax consequences of having fewer children.

10. Temporary Taxes and Aggregate Consumption

1 Many authors have made this observation. Among them are Dolde (1978), Fleming (1973), Heller and Starr (1979), and Tobin (1972).

2 Heller and Starr (1979) point out that liquidity constraints cause the propensity to consume temporary tax changes to be dependent on the sign and magnitude of the tax change.

3 Dolde (1978) also uses a simulation methodology. His treatment of liquidity constraints is somewhat more general but less tractable. He allows the borrowing rate to vary according to the family's circumstances, and the model is solved using nonlinear programming methods. Dolde does not attempt to estimate the model's parameters. Instead he uses assumed parameter values.

4 We assume that the effect of the sequence of three unexpected taxes is additive. This is true as long as a previous tax does not change the cutoff dates associated with a current unexpected tax.

11. Life-Cycle Savings, Social Security, and Steady-State Capital Intensity

1 As in Chapters 9 and 10, we assume that the probability of death is zero up to age 45, after which the probability of being alive at each age is in accord with actual mortality probabilities. This assumption is made to ensure that no children are orphaned.

2 Summers (1981) demonstrates that the elasticity of steady-state life-cycle assets with respect to the real net rate of return is likely to be positive for reasonable values of the elasticity of intertemporal substitution.

Appendix D. Consumption under Uncertainty

1 The Hakansson model is, of course, only a special case. More general conclusions regarding the effect of capital risk on consumption have been derived in the context of two-period models. The principal contributions are Levarhi and Shrinson (1969), Mirman (1971), Phelps (1962), Rothschild and Stiglitz (1971), and Sandmo (1970).

2 Rothschild and Stiglitz (1971) argue persuasively that this is the appropriate concept of "an increase in risk."

References

Advisory Commission on Intergovernmental Relations. 1962. *Measures of state and local fiscal capacity and tax effort.* Washington, D.C.: Government Printing Office.

Ando, Albert, and Franco Modigliani. 1960. The permanent income hypothesis and life cycle hypothesis of saving behavior: comparison and tests. In *Consumption and saving, vol. 2,* eds. Irwin Friend and Robert Jones. Philadelphia: University of Pennsylvania.

———— 1963. The life cycle hypothesis of saving: aggregate implications and tests. *American Economic Review* 53: 55–84.

Arrow, Kenneth. 1971. *Essays in the theory of risk-bearing.* Chicago: Markham Publishing Co.

Atkinson, Anthony B. 1971. The distribution of wealth and the individual life cycle. *Oxford Economic Papers* 23: 239–254.

Auerbach, Alan J., and Laurence J. Kotlikoff. 1983a. An examination of empirical tests of social security and saving. In *Social policy evaluation: an economic perspective,* ed. Elhanan Helpman, Assaf Razin, and Efraim Sadka. New York: Academic Press.

———— 1983b. National savings, economic welfare, and the structure of taxation. In *Behavioral simulation methods in tax policy analysis,* ed. Martin Feldstein. Chicago: University of Chicago Press.

Barro, Robert J. 1974. Are government bonds net wealth? *Journal of Political Economy* 82: 1095–1117.

———— 1978. The impact of social security on private saving, evidence from the U.S. Time Series. AEI Studies 199. Washington, D.C.: American Enterprise Institute for Public Policy Research.

———— 1979. Social security and private saving: another look. *Social Security Bulletin* 42: 33–40.

Bernanke, Ben. 1984. Permanent income, liquidity, and expenditure on automobiles: evidence from panel data. *Quarterly Journal of Economics* 99: 587–614.

257

REFERENCES

Bernheim, Douglas B., Andrei Shleifer, and Lawrence H. Summers. 1984. *Bequests as a means of payment.* National Bureau of Economic Research Working Paper no. 1303.

Bevan, D. L. 1979. Inheritance and the distribution of wealth. *Economica* 46: 381–402.

Bixby, Lenore. 1970. Income of people aged 65 and older: overview from the 1968 survey of the aged. *Social Security Bulletin* 33: 3–34.

Blinder, Alan. 1975. Distributional effects and the aggregate consumption function. *Journal of Political Economy* 83: 447–475.

——— 1976. Intergenerational transfers and life cycle consumption. *American Economic Review* 66: 87–93.

Blinder, Alan, Roger Gordon, and Donald Wise. 1980. Reconsidering the work disincentive effects of social security. *National Tax Journal* 33: 431–442.

——— 1983. Social security, bequests and the life-cycle theory of saving: cross-sectional tests. In *The Determinants of national saving and wealth,* ed. Franco Modigliani and Richard Hemming. London: Macmillan.

Bloomquist, N. S. 1979. The inheritance function. *Journal of Public Economics* 12: 41–60.

Chow, Gregory C. 1983. *Econometrics.* New York: McGraw-Hill.

Crockett, Jean. 1964. Income and asset effects on consumption: aggregate and cross-section. In *Models of income determination,* Studies in Income and Wealth, vol. 28. Princeton: Princeton University Press.

Crockett, Jean, and Irwin Friend. 1967. Consumer investment behavior. In *Determinants of investment behavior,* ed. R. Ferber. New York: National Bureau of Economic Research.

Davies, James B. 1981. Uncertain lifetime, consumption, and dissaving in retirement. *Journal of Political Economy* 89: 561–577.

Diamond, Peter A. 1965. National debt in a neoclassical growth model. *American Economic Review* 55: 1126–50.

——— 1977. A framework for social security analysis. *Journal of Public Economics* 8: 275–298.

Dolde, Walter. 1978. Capital markets and short run behavior of life cycle savers. *Journal of Finance* 33: 413–428.

Drazen, Allan. 1978. Government debt, human capital, and bequests in a life cycle model. *Journal of Political Economy* 86: 505–516.

Dreze, Jacques, and Franco Modigliani. 1972. Consumption decisions under uncertainty. *Journal of Economic Theory* 5: 308–335.

Eisner, Robert. 1969. Fiscal and monetary policy reconsidered. *American Economic Review* 59: 897–905.

Fama, Eugene F. 1970. Multiperiod consumption-investment decisions. *American Economic Review* 60: 163–174.

Feldstein, Martin. 1974. Social security, induced retirement, and aggregate capital accumulation. *Journal of Political Economy* 82: 905–926.

———1976a. Social security and saving: the extended life cycle theory. *American Economic Review* 66: 77–86.

———— 1976b. Social security and the distribution of wealth. *Journal of the American Statistical Association* 71: 800–807.

———— 1978. Welfare loss of capital income taxation. *Journal of Political Economy* 86: S29–S51.

———— 1982. Social security and private saving: reply. *Journal of Political Economy* 90: 630–642.

———— 1983. Social security benefits and the accumulation of preretirement wealth. In *The determinants of national saving and wealth,* ed. Franco Modigliani and Richard Hemming. London: Macmillan.

Feldstein, Martin, and Anthony Pellechio. 1979. Social security and household wealth accumulation: new microeconomic evidence. *Review of Economics and Statistics* 61: 361–368.

Flavin, Marjorie A. 1981. The adjustment of consumption to changing expectations about future income. *Journal of Political Economy* 89: 974–1009.

Fleming, J. S. 1973. The consumption function when capital markets are imperfect: the permanent income hypothesis reconsidered. *Oxford Economic Papers* 25: 160–172.

Friedman, Milton. 1957. *A theory of the consumption function.* Princeton: Princeton University Press.

————. 1963. Windfalls, the "horizon," and related concepts in the permanent income hypothesis. In *Measurement in economics: studies in honor of Yehuda Grunfeld,* ed. Carl Christ, Stanford, Calif.: Stanford University Press.

Friend, Irwin, and Marshal Blume. 1975. The demand for risky assets. *American Economic Review* 65: 900–922.

Ghez, Gilbert, and Gary Becker. 1975. *The allocation of time and goods over the life cycle.* New York: National Bureau of Economic Research.

Glezser, H. 1969. A new test for heteroscedasticity. *Journal of the American Statistical Association* 64: 316–323.

Gollop, Frank, and Dale W. Jorgenson. 1980. U.S. productivity growth by industry, 1947–1973. In *New developments in productivity measurement and analysis,* Studies in Income and Wealth, vol. 41, ed. J. W. Kendrick and B. Vaccara. Chicago: University of Chicago Press.

Hakansson, Nils H. 1970. Optimal investment and consumption strategies under risk for a class of utility functions. *Econometrica* 38: 587–607.

Hall, Robert. 1978. Stochastic implications of the life cycle–permanent income hypothesis: theory and evidence. *Journal of Political Economy* 86: 971–987.

————. 1981. Intertemporal substitution in consumption. National Bureau of Economic Research Working Paper #720.

Hall, Robert, and Frederic Mishkin. 1982. The sensitivity of consumption to transitory income: estimates from panel data on households. *Econometrica* 50: 461–482.

Hansen, Lars P. 1982. Large sample properties of generalized method of moments estimators. *Econometrica* 50: 1029–54.

Hansen, Lars P., and Kenneth J. Singleton. 1982. Generalized instrumental variables: estimation of nonlinear rational expectations models. *Econometrica* 50: 1269–86.

Hayashi, Fumio. 1982. The permanent income hypothesis estimation and testing by instrumental variables. *Journal of Political Economy* 90: 895–916.

———— 1984. The permanent income hypothesis and consumption durability: analysis based on Japanese panel data. Mimeographed.

———— 1985. The effect of liquidity constraints on consumption: a cross-sectional analysis. *Quarterly Journal of Economics* 100: 183–206.

Heckman, James. 1974. Life cycle consumption and labor supply: an explanation of the relationship between income and consumption over the life cycle. *American Economic Review* 64: 188–194.

Heller, Walter P., and Ross M. Starr. 1979. Capital market imperfection, the consumption function, and the effectiveness of fiscal policy. *Quarterly Journal of Economics* 93: 453–463.

Keynes, John M. 1936. *The general theory of employment, interest, and money.* New York: Harcourt, Brace, and World. (Reprinted, 1964.)

King, Mervyn, and Louis Dicks-Mireaux. 1981. Asset holdings and the life-cycle. *Economic Journal* 92: 247–267.

Kochin, Levis A. 1974. Are future taxes anticipated by consumers? *Journal of Money, Credit, and Banking* 27: 385–394.

Kormendi, Roger C. 1983. Government debt, government spending, and private sector behavior. *American Economic Review* 73: 994–1010.

Kotlikoff, Laurence 1979a. Social security and equilibrium capital intensity. *Quarterly Journal of Economics* 93: 233–255.

———— 1979b. Testing the theory of social security and life cycle accumulation. *American Economic Review* 69: 396–410.

Kotlikoff, Laurence, and Avia Spivak. 1981. The family as an incomplete annuities market. *Journal of Political Economy* 89: 372–391.

Kotlikoff, Laurence, and Lawrence Summers. 1981. The role of intergenerational transfers in aggregate capital accumulation. *Journal of Political Economy* 89: 706–732.

Kurz, Mordecai. 1985. The life-cycle hypothesis as a tool of theory and policy. In *Arrow and the foundations of the theory of economic policy,* ed. George R. Feiwel. London: Macmillan.

Laitner, John. 1979. Bequests, golden-age capital accumulation and government debt. *Economica* 46: 403–414.

Leimer, Dean, and Selig Lesnoy. 1982. Social security and private saving: new time-series evidence. *Journal of Political Economy* 90: 606–629.

Leland, Hayne E. 1968. Saving and uncertainty: the precautionary demand for saving. *Quarterly Journal of Economics* 82: 465–473.

Levhari, David, and T. W. Srinivasan. 1969. Optimal saving under uncertainty. *Review of Economic Studies* 36: 153–164.

MaCurdy, Thomas E. 1981. An empirical model of labor supply in a life-cycle setting. *Journal of Political Economy* 89: 1059–85.

Mankiw, N. Gregory, Julio J. Rotemberg, and Lawrence H. Summers. 1985.

Intertemporal substitution in macroeconomics. *Quarterly Journal of Economics* 100: 225–251.

Mayer, Thomas. 1972. *Permanent income, wealth, and consumption: a critique of the permanent income theory, the life cycle hypothesis, and related theories.* Berkeley: University of California Press.

Merton, Robert. 1971. Optimal consumption and portfolio rules in a continuous time model. *Journal of Economic Theory* 3: 373–413.

Mirer, Thad. 1979. The wealth-age relation among the aged. *American Economic Review* 69: 435–443.

Mirman, Leonard J. 1971. Uncertainty and optimal consumption decisions. *Econometrica* 39: 179–185.

Modigliani, Franco, and R. Brumberg. 1954. Utility analysis and the consumption function: an interpretation of cross section data. In *Post Keynesian economics,* ed. K. Kuriha. New Brunswick, N.J.: Rutgers University Press.

Nagatani, Keizo. 1972. Life cycle saving: theory and fact. *American Economic Review* 62: 344–353.

Oulton, Nicholas. 1976. Inheritance and the distribution of wealth. *Oxford Economic Papers* 28: 86–101.

Phelps, Edmund S. 1962. The accumulation of risky capital: a sequential utility analysis. *Econometrica* 30: 729–743.

Pollak, Robert A. 1968. Consistent planning. *Review of Economic Studies* 35: 201–208.

Projector, Dorothy. 1968. *Survey of changes in family finances.* Washington, D.C.: Board of Governors of the Federal Reserve System.

Projector, Dorothy, and Gertrude Weiss. 1966. *Survey of financial characteristics of consumers.* Washington, D.C.: Board of Governors of the Federal Reserve System.

Rothschild, Michael, and Joseph E. Stiglitz. 1971. Increasing risk II: its economic consequences. *Journal of Economic Theory* 3: 66–84.

Samuelson, Paul A. 1958. An exact consumption-loan model of interest with or without the social contrivance of money. *Journal of Political Economy* 66: 467–482.

Sandmo, A. 1970. The effects of uncertainty on saving decisions. *Review of Economic Studies* 37: 353–360.

Shorrocks, Anthony F. 1979. On the structure of inter-generational transfers between families. *Economica* 46: 415–425.

Strotz, Robert H. 1955–56. Myopia and inconsistency in dynamic utility maximization. *Review of Economic Studies* 23:165–180.

Summers, Lawrence. 1981. Capital taxation and accumulation in a life cycle growth model. *American Economic Review* 71: 533–544.

—— 1982. *Tax policy, the rate of return, and savings.* National Bureau of Economic Research Working Paper no. 995.

Tax Foundation, Inc. 1964. *Facts and figures on government finance.* Englewood Cliffs, N.J.: Prentice-Hall.

Theil, Henri. 1971. *Principles of econometrics.* Santa Barbara, Calif.: John Wiley and Sons.

Thurow, Lester. 1969. The optimum lifetime distribution of consumption expenditures. *American Economic Review* 59: 324–330.

Tobin, James. 1967. Life-cycle saving and balanced growth. In *Ten economic studies in the tradition of Irving Fisher,* ed. W. Fellner et al. New York: Wiley.

—— 1972. Wealth, liquidity, and the propensity to consume. In *Human behavior in economic affairs (essays in honor of George S. Katona),* ed. J. Morgan and E. Zahn. Amsterdam: Elsevier.

Tomes, Nigel. 1981. The family, inheritance, and the intergenerational transmission of inequality. *Journal of Political Economy* 89: 928–958.

—— 1982. On the intergenerational savings function. *Oxford Economic Papers* 34: 108–134.

U.S. Department of Commerce, Census Bureau. 1963. *Income of persons in the United States: 1963,* Series P-60. Washington, D.C.: Government Printing Office.

U.S. Department of Health, Education, and Welfare, Social Security Administration. 1964. *Social Security Bulletin, Annual Statistical Supplement.* Washington, D.C.: Government Printing Office.

Watts, Harold. 1958. Long-run income expectations and consumer saving. In *Studies in household economic behavior,* ed. R. Rosett and H. Watts. New Haven: Yale University Press.

White, Betsy B. 1978. Empirical tests of the life cycle hypothesis. *American Economic Review* 68: 547–560.

Wonnacott, Thomas H., and Ronald J. Wonnacott. 1977. *Introductory statistics for business and economics.* Santa Barbara, Calif.: John Wiley and Sons.

Yaari, Menahem. 1964. On the consumer's lifetime allocation process. *International Economic Review* 5: 304–317.

—— 1965. Uncertain lifetime, life insurance, and the theory of the consumer. *Review of Economic Studies* 32: 137–158.

Index